PRIVATE EQUITY'S
PUBLIC DISTRESS

The Rise and Fall of Candover

and the Buyout Industry Crash

SEBASTIEN CANDERLE

CONTENTS

POST-MORTEM

APPENDICES

Foreword

This is a true story. All the events related in this book took place and every effort was made to ensure their accurate description. Still, as with any undertaking attempting to report actual circumstances, this volume only reflects one interpretation of what happened. The output represents several months of fact-based research, analysis, interviews and investigation.

The author signed a confidentiality agreement at the time of his departure from Candover in the summer of 2005. Although the entity he used to work for no longer operates under that name, he has nonetheless decided to abide by this agreement. He undertook not to reveal information referring to, inter alia, the specific performance of the Candover funds, unless publicly available, the inner workings of the firm's investment and executive committees, and the terms and conditions of his employment during his time at the firm's London office between 2002 and 2005. Equally, individual remuneration and incentive packages of senior executives were left out in order to preserve people's privacy. Details regarding the investment returns on particular portfolio companies were intentionally omitted to respect contractual requirements except when such information was made available in Candover Investments plc's annual reports and accounts or via other public records. Material related to the performance of Candover's investments was also sourced from financial data providers and cross-examined or confirmed by third parties.

A large number of conversations with private equity investors, advisers, bankers and various industry experts form the genesis of this book. Other parties that had relevant knowledge of the events described hereinafter, including equity analysts and hedge fund managers, also contributed to this work. To ensure their complete and unrestrained participation, the identity of these collaborators has not been disclosed.

Undeniably, the author is grateful to the financial and business journalists whose various articles published in newspapers and magazines and on the Internet helped support his findings. A long list of articles and reports published over a thirty-five-year period was reviewed, so it would be impossible to name all these valued contributors.

The author did not approach the main protagonists mentioned in these pages. He took the view early on that, because of contractual obligations or other personal reasons, it was unlikely that any of them would want to contribute to an account relating the collapse of their company and the shortcomings of some of their decisions. There was also the risk that such discussions would turn into an exercise of finger-pointing.

Private equity is a niche financial trade with its own jargon. Some technical practices can be difficult to understand for someone outside the industry but are also hard to explain in simple terms. It was a challenge to provide the right description of some of the industry's processes, practices and trends without oversimplifying. A glossary can be found in appendix A. In advance, the author apologises if parts of this book still come across as esoteric. In a sector that prides itself on its secrecy, industry data are not always reliable or consistent from one source to the next. When needed, the author used his judgement to select the most appropriate material.

To avoid breaching the very stringent libel laws in force in the UK, it was decided to exclude many second-hand comments and details explaining the matters covered. Furthermore, internal politics and personality clashes are not related in this volume. It makes for a somewhat incomplete, mildly inaccurate and assuredly less entertaining description of the reasons behind Candover's and the industry's setbacks and trials over the years, but the law is the law.

Reporting on a former employer and in particular the last few years of its existence is always going to be a tricky enterprise; one open to criticism regarding the true motives behind it. The fact is that

Candover is the only buyout group to have made extensive and consistent disclosures about its performance and strategy over the last three decades so it was the obvious candidate for a case study. It serves as a magnifying glass for the whole sector's modi operandi. Keeping a neutral stance in the face of such a delicate task is essential in order to ensure that any personal or emotional opinion does not put into question the credibility of the arguments brought forward. Luckily, in the present case the public profile of the company made the evidence irrefutable.

The intention was initially for the manuscript to be published by Oneworld Publications. A couple of intimidating letters sent by Arle Capital and Candover to Oneworld led to the decision to self-publish. It is in the interest of the public to gain a better understanding of the way the buyout sector operates. Candover's history helps explain the events that shaped the enigmatic world of private equity over the last thirty years. The aim of this chronicle is not to lay the blame on particular individuals but rather to analyse where the company's strategy went wrong, thereby assessing the flaws of the industry's fundamental principles, and to suggest remedies to help sector specialists, bankers and financial regulators draw the appropriate lessons in order to avoid making similar mistakes in the future.

The story of Candover's untimely downfall contains many ingredients of a corporate tragedy: job losses, the destruction of significant economic value and the eventual break-up of the business. In the aftermath of the recent financial crisis, it will rightly or wrongly be interpreted by some as a typical account of life in the City of London. Candover became a victim of all the excesses of the mid-2000s buyout bubble; it certainly won't be the only one.

December 2011

Main Characters

John Arney

Joined Candover as a Director in 2002. Managing Director of Candover Partners Limited (CPL) between 2006 and 2009. Managing Partner of CPL from June 2009 and of Arle Capital Partners since December 2010

Roger Brooke

Founder of Candover in 1980. Chief Executive from 1980 to December 1990. Chairman from January 1991 to May 1999. Honorary Life President of Candover Investments plc (CIP) since 1999

Colin Buffin

Joined Candover in September 1985. Director of CPL from 1995. Managing Director from March 1998 to 2006. Senior Managing Director of CPL from 2006 until June 2009. Senior adviser until his departure in the second half of 2009

Stephen Curran

Joined Candover in May 1981. Deputy Chief Executive from July 1982 to 1991. Chief Executive of Candover from 1991 to 1999. Executive Chairman between May 1999 and May 2006. Non-executive Director of CIP from May 2006 to December 2007

Doug Fairservice

Joined Candover in March 1984. Deputy Chief Executive of Candover from 1991 to 1999. Deputy Chairman between May 1999 and May 2004. Director of CIP from May 2004 to May 2006

Gerry Grimstone

Non-executive Director of CIP from July 1999. Non-executive Deputy Chairman from May 2004 to May 2006. Non-executive Chairman of CIP from May 2006 until his resignation in April 2011

Marek Gumienny

Joined Candover in January 1987. Director of CPL from 1995. Managing Director from March 1998 to 2006. Senior Managing Director from 2006 to June 2009. Chairman of CPL from June 2009 and of Arle Capital Partners from December 2010 to December 2011

Introduction

It was past 3 p.m. I had been waiting for some time now, sitting on a comfortable chair at the centre of the varnished wooden table and scanning the room. It was a surprisingly small and low-key meeting room, with fading lavender blue wallpaper and dark wall-to-wall carpeting. Not what I had come to expect from one of the most prestigious buyout firms in Britain. And I liked it. It suited me. I had always reviled the ostentatious offices that some of the investment banks and other buyout players had built for themselves. It was promising.

It was my seventh meeting with as many people and I had been told that it would be my last. They would take a decision shortly afterwards.

I had done some background research on the company. They had been active in the UK for over twenty years and had recently started taking a stab at the rest of Europe. They were in fundraising mode, always a good time to join a private equity firm.

Marek Gumienny walked in. He was a shorter than average, dark-haired individual. I had read on the company's web site that he was one of the joint Managing Directors heading the firm and that he had been working there for fifteen years. From the photo posted on the site, I had guessed that he was in his mid-forties. In our meeting, he came across as very enthusiastic, giving the unmistakable impression that private equity investing was one of the most dynamic occupations in the world. He was an engaged, straight-talking and entertaining communicator. You could tell that he was in the right job. To source and close deals, you need to have a lively, confident personality. You also need to have the ability to click with people, irrespective of their temperament. Quick thinking is a must. An open mind does help. A good sense of humour does not hurt.

Our conversation was as much about my qualifications and skill set as about my eagerness to join the team. It covered what Gumienny had achieved for the partnership and what the firm's strategy was for the coming years. Their plans were ambitious. They wanted to expand overseas, to become one of Europe's undisputed top-tier private equity investors. It was a formidable project. I wanted to be part of it.

As the interview was drawing to a close, Gumienny asked me one final question: 'What is your favourite wine?'

'It would have to be a Saint Emilion', I replied without hesitation.

'Which one?' he enquired.

'Probably Cheval Blanc'.

He smiled approvingly. Like me, he enjoyed his wine. He acknowledged that I had good taste and called the end of the meeting. I was in.

It was April 2002 and I had just received an offer to join Candover, one of the most respected institutions in the European buyout industry. I did not suspect then that the firm's expansion plans would go horribly wrong.

BROOKE'S VISION

Chapter 1 - The Harsh Reality

If I describe to you a country afflicted by incessant trade union strikes, deep-rooted hyper-inflation, permanently low productivity and an income per capita a third below the level recorded by France or Germany, you would be forgiven for reaching the conclusion that I am referring to a Third World nation. But you would be badly mistaken. The above country is none other than Britain in the 1970s. All joking aside, it is no surprise that by the time Margaret Thatcher was elected to the premiership in 1979, Britain had been nicknamed the 'sick man of Europe'. How had one of the most powerful industrial economies in the world only half a century before become such a basket case?

Immediately after the Second World War, the national governments of all western European economies had tackled the urgent task of their reconstruction. Britain's was no different, following a centralised Keynesian policy to inject capital in all major sectors of the economy. Labour governments had nationalised vast chunks of the country's industry, including the railroads, coal mining and public utilities, in some sort of major national bail-out. The heavy involvement of the government was essential and indispensable, such was the derelict state of the nation after the war. Unfortunately, while contributing positively to the prosperity of the population, it was evident by the early 1970s that centralised policies had not produced benefits as great for Britain as for France and Germany. The two continental countries kept displaying much higher gross domestic product (GDP) growth and productivity improvements.

And as the world was going through the oil shock of 1973, it was becoming clear to all that the welfare state, so important in the post-war years to provide the whole population with health cover, universal education and job security, was now proving too expensive to run - in part due to the high-inflation environment - and was somewhat to blame for throttling the economy. Britain's successive governments had overspent for many years and had run a budget deficit almost consistently between the late 1950s and the early 1970s. In order to tame inflation, which was partly fuelled by the cost of running such an overgrown state, the Bank of England had raised its base rate continuously since the late 1950s. A 4 per cent interest rate in 1959 had reached over 14 per cent in 1976. Under the Tory leadership of Edward Heath, government spending had more than doubled between 1970 and 1974. From 1955 to 1975 general government expenditure had mushroomed, going from 35 per cent of GDP to just shy of 50 per cent. This oppressive state influence had frequently been accentuated by the various Labour governments' tendency to nationalise corporations or entire industries as soon as they faced the risk of going broke. The nationalisation of the steel industry in 1967 and, eight years later, that of British Leyland - the 170,000-employee-strong manufacturer of several famous car brands like Jaguar, Rover and MG as well as trucks and buses - were two of many examples of the state's interventionist policy.

Chronic budget and balance of payment deficits had eventually led international investors to ditch the pound, leading sterling's value to plummet by a third against the US dollar between late 1974 and the autumn of 1976. In order to avoid national bankruptcy, in another sign that Britain in those days was more akin to an emerging economy than to a great European power, its government had had little alternative but to request a $3.9 billion-loan from the International Monetary Fund (IMF) in late 1976. In exchange, the IMF had insisted on deep cuts to public spending. In order to refill the nation's coffers, Prime Minister Jim Callaghan had attempted from then on to raise taxes, reduce the government budget and introduce salary caps in the public sector. Confronted by the ripple effects of the 1973 oil embargo and a growing number of unemployed workers, Callaghan had also tried to revive the economy by finally dropping the central bank's interest rate from 14 per cent in January 1977 to 6.5 per cent in January 1978. While it helped support the economic recovery, it was not sufficient to erase two decades of structural underperformance.

It seems hard to believe today, but in 1980 Britain was one of the poorest of Western Europe's large industrialised countries, with a GDP per head almost 40 per cent below that of West Germany and 20 to 30 per cent below France's. It had just gone through the 1970s struggling with the unstable energy context and, as a consequence, its coal mining and steel manufacturing industries were overdue a serious restructuring.

Between 1970 and 1980 its economy had witnessed an average annual growth rate of 1.9 per cent, the lowest by a long margin among the largest industrialised countries, and one full percentage point below the OECD average. By comparison, over that period, Italy's GDP rate of growth had been 3.1 per cent, West Germany's 2.7 per cent and France's 3.7 per cent.[1]

During the 1970s, Britain had also suffered from the most harmful of inflationary circumstances. As the world was striving through two oil crises, inflation had turned into a global economic plague. However, the country's trade partners had overcome the problem more effectively than its successive leaders, primarily by containing the wage gains of public servants and introducing strict consumer price controls. In 1975, according to the IMF, Britain's rate of inflation was 24.2 per cent, more than twice that of France and four times that recorded in West Germany. Between 1970 and 1980, overall prices in Britain had risen by 261 per cent. Annual inflation had exceeded 10 per cent in each year between 1974 and 1980, with the exception of 1978, which still endured a punishing rise of more than 8 per cent.

As mentioned, in such a hyper-inflationary world the Bank of England did its best to cope. Throughout the 1970s, it kept raising its base rate to try and control price increases; the central bank's interest rate reached 14.75 per cent in late 1976, and after Callaghan's late 1970s loosening policies, it was back up at 17 per cent by November 1979 as Thatcher's first move to bring down inflation. With such frantic retail price jumps, though, the country remained unattractive to investors. And for savers and consumers, the weight of tax levies, including the introduction of the value-added tax in 1973, made things even more hopeless.

To highlight how desperate British politicians had got to turn things around, the most Euro-sceptic nation had joined the European

Economic Community (EEC) in 1973, wrongly hoping that it would be sufficient to turn its fortune around. Under Edward Heath's premiership, between 1970 and 1974 the country had lost over nine million days in strike action. Unemployment had even started to rise sharply, reaching 5.8 per cent in 1978 compared to a rate of 3.5 per cent four years earlier. During the winter of 1978 and 1979, social unrest was so widespread that Callaghan referred to it as the 'Winter of Discontent' It surprised no one when, in the spring of 1979, his Labour government lost the elections after he had been forced to dissolve Parliament following a vote of no confidence in the House of Commons. Margaret Thatcher had been elected Prime Minister on a liberal programme. She had promised reforms; that's what the British people would get.

In May 1979, she had come to power following a hard-fought campaign against a Labour party universally considered incapable of reforming the country. She was proposing a remodelling of the economy based on a drastically different agenda. This effectively meant moving away from a state-controlled system in favour of a more entrepreneurial private sector. Thatcher also wanted to shift away from the traditional unionised setting in large corporations and to encourage individuals to take the initiative. She certainly had her work cut out for her, and people who thought that she would not dare put in place such a radical programme would prove seriously mistaken. She would succeed where all governments had failed for the last ten years.

And the fact that Britain had endured the dreadful decade of the 1970s did not prevent the country from feeling the brunt of the worldwide economic recession in 1980-81. Britain's GDP fell by over 2 per cent in 1980 alone. Double-digit inflation was still rife as that same year registered a rampant increase in retail prices of 18 per cent. In the first quarter of 1982, the country's GDP was at the same level as in the third quarter of 1978.[2] But Thatcher's reforms would start yielding results soon.

The new Prime Minister did not have much room to manoeuvre. Still she went ahead with her reform agenda, implementing a vast programme of privatisations of the large state-owned enterprises, starting with British Petroleum and British Aerospace. Deregulation of the big utilities (water, electricity and gas) was also introduced. The government's strategy was essentially aimed at modernising its industry and making it more competitive by getting British companies' growth projects financed by private funding or the stock markets rather than public money. Competition policy would replace the industrial initiatives of the last thirty years.

Her intention was also to curb consumer price increases through monetarist policies. Championed by US economist Milton Friedman, monetarism aimed at controlling the supply of money in order to keep consumer prices under control. Tackling inflation would become Thatcher's economic *raison d'être*. Until then, politicians had always paid more attention to unemployment.

To finance the welfare state, Britain's successive governments had raised taxes and invented new tax levies. Many of these had obviously proved inflationary. In 1973, VAT had been introduced at a standard rate of 10 per cent. In 1974, the newly elected Labour government had introduced a punitive top rate of income tax of 83 per cent. When you added the 15 per cent tax imposed on dividends and investments, a top earner could potentially face a marginal tax rate of 98 per cent. It was not just vindictive, it also affected labour productivity, which was already much lower than in neighbouring countries due to the country's heavily unionised and therefore relatively expensive labour. In 1979, in its first budget Thatcher's government would immediately bring the top income tax rate down to 60 per cent and would choose instead to follow a fiscal policy focused on indirect taxation such as VAT, excise duties and housing tax.

But her biggest battle, and the one Thatcher is most often remembered for nowadays, was the one she fought with the then very powerful trade unions. It culminated in the Miners' Strike of 1984. For the first time after more than fifteen years of almost uninterrupted industrial action, a British government would not accede to the requests of the union barons. Thatcher would win the contest but her image would suffer greatly, not just in the eyes of the mining industry, not just among union members, but with the whole population. The number of miners employed in the UK would go from over 200,000 in 1984 to 20,000 ten years later, but by then, in some form of justice, Thatcher would also have lost her job.

Not all of her policies yielded immediate results. But she singlehandedly introduced fundamental and painful changes that would transform the very fabric of Britain's economy. Back then, she came across as a selfish neo-liberal politician with no respect for the social suffering inflicted by her drastic measures. Her poll ratings throughout her time in power support that fact. In hindsight, she proved one of the most courageous leaders of modern politics, recognising that the country needed to be restructured to be able to start afresh. Looking at the vast project of institutional changes she launched throughout the 1980s, she certainly suspected that she would not get the chance to witness the full impact of her reforms while in government.

The purpose of this book is not to discuss the merits and shortcomings of Thatcherism but rather to demonstrate that the structural transformation introduced by the successive Conservative governments during the 1980s and 1990s help explain why the buyout industry not only grew and thrived in the UK but also why several British firms quickly became a dominant force behind the development of buyouts in continental Europe.

Moving away from the traditional textile, steel manufacturing and coal mining industries in which it had become uncompetitive due to high wages and chronic underinvestment, the nation would convert into a modern service economy. Of course, as has been widely documented and commented upon, the financial industry in particular would greatly benefit from Thatcher's reforms.

In the 1970s, the financial sector in the UK was rigorously regulated and protected. Each segment, be it retail banking, merchant banking (as investment banking was then called), mortgage lending, stockbrokerage, insurance or investment management, was neatly separated and safeguarded from competition by a strict regulatory framework. Outsiders could not become members of this selective circle and no foreign institution could readily acquire a British bank or brokerage house for instance. The industry's identity was that of an old gentlemen's club. It was protected but was also trailing its US and European counterparts. The UK's financial industry lacked any innovative or entrepreneurial spirit. But it had one major advantage: the absence of conflicts of interests that would creep in post-deregulation.

Nonetheless, as successive governments had failed to restore confidence in the country's economic prospects, the private sector was coming up with its own solutions. The mid-to-late 1970s had seen the emergence of a new breed of financiers. Then called venture capitalists or VCs, these investment specialists focused on backing small private enterprises in their expansion strategies. While originally such investment programmes had been government-backed – in the UK, 3i or Investors in Industry, had been active since 1945 under the names ICFC (Industrial and Commercial Financial Corporation) and FCI (Finance Corporation for Industry), and was at the time under direct supervision from the Bank of England – more recently private institutions had been established with corporate and bank funding.

Since the 1960s, the Charterhouse Group had developed a strong financial arm that included a merchant bank called Charterhouse Japhet but also investment trusts and a VC-type activity under the name Charterhouse Industrial Development. Financial institutions such as investment firms Apax and Electra Investment Trust and banks National Westminster and HSBC had already set up venture capital activities. Electra and both banks had launched their first VC funds in 1976. Independent fund manager CINVen had also emerged in 1977 under the sexy-sounding name National Coal Board Pension Fund. CINVen, which stands for Coal Investment Nominees for Venture capital, was backed by British Coal, British Rail and Barclays Bank.

In those days, between 100 and 150 VC transactions were executed each year in the UK. The average deal size was lower than £1 million, an amount for which no early-stage investor would get out of bed today. Many equity tickets did not in fact exceed £100,000. Growth capital represented the bulk of the deal flow, meaning that transactions were primarily equity financed. Leverage was very rarely part of the equation. A company looking for financing would run an overdraft, go to its bank for an expensive loan or raise equity from venture capitalists. And given how tricky the economic conditions were in the 1970s, ICFC and its peers often provided a last lifeline for companies which would otherwise have gone under. Stock markets were not really an option as they were only accessible to large corporations. The high rates of taxation and hyper-inflation prevalent at the time did not leave much saving for individuals to invest in the stock market so pension funds held most of the capital, and they were only interested in taking positions in large corporations. Tickets of £1 million or less did not attract institutional investors. Buyout transactions did not properly exist, simply because debt structuring and the regulatory framework were not sophisticated enough to allow them to take place. Also, in such an unstable, unpredictable economic context, which banker would have been so bold as to offer venture capitalists any leverage? The inflationary late 1970s and recessionary early 1980s would change the nature of VC transactions, offering plenty of opportunity to shore up bankrupt companies and restructure firms in trouble. In 1980 a second-tier stock market, the Unlisted Securities Market (USM), was opened to provide an exit opportunity for small VC-backed companies. From then on, a large number of management buyouts (MBO) would take advantage of a stock market listing to realise an exit. Thanks to the numerous reforms that the Tories would introduce, the market conditions would eventually move in the right direction.

In the meantime, the bulk of all acquisitions in the UK, and definitely the sizeable ones, were carried out by large corporations. Many of these trusts or conglomerates, as they were known, had been built through external growth, that is by acquiring many, often unrelated activities. Thorn, which would acquire music publisher EMI in 1980, was one of these singular corporate entities. These conglomerates aimed at generating value by buying troubled businesses to turn them around or by injecting further capital in promising technologies or products. BTR, formerly British Tyre & Rubber, was a vast organisation operating in engineering, packaging, building products and materials. But the most formidable of the lot was Hanson Trust, an industrial concern which had built a reputation as an asset-stripper. Set up in 1964 as a sack hire and fertiliser manufacturing concern and introduced on the public market under the Wiles Group name for a market capitalisation of less than £1 million, the business had reached a £250 million valuation by 1980. That same year, it had acquired US-based McDonough for £74 million, a big ticket in those days. The business worked closely with the illustrious house of Rothschild. For many years, the latter would handle almost exclusively all the money-raising operations to finance the conglomerate's huge appetite for external growth. Hanson Trust aimed at maximising return on capital employed in a way similar to the buyout investors' focus on internal rate of return (IRR) nowadays. At the time, Hanson was the best at that game.

There was a wide variety of smaller holding companies and mini-conglomerates in all sectors of the economy. In that pre-globalization period, high trade tariffs and stringent regulation often helped businesses establish national leadership in their field without the fear of competition from more sophisticated or powerful foreign groups. Building scale across various industries was the main strategic tool to establish a company's competitive advantage. Horizontal and vertical consolidation was a key objective of business managers. Revenues were more important than profits; sales growth prevailed over margin improvements. Scale was believed to constitute an unassailable barrier to entry and bring bargaining power over suppliers and customers; higher profits would be naturally derived from a leading market share. And just like some of their private equity (PE) successors two decades later, the founders and managers of these conglomerates – who were often colourful characters – would be rewarded for their contribution to society by being granted a title. Enter Sir Jules Thorn and Sir James Hanson.

As we have seen, by the time Thatcher had won the general election of 1979 Britain was a hopeless basket case. Hyper-inflation, crippling income tax rates, ever-increasing tax levies, anaemic economic growth, rising unemployment and influential unions blocking any political reform had turned the country into an isolated, lifeless economy. But it is often from burnt fields that the best crops are won. The 1980s would produce the best crop in decades.

In those prehistoric times, private equity, or rather venture capital, was almost a quaint activity. In Britain, it was a secluded financial trade and was not meaningful in a macroeconomic sense. On the scale of the corporate world, it did not weigh much. Roger Brooke's merit is to have foreseen that it was all about to change.

Chapter 2 - Humble Beginnings, Ambitious Goals

By 1980 Roger Brooke had worked many years in a corporate setting and like most businessmen he recognised that Thatcher's coming to power was an opportunity for Britain and the economy. Pushing 50, Brooke was ready for a career change. He had spent the last ten years as a senior executive in large corporations, including as Vice Chairman of conglomerate Pearson Longman between 1971 and 1979, and as Group Managing Director of record company EMI between 1979 and early 1980. When Thorn acquired EMI in 1980, the job that he had taken on the previous year to attempt to turn around the company was no longer his. He knew that he could leverage his contacts in the business world to take on a more entrepreneurial role. Away from the traditional stuffy corporate life, he certainly craved a more dynamic perspective. Still, immediately after leaving EMI, he was looking for the next opportunity.

He was not a financier but Brooke's experience as a Deputy Managing Director at the Industrial Reorganisation Corporation (IRC) between 1966 and 1969 had made him realise that the country's small and medium enterprises were in need of more private funding. The role of the government-backed IRC was to promote structural change to improve the efficiency and profitability of British industry. Between 1969 and 1971, Brooke had also been the chief executive of Scienta (short for Scientific Enterprise Associates), a Brussels-based company investing in European businesses developing new technologies. The time had come for privately-backed investment firms to orchestrate these structural changes.

As stated before, the UK's venture capital industry was so small in the 1970s that it had no real economic impact. Some small companies benefited from their financial support, but the British economy was so heavily regulated and controlled by the state that there was no need, no room, for private equity financing on a large scale. Across the Atlantic though, a revolution was in its infancy.

In the US, three financial professionals had set up shop in 1976 under the name Kohlberg, Kravis, Roberts & Co. (KKR). In the summer of 1980, as part of his information-gathering process on behalf of British investment firm Electra Investment Trust, Brooke met with KKR's co-founder, 36-year-old Henry Kravis, in New York. The latter, who by then had completed fewer than ten leveraged buyout (LBO) transactions including the ones executed when he worked at investment bank Bear Stearns, was probably the most enthusiastic salesman Brooke could have come across. The two men had been introduced through Michael Stoddart, the experienced financier who four years earlier had founded Electra, one of Britain's very first independent investment firms. Electra's founder and Chief Executive was considering investing in KKR and had asked Brooke to look into it. LBOs were very much in their infancy then and it was unclear, even to seasoned venture capitalists like Stoddart, whether such acquisitions, financed via a mix of debt and equity, were just a fad or a viable alternative to conventional VC funding.

The meeting with Kravis convinced Brooke that LBOs were the way forward for the industry. When he came back from the US, he persuaded Stoddart that they should launch a similar activity in Britain. Although it might seem like a no-brainer today, back then, it was real foresight. Before 1980, the UK had witnessed very few buyout transactions. By 1985, the country would have recorded 300 of them in that year alone. His timing was perfect.

The decision to enter the somewhat secretive and cliquey world of venture capital was a risky career move for someone with no professional history in the City, London's financial district. Brooke certainly realised that it was a hermetic world where executives with a background in large corporations did not have easy access. In spite of that hurdle, recognising that his unrivalled corporate credentials offered a unique selling point, in September 1980 he set up a buyout investment firm, having managed to raise £2.1 million of equity and debt from institutional investors, including Electra, FCI, Globe Investment Trust, insurer Prudential and BP Pension Fund. For Stoddart, backing this project was a way of keeping Electra focused on its core venture capital activities while dabbling at the same time on the new emerging trend of LBOs. Through business associates in the US, the VC investment trust had already been able to study and participate in some management buyouts and had therefore enthusiastically supported Brooke's initiative to lead similar transactions in Britain.[3] At inception, Electra was believed to own 40 per cent of the newly established buyout business.[4]

But we should not assume that Brooke's decision process had occurred in a vacuum. Other entrepreneurs had identified the trend and had already jumped on the bandwagon. In December 1979, Birmingham-based broker Albert Sharp had set up SUMIT (Sharp Unquoted Midland Investment Trust), with the backing of eleven institutions and an initial capital injection of £1 million in equity and £4.1 million in performance stock. Similarly, two former Rothschild bankers had established Guidehouse in August 1980 to raise funds under a Business Expansion Scheme, a government-backed initiative that allowed individual investors to invest in unquoted companies. Both of these new institutions were targeting minority positions in MBOs.

Brooke chose to call his new firm Candover Investments Limited. The name was a direct reference to a remote picturesque valley in Hampshire, a county in southern England, where he was living at the time. Despite his successful career in business and the public sector, he had elected to give his company an original, almost humble identity in homage to the country life he enjoyed so much. The Candover valley abounded in thatched cottages with acres of land, walled gardens with enough space to train horses, classic Georgian red-brick houses with verandas, top local schools for the children, and peaceful riverbanks to go trout fishing at the weekend. Hampshire was and would increasingly become a favourite spot for City high-flyers looking for a spacious property within a one-hour train ride of London.

In keeping with its name, the firm's beginnings were understated. Operating out of a small single-room office at 4–7 Red Lion Court, just off Fleet Street on the west side of the City, it nonetheless managed to close its first deal by year end. It invested with ICFC and SUMIT in Truflo, a gas turbine blade manufacturer and a subsidiary of

US group Rockwell International, in December 1980. The deal was worth £6.8 million, £3.5 million originating from a club of institutions with Barclays Bank providing the debt.[5] The transactions that the firm carried out in 1981 were of similar size: Gower, a manufacturer of flat-packed fitted furniture was acquired for £2.85 million from its parent PMA Holdings in February of that year,[6] and Cavenham's confectionery activities, renamed Famous Names, had been acquired from financier Sir James Goldsmith[7] for approximately £6 million. Candover was in business.

After so many years in the corporate world and in government, Brooke's network of contacts could be used to source and finance deals while his operational training could be put to contribution when managing portfolio companies. For instance, he would bring in food specialist Michael Vernon to take on the Chairman duties at Famous Names; Vernon had previously worked at EMI. At the same time, Brooke realised that investment firms were run by financiers who did not care exclusively about the functional aspects of running companies but also about financial management. Thankfully, he had enough humility to acknowledge that his investment analytical skills were not the strongest; he had a limited grasp of complex financial transactions, having studied classics at Oxford University's Trinity College. His forte was deal origination.

He decided to bring in individuals with the appropriate competence to assess and execute investment opportunities. His first recruit in May 1981 was Stephen Curran, then a 38-year-old project finance manager working for the National Coal Board Pension Fund,[8] a predecessor to CINVen as mentioned. We will see later that Candover and CINVen would go on to build a strong tie, jointly acquiring companies in the early and mid-1990s and again in the early 2000s. As Deputy Chief Executive,[9] Curran would bring in the analytical ingenuity that would complement Brooke's management and operational expertise. Curran was a graduate of the illustrious Sandhurst military academy, a certified accountant and a former consultant from accountancy firm Coopers & Lybrand. He was a slick, level-headed individual whose command of investment execution would perfectly blend with Brooke's charm as a networker.

Because the concept of management buyout was so unfamiliar to the industry specialists' potential clients, LBO firms started advertising in national newspapers. It might seem incongruous today but throughout the 1980s ICFC, Barclays Development Capital, Charterhouse and naturally Candover vied for advertising space in the business section of major newspapers. These classified ads started initially to explain the concept of MBOs to attract business owners who might be interested in selling, corporate managers who might want to acquire the division they were running or even institutional investors looking for a new way to diversify their portfolio. Progressively, as the competitive landscape became more crowded, the LBO experts would praise their track record by mentioning successful investments and exits or the number of deals they had completed.

Brooke spent his time not only marketing the firm to potential clients and investors but also the concept of a management buyout itself, which was as I mentioned still little known. From the outset, he spent a considerable amount of time with financial journalists to explain how each 'project', as he referred to them, worked. His buyouts were to be financed largely with loan capital, split into different classes according to security, yield and maturity. In addition, preferred stock could be issued. Equity would rarely exceed 10 per cent of the total transaction value. It was a real education exercise. In October 1981, he chaired a two-day conference on buyouts in London where the UK's Industry Secretary, Sir Keith Joseph, was one of the key speakers. It was a great way to show that this nascent industry was getting the backing of the government. The notion of buyouts, or 'incentive financing' as they were sometimes labelled, fitted perfectly with Thatcher's policies to encourage entrepreneurs and businessmen to contribute to her national 'restructuring' programme.

And the industry got another boost when in 1981 the government introduced new legislation on financial assistance, enabling a company to use its own assets as part of the collateral to finance a buyout. Until then, it was difficult to raise significant amounts of debt as the banks were reluctant to make unsecured loans and business managers were not prepared to use their own assets, usually their own house, as collateral. The new provision made it easier for banks to lend money and back

MBOs and for management teams to pledge security on the assets of the company. One stone at a time, the buyout revolution was taking shape.

Very soon the LBO market was experiencing vigorous growth. Until 1978, ICFC, by far the most active buyout engineer, had only closed four to five MBOs a year, but in its fiscal year to 31 March 1978, it had executed ten of them. And as the Conservatives encouraged the private sector to take the initiative, ICFC's deal list rose from twenty LBOs in the 1979 fiscal year to over 100 in the twelve months to 31 March 1982. It was frenetic.

ICFC was an exception in closing so many transactions. Most funds did not have the government-backed agency's influence. Also, in those days, Candover and its peers were committing capital as the investment opportunities arose rather than from a dedicated fund. Even Barclays Development Capital, Midland Bank Industrial Finance and Midland Bank Venture Capital only closed a handful of deals in 1980 and 1981. Barclays's buyout unit tended to take majority control of the companies it acquired, purchasing for example 51 per cent of DIY retailer and paint manufacturer Jacoa and a similar stake in Wilmot Breeden Electronics, a manufacturer of electronic equipment and components. The amounts they invested were small: £4.75 million in Jacoa and £2 million in Wilmot. In the same vein, Charterhouse had acquired minority stakes in cash and carry warehouse M6 for £2.25 million and in insurance brokers Cambers and Newman for £0.75 million. MBO investors were the minnows of the world of mergers and acquisitions (M&A).

Brooke had decided that he wanted to register Candover as an investment trust in order to take advantage of the favourable tax legislation derived from this type of structure. There was one main drawback with it, though: the investment trust had to be a minority shareholder in any investee company. This helps explain why in those days Candover completed primarily minority buyouts and why it systematically syndicated its transactions. Looking at the list of deals carried out by the firm in the first twelve months of operation, the shareholding varied from 10 per cent in Ansafone, a manufacturer of telephone answering machines backed alongside investors Equity Capital for Industry (ECI) and Montagu in March 1981, to just shy of 50 per cent in Famous Names.[10]

Early on, Brooke had staked everything on the belief that the opportunities were virtually limitless. In 1982, he expressed the idea that there were thousands of subsidiaries of US companies in the UK, and some of them were unwanted by their parent companies. His view was that the buyout situation in Britain was where it had been in the US in the late 1960s.[11] He was following closely what was happening in the American market, not just due to his initial conversations with Kravis but because he knew that they were trend-setters just as they had been for the VC segment. Having been based in Washington in the early 1960s during his spell with the British Diplomatic Service, Brooke admired the American way of doing business. Also, incidentally, Brooke's wife Nancy was American.

For the first few years of Candover's life, Brooke would in fact participate in US leveraged transactions alongside Forstmann Little in New York and provide venture capital funding in advanced technologies with Chappell in San Francisco.[12] He knew of course the technology space from his two years at Scienta so he must have felt that he was competent enough to analyse these opportunities. As already explained, it also gave him a chance to keep up with developments across the Atlantic.

Initially, due to the novelty of buyouts but also partly because of the challenging economic climate of the early 1980s, Candover executed transactions on an ad hoc basis. As touched upon before, it did not raise a fund but instead assembled a syndicate of institutional investors each time it wanted to buy out a company. It was a painstaking exercise but Brooke and his team had still managed to invest in eleven British businesses between December 1980 and December 1983, seven of them in the first nine months, exceeding their most optimistic predictions. A typical transaction at the time was the £4.2 million MBO of brokers Vickers da Costa. Brooke had brought in many of his own investors, including Electra, ICFC and Prudential Assurance, to invest alongside the firm.[13]

The amount of equity invested in those deals (less than £10 million per deal) would make one smile in today's environment of multi-billion-euro transactions, but in those days they were a clear signal that Candover was able to make room for itself in a promising, fast-expanding segment of the investment industry. In these sluggish economic times, most targets were subsidiaries of large corporations that were going through a restructuring process or were no longer considered core to the parent company's strategy. Many of these investment opportunities were syndicated by Candover or by its peers or seed investors, indicating that the market opportunities were so many in relation to the number of LBO funds that collaboration was far more prevalent than competition. Auctions were rare as investment opportunities were often intermediated by merchant banks that had close relationships with their clients and played an introductory role between corporate managers and venture capitalists. It might seem bizarre but back then managers who were interested in buying out their own business or division, often from a parent company that had shown little interest in it for many years, would themselves approach buyout specialists like Candover to help them put the financing in place.

Because of the recessionary background, these transactions required hard work from the investment team. Cash management was obviously very important to make sure that the company could pay back its debt and equity obligations. Leverage was not the key to success; turning the business around was. Brooke and his team had to work relentlessly to improve the way operations were run. Shortening production runs, reducing idle time, improving capacity utilisation and managing stock levels often had more impact on the success of the buyout and the ultimate rate of return on the original equity invested than the structure of the financing. While Candover's early buyouts were in the industrial sector, quickly the firm broadened its spectrum to the services sector. Sure, Britain was a big industrial nation but it had already begun its mutation into a service-centred economy and that would create many opportunities for LBO shops. Operational improvements were easier to implement in the industrial sectors because they had been well documented thanks to the Japanese economic miracle. The just-in-time production planning revolution and the introduction of the kaizen method of continuous improvement were gaining in popularity. But many enhancements could also be introduced in the financial and business services, media and leisure segments of the economy.

Brooke had from day one indicated that he was not interested in businesses that were on the rocks. He was looking for parent companies wanting to 'deglomerate' or for family businesses with a succession issue. Still, because he had set up the firm in the fiercest post-war recession, he and his team could not afford to be too picky. Focusing on improving operations was time-consuming but it was often a very rewarding exercise, not just from a monetary point of view but also from a personally gratifying angle. The companies that Candover acquired were small. Frequently, the deal team was closely in touch with not only the target's management team but many of its employees. Improving the operational performance of a business sometimes implied cutting headcount but more often than not the ultimate survival of the company meant saving jobs. Compared to today's ruthless dealmakers sitting in an office and looking at monthly management reports, Brooke and his team really had to roll up their sleeves to deliver superior returns. Having come out of the 1970s, corporate management teams were reluctant to change. In an economy that was dominated by the state, competition was sometimes restricted by red tape and protectionist measures so it was a challenge to motivate people to change the status quo. Companies were production-led. They were used to paying attention to their customers' orders but not to the way they managed cash. And if management was incompetent, it was difficult to replace them as, unlike today, you did not dispose of a large pool of tried and tested operational experts. There was little literature providing tools to improve efficiency and cash management. We were still in the early years of management books written by gurus like Peter Drucker and Charles Handy and there were even fewer experience-based accounts like the ones reported in the late 1980s and the 1990s by more hands-on corporate troubleshooters like former Imperial Chemical Industries (ICI) Chairman John Harvey-Jones. Venture capitalists and buyout professionals brought in the necessary discipline to reduce production times, manage stock levels and collect cash from customers. They were very much going through trials and errors. It is by demonstrating that they were first-class cash managers that, gradually, MBO specialists managed to obtain the kind of debt quantum that had so far been reserved for industrial conglomerates. In the early 1980s, newly created Candover and other buyout firms had to prove themselves; leverage remained moderate.

As a consequence of the efforts and changes required to improve the investee companies' situation, holding periods – that is the number of years the companies were been kept in portfolio – frequently exceeded five years. For instance, Candover's very first investment was kept more than seven years. The average holding period of the firm's first ten investments was just short of five years. Still, in some cases, when the business was performing strongly, they were able to exit sooner. The £2 million buyout of computer service group DPCE, executed in February 1981, lasted a bit more than two years, Candover (with a 9 per cent stake), Thompson Clive, Electra and the other investors eventually floating the company and selling part of their holding in July 1983. Merchant bank Lazard, which was also one of the co-investors on the buyout, had run the Initial Public Offering (IPO) of a company valued at *c.* £20 million,[14] or ten times its original buyout valuation.

During those early years, the firm closed two high-profile deals. The carve-out of Stone Platt's specialist electrical division was an £18 million buyout executed with Electra, ICFC and Charterhouse in May 1982. And more importantly, Candover led the acquisition of shoe retailer William Timpson from Hanson Trust in 1983. Managing 250 repair shops, the company was bought alongside Electra, Murray Caledonian, BP Pension Fund and Fleming Enterprise Investment Trust for £40 million, the largest ever buyout in Britain at the time.[15] For both of these transactions, as for its DPCE buyout, the firm only held a small minority stake. Importantly, while others continued to focus on small transactions, Candover was purposefully targeting larger LBOs. Industry data reveal that in 1981, its first full year of activity, the firm's average buyout size was more than twice as large as that of Barclays Development Capital and seven times bigger than Charterhouse's.[16] The capital gains were not life-changing for Brooke and Curran, but they contributed to establishing strong foundations on which to build a solid reputation.

Surprisingly, in this challenging economic context the industry did not record many casualties among its portfolio companies. Some, like Ansafone and the original Stone Platt Industries buyout backed by FCI and ECI in May 1981, would ultimately fail but LBO specialists usually followed a prudent and selective approach. It was essentially solid businesses that were getting bank financing. By the end of 1981, out of approximately 200 MBOs completed by ICFC in its entire history, only nine had reportedly been failures.[17] There was also one key reason behind such strong results: there was little competition to bid for assets that were publicly known to be non-core for their cash-constrained parent companies. The seller did not have many options to dispose of small activities. Big divisions were gobbled up by conglomerates but sub-£50 million businesses were prime contenders for MBOs. While during the recession years some buyouts were taking place because of distressed reasons – Stone Platt's railway carriage air-conditioning activities, for instance, were bought by Candover from the receivers – most candidates were corporate strategic divestments. In contrast, younger companies that attracted VC funding had a higher rate of failure: in the twelve months to June 1984, Stoddart had reported four liquidations out of its Electra Risk Capital I fund, a £8.7 million investment vehicle set up under the government's Business Start-up Scheme and aimed at backing businesses in activity for less than five years.[18]

In line with the growth of the business, Candover added two other individuals to its leadership team. 39-year-old Philip Symonds joined in 1983, bringing with him his accountancy background. This profile would, for most of the 1980s and 1990s, be the entry ticket not only to Candover but to most British PE outfits. Such financial management skills were in high demand to carry out thorough due diligence of target companies. In March 1984, Candover recruited as senior manager Doug Fairservice, a 37-year-old accomplished dealmaker who had spent ten years working for venture capital firm ICFC and for the British Technology Group.[19] Fairservice would prove one of the most productive deal originators in Candover's early years.

But hiring investment professionals was only half the trick. Brooke knew that if he wanted to establish a long-term franchise, he needed to extend his web of contacts across the City. Several of Candover's board members naturally came from the firm's initial backers. Stoddart was on the board and so was Lawrence Tindale, Deputy Chairman of FCI. Brooke had also brought in veteran Scottish industrialist Angus Murray as Chairman in order to build the firm's credibility within the corporate managers' community. Murray had been introduced by Electra, where he was a member of the advisory panel. To replace Murray after his unexpected death in 1982, Candover had hired Peter Wreford in January of the following year. A former Chairman of

Gresham Trust, Wreford was a director of several financial and investment firms. His profile was what Brooke needed to get the right introductions among institutional investors.

Eventually Candover managed to raise a fund in 1984 with the collaboration of the esteemed British brokerage house Hoare Govett. Called the Hoare Candover Exempt Trust, this first fund closed with £7.5 million of commitments from twenty-five institutions. Its prospectus stated that it would be investing in companies aiming to float on the USM within five years.[20] Although the Hoare Candover fund was small, even by those days' standards, it opened the door for upcoming transformational, trend-setting fundraises.

As previously explained, Brooke wanted to set up the firm as an investment trust in order to be exempt from UK corporation tax on chargeable gains realised on portfolio exits. A listing was one of the conditions to fulfil for any company to qualify for such a status. In December 1984, via a flotation on the London Stock Exchange (LSE), Candover Investments plc (CIP) was born. Valuing the company at £11.45 million, the institutional and management owners had chosen to list the business slightly below its net asset value (NAV) of £12.2 million on 26 November. It was a pretty impressive progression from the original £2.1 million put in by its seed investors four years earlier. That jump in value had essentially occurred in 1984 itself, thanks to three portfolio exits, including the listings of DPCE and Stone International. At the end of 1983, the firm's net assets were only worth £5.9 million but thanks to its residual stakes in DPCE and Stone, which were worth £4.6 million at market prices, and significant appreciation in unlisted investments, Candover's valuation had more than doubled in just twelve months.[21] Brooke had marketed the float actively. The firm had already made over forty investments, typically taking a 5 to 15 per cent stake in the investee companies. A quarter of the company's shares had been offered but the flotation would have passed unnoticed for most people, not just due to its size, but because two-thirds of the shares were allocated to the firm's directors and employees and to a few institutional investors carefully selected by placement agent Cazenove.

With his senior team in place, Brooke focused his attention on what he was good at: building relationships with the other investment houses. His years in the Foreign Office between 1955 and 1966 had certainly taught him that personal contacts can go a long way. Following the establishment of the firm's first fund in 1984, Candover had had the benefit of public exposure. With a trust publicly listed, the firm could move up a gear. Electra Investment Trust plc was already a well-established British VC investor and, in a bid to raise Candover's profile, Brooke once again called upon the services of his friend Stoddart and negotiated a partnership with Electra. In late 1985, the Electra Candover Direct Investment Plan was set up, collecting £260 million of commitments from thirty-six separate institutional investors in what was the largest LBO fund ever raised in the country. It dwarfed the UK's second largest fund, the one closed that same year by Citicorp Venture Capital (CVC) with a total £100 million of equity. Sixty per cent of the Electra Candover Plan's capital originated from Britain while the rest came from American investors such as General Electric's pension fund and insurance companies Prudential and Travelers.[22] With such a sizeable fund, Candover would be able to close more complex deals and build a reputation as an investor to contend with. In November, as he had announced the successful completion of the fund-marketing initiative, Brooke had proudly admitted that the stand-by facility's purpose was to promote large management buyouts requiring £200 million or even more in funds, including bank and intermediary finance. Its aim was also to speed up deal execution; it would address the primary drawback that the industry had faced until then: the need to set up a club of institutional investors each time an MBO was being financed.

The timing could not have been better; for the first time in its history, the UK had recorded over £1 billion worth of buyouts across 230 transactions. The view was that the industry would only grow stronger from there. The value of UK buyouts in 1985 was reported to have exceeded the combined total of the previous five years.[23] It might seem preposterous but as more and more MBO transactions were taking place and in view of the heavy use of leverage, commentators were already lamenting the climate of euphoria surrounding LBOs.[24] Let's hope these observers did not live long enough to witness the deal frenzy of the mid-2000s.

After only five years operating in a financial industry in which he had had no extensive previous exposure, Brooke had managed to turn his company into a credible buyout specialist and had set the pace to the industry's foray into more sizeable transactions. He had made it into the very exclusive club of venture capitalists. The strong economy and Thatcher's reforms would help the firm put the 1985 Fund to work.

Chapter 3 - A Small Club of Like-minded People

Just like their comrades across the Atlantic, throughout the 1980s the British LBO firms were constantly defining the rules of the game as they went along. Carve-outs, turnarounds, or re-engineerings as they were then called, syndicated deals, ever-larger transactions; anything seemed possible.

By the middle of the 1980s, a handful of venture capitalists had already imposed themselves as the emerging leaders of the nascent but fast-growing European buyout industry. Candover had been one of the very first pure buyout investors but by the mid-1980s new firms had followed suit. For instance, Citicorp Development Capital, a predecessor to Citicorp Venture Capital and the US bank's European LBO activities, had been founded in 1981; Schroder Ventures, Mercury Private Equity and Doughty Hanson had emerged in 1985, and Baring Capital Investors (later rebranded BC Partners) in 1986. The private equity arms of British banks HSBC and National Westminster had both executed their first buyout transactions in 1982. As mentioned, Barclays had a Development Capital division since 1980 and Midland Bank was equally active in that field through its Industrial Finance and Venture Capital subsidiaries. While it had done MBOs alongside Candover, Electra would not set up a separate buyout entity until 1989. The popularity of buyouts was not so surprising. It was easier to assess the potential of an established business than that of a start-up. Over the years, the growth of the leveraged buyout market would exceed that of the VC sector many times over.

On the European continent, even if no government was inclined to deregulate its financial industry as drastically as Britain had, several state-backed and private initiatives had taken shape.

Just across the Channel, Eurafrance, an investment firm, had seen the light in 1974. Its investment strategy was to take minority or controlling stakes in industrial companies in a hands-off manner. In 1983, it transformed itself into an investment fund, taking stakes into financial institutions like the French arm of Lazard, French insurer UAP, and various investment firms. Nowadays renamed Eurazeo, it executes both minority investments and buyouts. In 1974, in France as well, the very industrious Wendel family had set up a company, Compagnie Générale d'Industrie et de Participations (CGIP), following the forced nationalisation of their steel manufacturing activities by the French government. In the early 1980s, CGIP (later renamed Wendel) and Eurafrance were not specifically considering buyouts. Their structure was more that of a holding company, taking minority and controlling stakes in companies that they regarded as strategically well positioned for expansion. Several French banks had also established their in-house investment fund; Paribas was managing what would later become Paribas Affaires Industrielles (PAI) but it also played the role of a holding company. PAI would not raise its first buyout fund before 1999.

In Sweden, the Wallenberg family, part-owner of Stockholms Enskilda Bank, had spun out the investment arm of SEB, appropriately named Investor AB, in the 1970s. Investor AB had a similar investment strategy to its French counterparts, taking stakes in Swedish companies and funding their development. Packaging company Stora Enso, airline SAS, telecom giant Ericsson, and clearly SEB, all benefited from Investor AB's backing, but buyouts were not part of the investment firm's mission. It was only in 1994 that the Wallenbergs would set up a specific LBO firm: EQT.

The Flanders government, in the northern half of Belgium, created investment firm GIMV* in 1980 to provide capital to the Flemish industry. Whereas Wallonia, the southern region of Belgium, had been until the 1970s the economic engine of the country with traditional industries like steel manufacturing, Flanders was taking a more liberal, entrepreneurial approach to foster new segments such as automotive, chemicals and pharmaceuticals, eventually outpacing Wallonia in terms of wealth creation and economic performance. It was also in 1980 that

---

* Gewestelijke Investerings Maatschappij Vlaanderen

Flemish company Gevaert had started operating as an investment firm, taking stakes in publicly listed as well as private companies. But it was the Dutch market that seemed to take its cue from the UK. Gilde, for instance, was created in 1982 and would from day one act like a VC fund. Many other bank-sponsored or family-backed initiatives would see the light across Europe but the buyout revolution in most European countries would come ten to fifteen years later.

Indeed, a handful of investment firms had been set up on the Continent but none of these countries were experiencing the entrepreneurial innovation that was sweeping the UK's VC and buyout sectors. Industry data reveal that by mid-1987, while Britain only had a fifth as many VC firms as the US, it had over twice as many as France did and 4.5 times more than West Germany's. Its capital pool totalled $4.5 billion compared to $20 billion for the US, France's $750 million and West Germany's $500 million.[25]

Since 1979, Thatcher's government had resolutely unrolled its liberal economic agenda. In the mid-1980s, it had imposed a complete reform of the financial and banking industries. The deregulation of the London Stock Exchange and of all the professions living off it was introduced in October 1986. Called the 'Big Bang', it abolished the fixed minimum commissions charged by stockbrokers and opened access to the capital markets to all financial institutions, be they brokerage houses, merchant banks or investment managers. Frankly it was a bit of a misnomer as the deregulation process had been encouraged by the Bank of England for over three years by the time it was declared official. The Big Bang had more similarities with a slow-motion hatching than with a quick explosion. Regardless, it encouraged merchant banks to acquire or partner with stock exchange operators. And it would have far-reaching consequences by also opening the door to non-UK institutions. Increased competition forced pricing down and announced a wave of innovations. The stock market crash of October 1987 would only accelerate this transformation process. Over the following years, foreign banks, and in particular American ones, would revolutionise the cosy world of capital raising, stock trading and investment management in the City. Investment banks would merge with stockbrokers, and over time large international financial institutions like Citicorp, Deutsche Bank, UBS,

Merrill Lynch and JP Morgan would come to dominate the UK financial industry, replacing honourable names like Morgan Grenfell, S.G. Warburg, Fleming and Kleinwort. The blue-blooded old guard would be supplanted by the brash golden boys.

In November 1986, the Building Societies Act and the Financial Services Act were also passed by Parliament. Building societies were very much a British particularity. These mutual institutions often held local monopolies for the marketing and selling of mortgages. After the Acts were adopted, retail banks could offer mortgage loans and building societies could demutualise to take the public limited company (PLC) status and sell banking products. It led to a wave of consolidation across those two retail sectors of the financial industry in the late 1980s and throughout the 1990s. It also contributed to the biggest housing boom Britain had ever seen. Creativity and rivalry were two words that had never before been associated with mortgage lending. Whereas 55 per cent of British households were homeowners in 1979, fifteen years later 68 per cent of them would be. That was also helped by Thatcher's decision to sell low-rent public housing to their tenants at reduced valuations. House prices doubled relative to retail prices between 1982 and 1989, and housing transactions swelled from 1.2 million in 1981 to two million in 1988. The British population was getting richer.

The Big Bang and the two Acts of 1986 introduced competition and self-regulation to the country's financial services industry. They would be a tremendous boost for Britain's buyout industry, not just for deal financing, but also for fundraising. In fact, the US buyout industry was going through a phase of hysteria. Multi-billion-dollar deals were already the norm in North America by 1985-86, so US banks taking advantage of the UK deregulation would bring in a fresh dynamism from which the British economy and its buyout market would greatly benefit. By the late 1980s, the abolition of exchange controls that had taken place on 23 October 1979 was helping the City assume a leading role in the nascent internationalisation of the financial industry.

In 1986, the total PE market in the UK was still only worth £1.2 billion, representing approximately 310 transactions.[26] By that stage, Thatcher's Britain was showing encouraging signs of revival. A country that had started the decade as one of the poorest among the industrialised nations was displaying symptoms of revitalised hope. Across Europe,

Britain's dynamism and economic growth were shown as proofs that the neo-liberal model worked. After a painful set of reforms, GDP was expanding at a rate close to 5 per cent by the middle of the decade. By the summer of 1986, the annualised inflation rate was as low as 2.4 per cent. It was a temporary victory over the plague of the 1970s, but a victory nonetheless. The effects of the 1980–81 recession were long gone but investors were only just starting to believe that the government's liberal programme was finally working. Due to the ongoing restructuring of Britain's traditional industries such as textiles, mining and metallurgy, the country still had over three million unemployed by early 1986, representing more than 10 per cent of the working population. To many British people at the time, life remained hopelessly dire. However, as a sign that things were taking a turn for the better, while in the early 1980s buyout investors had primarily put money to work in restructuring situations, the second half of the decade was more favourable to expansion capital opportunities as the country was experiencing strong economic growth. Between 1982 and 1988, the annual rise in Britain's GDP had averaged 4 per cent thanks to the combination of a booming world economy and the deregulation of the country's industrial fabric. Even in Thatcher's Britain, it is fair to say that venture capitalists and buyout investors were not always the most popular bunch. As the economy was experiencing a major switch from broken industries and into the more dynamic and less regulated service sector, private equity investment often meant layoffs, restructuring and cost cutting. With the economy back on track though, the second half of the 1980s had the potential to give the industry a better image. LBOs of growing, healthy businesses were becoming more prevalent, and sophisticated financing from US banks made larger transactions possible.

Naturally, Candover and its peers would produce some incredible returns out of their mid-1980s funds. In such a positive setting, the Hoare Candover Exempt Trust was finding plenty of opportunities to go after. In 1985 alone, CIP had made sixteen investments including Caradon, the former building products division of Reed International acquired for £61 million,[27] which was the firm's largest transaction to date. Candover's NAV had reached £14 million at the end of 1985, a healthy 18 per cent annual increase, thanks in part to the realisation of its investment in

Famous Names on which it had returned 10 times its original equity after selling it to Imperial Tobacco in September 1985. The firm had even taken advantage of Thatcher's privatisation programme by acquiring strike-plagued warship yard Swan Hunter for £5 million in early 1986.[28] A year later, it had also financed the privatisation of Istel, an information technology division of the Rover Group in which more than 1,000 employees had been invited to invest alongside management and Kleinwort Benson, Candover, CVC and Thompson Clive,[29] initiating as a result a new form of MBO: the employee buyout.

To cope with the increasing deal flow, Candover recruited two young professionals who would, for most of the second half of the 1980s, be doing the grunt work of the investment process: financial analysis and valuation assessment. In September 1985, Colin Buffin was recruited from accountancy firm Deloitte, Haskins & Sells where he had worked in the audit, investigations and corporate finance departments. A 28-year-old chartered accountant and chemistry graduate from Oxford University, Buffin had the relevant training to carry out the analytical tasks required from venture capital investment. Again, in those days, VC investors carried out the simple role of equity finance provider to small and medium-sized enterprises (SMEs) and needed a solid understanding of financial management. In a similar vein, in January 1987, the firm recruited Marek Gumienny, a 28-year-old British national of Polish descent with an undergraduate degree in maths from Warwick University. Also a chartered accountant, Gumienny had spent the previous seven years with auditors Price Waterhouse. A bright individual with a knack for numbers, he would over time become Candover's top deal originator. For now he had to spend time proving that he had the analytical aptitude to execute transactions. Soon enough, he would move to the more noble trade of deal sourcing.

After several months on the road, in early 1986 Electra and Candover had a final closing for their Electra Candover Direct Investment Plan. But it would experience a very slow start, striving to find appropriate LBO targets. Throughout its first two years, the two fund managers would need to advertise in the financial press to raise awareness of their firepower. It would take until December 1986 for the fund to close its first deal: the £51.5 million buyout of Fairey Holdings Limited.[30] Brooke's knack for building a strong network from day one was showing its full benefit. That transaction was not sourced out of the blue: Fairey was the engineering division of Pearson plc where Brooke had spent a fair amount of time in his previous corporate life. Also, I referred to the fact that Candover's first Chairman was Angus Murray. What I did not specify was that Murray had been formerly Chairman of Fairey. Even though Murray had died in August 1982, that connection and Brooke's long spell at Pearson had enabled Candover to build a strong bond with the target's management team. In a sign that the 1985 Fund was getting some traction, in January 1987 Electra Candover Partners also acquired the UK paper activities of Bowater International plc.[31]

The year 1986 had been as active as the previous one, with Candover closing eighteen investments, including thirteen management buyouts in the UK, three US investments, one in Italy and one in the Netherlands. The firm's net assets had risen 27 per cent, to £18 million.[32] To cope with its own team expansion, the firm had moved to new offices on East Harding Street, within two hundred yards of the old premises. There was no looking back, Brooke and his team were taking full advantage of the ascending LBO trend. But the market was progressing slowly in the large buyout segment. For that reason, Brooke and Curran decided that given how successful the 1984 Hoare Candover fund had been, they should raise a similar investment vehicle to target smaller situations requiring tickets below the £10 million mark.

They launched the marketing campaign for the Candover 1987 Fund in March 1987. It was also at the time that they entered into joint ventures (JVs) to start investing more actively in West Germany and the Netherlands. In Germany, the investment firm partnered with London and Continental Bankers, a merchant bank partly controlled by local institution DG Bank, to form LCB-Candover. Recognising that the main continental market was almost untapped and offered the opportunity of a first-mover advantage for British LBO firms willing to make the jump, many of Candover's rivals were even more adventurous, with 3i opening its own Frankfurt office and Schroder Ventures raising a DM 140 million fund* to invest locally from Hamburg. In 1987, its first year of operation, Baring Capital opened permanent French and German outposts and

---

* DM = Deutsche Mark

raised an ECU 60 million fund* to invest on the Continent.[33] Publicly, Brooke acknowledged that MBOs remained a new idea in continental Europe so a JV was seen as the most prudent approach. He even announced a roadmap for similar structures in France, Scandinavia and Italy.[34] The Dutch JV partner had already sourced the £38.4 million buyout of cable maker NKF Holding BV in late 1986, a business that would be floated on the Amsterdam stock exchange in May 1988 with a healthy profit. And in December 1987, LCB-Candover would originate the DM 55 million Heidemann-Werke transaction. The firm's management had ambitious plans for Europe.

Post-1986, the highly visible Fairey and Bowater Paper deals made things easier to market the Electra Candover fund. The buyouts of Humberclyde Finance from the Australia and New Zealand Banking Group in September 1987, of professional services provider Hays and kitchen and bathroom furniture retailer MFI (in which Candover had taken a small £1 million syndicated ticket[35]) in November 1987, and of Bricom alongside Baring Capital in July 1988 all had a transaction value in excess of £200 million, turning Candover instantly into a major player. In particular, the acquisition from Asda of a 75 per cent stake in MFI for £750 million, led by CVC and Charterhouse, was Britain's largest buyout in 1987.

Across the industry, buyout fund managers were closing more sizeable deals, often worth hundreds of millions of pounds, such as the ones above or Schroder Ventures's £250 million LBO of Parker Pen in 1987, but the mega-transactions worth over £1 billion remained the hunting ground of the conglomerates. Hanson Trust's market capitalisation had increased ten-fold since 1980 to reach an impressive £2.5 billion by the middle of the decade. The industrial holding managed a total of 67,000 employees. Despite the larger deal values, its Chairman, by then Lord Hanson, and his business partner and co-founder Sir Gordon White (Chairman of the group's US subsidiary Hanson Industries Inc.), had not slowed down the pace and would go on to acquire Imperial Tobacco in 1986 and Consolidated Goldfields in 1989, thus assembling one of Britain's ten largest listed companies. By the end of the 1980s, Hanson had operations in the retail, building materials,

---

* ECU = European Currency Unit, precursor to the euro

chemicals, paper, mining and tobacco sectors. It was at the pinnacle of its reign. Thorn EMI itself was now active in TV broadcasting, retail, defence, music recording and consumer electronics. Similar organisations were equally acquisitive in America, with General Electric, ITT Corporation and Tyco being the most visible. Their power would eventually fade, but by 1990 industrial conglomerates were the kings of deal-making.

Hays had turned out to be a good investment for the firm, but it had been a bit of a lucky escape. In late 1987, Candover had backed the company's chief executive Ronnie Frost together with over 100 senior managers and staff members to buy the business off their owners Kuwait Investment Office for £255 million.[36] With a strong economy throughout 1988 and the first half of 1989, Candover had pushed for a listing on the LSE in October 1989, probably anticipating that the business might not perform so well in the widely expected recession. The IPO, valuing the company at £400 million, had taken place on the day the UK's Chancellor of the Exchequer Nigel Lawson had resigned, shaking the stock market's confidence and leaving Candover's stake in the hands of the underwriters.[37] Candover was home and dry. Hays's stock would linger below its introductory price for most of the next two years.

Despite such occasional inconvenience, by investing in large companies across a whole range of sectors the Electra Candover fund would firmly position the company as a leading buyout player in Britain. Candover's success was not fortuitous. It stemmed from a disciplined investment strategy followed by the original quartet. As already mentioned, Brooke had strong commercial skills and Curran had an indispensable operational mind but Symonds and Fairservice were equally relevant in their respective roles. Finance Director Symonds was an extremely calm and assured individual. Sharp yet humble, very analytical and soft-spoken, it was easy to understand why Brooke had hired him. He fitted the Candover profile perfectly. As for Fairservice, he had led or co-led several important transactions for the firm. He was a hard-nosed investor. Each of the firm's top executives was excellent in his role and respected the others for what they brought to the business. People who knew them at the time confirm that they worked jointly for the good of Candover and with the same objective of turning it into a trailblazer of the UK buyout industry. By the end of the decade, it was obvious that they had achieved their common goal.

At the lower end, the small-MBOs-dedicated Candover 1987 Fund had managed to raise £30 million. It was meant to take advantage of the thriving UK economy and its beneficial impact on entrepreneurial businesses. It looked like an obvious decision. In 1987, Britain's GDP had risen by 4.8 per cent and was to rise by a further 4.3 per cent the following year. Regrettably for Brooke and his team, the Thatcher miracle would suffer a setback; recession was just around the corner. The economy would go into reverse between 1989 and 1992, forcing many small British enterprises out of business. While the 1985 Fund had invested in large companies capable of using their market clout to survive, many of the 1987 vintage's investee businesses would require considerable efforts to stay afloat. The fund would take over fifteen years to be entirely realised and would eventually be closed in November 2002, five years after its originally intended termination date, yielding a return not much better than what its investors would have earned if they had placed their money in a savings account.[38] It would be a sobering experience for the Candover team. They were better off sticking to medium-sized enterprises if they could manage to structure more complex financing.

And more complex financing was exactly what the LBO industry had introduced in the mid 1980s. Led as one would expect by the more innovative and aggressive American market, a new type of debt had been coined over there to speed up the structuring process and enable buyout firms to complete larger acquisitions. Since 1985, leveraged transactions exceeding $1 billion were common practice in America thanks to the widespread use of high-yield bonds. Those were loans that could be raised more readily than conventional borrowing and made hostile takeovers possible. Importantly, such bonds were subordinated to the conventional asset-backed debt, meaning that in case of default of payment by the borrower, they would be redeemed only after all the secured debt-holders had been repaid. Because their quality and creditworthiness often proved questionable, those high-interest-bearing instruments soon came to be known as 'junk bonds'. That period culminated in November 1988 with a very public takeover battle to gain control of food and tobacco manufacturing giant RJR Nabisco. Buyout pioneer KKR had eventually prevailed thanks to the generous application of junk bonds.

The UK market had not made use of them, but by the late 1980s it had witnessed the development of another US-imported subordinated high-yield debt product called 'mezzanine', a form of hybrid financing between term loans and equity which gave the right to its holders to a share of the equity upside via instruments called warrants. Banks had pushed the product to help LBO groups structure deals more efficiently. Many of the largest transactions completed in the country between 1987 and 1989 were partly financed by mezzanine. In the summer of 1988, industrial group Bricom had been acquired for £405 million with the help of £30 million of mezz. In a sign that the UK market was overheating, the Americans had brought in some of their most offensive business practices: in mid-1989, one-year-old investment bank Wasserstein Perella had fought hard to acquire Britain's third largest food retailer Gateway in a £2.16 billion highly leveraged and hostile acquisition process, partly financed as one would expect with a £300 million mezzanine tranche. Bruce Wasserstein, who had left US institution First Boston in 1988 to set up his own M&A boutique, had been one of KKR's close advisers on the RJR Nabisco buyout only a few months earlier, so applying the same wheeling and dealing to eventually gain control of Gateway would have come naturally to him.

The availability of easier, quicker debt structuring had had an immediate impact on the size of transactions: in 1987, the total value of LBOs in the UK had climbed 170 per cent on prior year to reach £3.25 billion but volumes had only risen 7 per cent,[39] implying that the average deal size had been multiplied by 2.5 times to £10 million. Deal value for the year 1988 had reached almost £5 billion of MBOs and Management Buy-Ins (MBIs) – a term used to reflect the fact that external operating executives were brought in to help the VC firm acquire and manage the target – but as clouds gathered over the economy, 1989 had finally experienced a more modest increase of 3 per cent in volume even if the unusually big Gateway LBO had pushed total deal value up a further 50 per cent.[40] In this context, Candover saw its net asset value rise 250 per cent between the end of 1985 and December 1989 thanks to a long list of acquisitions and portfolio realisations carried out over that period.[41] The firm generated twice its original equity investment on the disposals of European trailer rental business Rentco, Dutch company NKF and agricultural finance specialist Humberclyde and was even reported to have made almost 20 times on the listing of Rechem.[42] In 1989 alone, the group had made seven acquisitions and the same number of exits. Brooke and his team had generally stayed clear of pushy M&A practices even if in January 1989 they had funded with the assistance of £40 million of mezz the largest Candover-led transaction to date, the £265 million buyout of the British Printing Corporation; a decision they would come to regret.

When Thatcher had come to power in 1979, the UK's general government expenditure* represented over 46 per cent of the country's GDP. By the time she left in 1991, it stood at 38 per cent. Through her programme of privatisation and deregulation, she had managed to scale back the influence of the state in Britain's economy. Despite her failure to win a vote of confidence from her own Members of Parliament and her forced departure in late 1990, her turnaround job was done. Between 1980 and 1989, the laggard of Europe had turned into a model of economic success, generating an average annual growth rate in excess of 2.7 per cent, the highest among the largest European industrialised countries, and half a percentage point above the OECD average.[43] The country would however suffer a great deal from the 1990–92 economic crisis, showing that its success was still based on fragile foundations and could not be taken for granted. Unemployment, which had almost reached 12 per cent in the mid-1980s, would be back down to 7 per cent by the time Thatcher left office in 1990,[44] the shift from old industries like coal mining to modern ones like pharmaceuticals and professional services having nearly been completed. Compared to the EEC average unemployment rate of 8.4 per cent in 1990,[45] Britain's seemed almost acceptable.

The whole economy was reaping the benefits of Thatcher's liberal reforms but strikes in specific sectors were as violent and prolonged in the 1980s as they had been in the previous decade. Old habits were proving resilient. Industrial action affected most sectors of

---

* An aggregate of spending by central government and local authorities

the economy and often anticipated deregulation or privatisation of old monopolies: steel workers in 1980, miners in 1984 and 1985, telecoms and postal employees in 1987 and 1988 respectively. Still, the country's attitude towards money was changing fast. High earners, who faced an 83 per cent top rate on their income until 1979, would be taxed at a maximum of 40 per cent from 1988 onward. A rate that was less than half what it was ten years earlier was considered so fair by the majority of the population that it remained the same until the Labour government of Gordon Brown decided otherwise in 2008. As for the British population as a whole, a staggering 25 per cent of Brits owned shares in a publicly listed company in 1989 compared to less than 8 per cent when Thatcher had come to power a decade earlier. One of the poorest countries of Western Europe in 1979 was becoming a haven for capitalists. When it came to money, over a ten-year period Britain had gone through a cultural revolution. That could only be a good thing for the buyout industry. I have already touched upon some of Candover's IPOs of portfolio companies, but with the likes of Caradon, floated in 1987, Fairey and Rechem in 1988 and Hays in 1989, the list was getting longer.

Although it was not Brooke's cup of tea, the firm occasionally funded turnaround strategies. In May 1989, Candover had backed engineering veteran John Crathorne, a former executive at Thorn EMI's domestic appliance division, in his buyout of cooker manufacturer Stoves. The company was producing low-end cookers in a declining market. It turned over £17 million but was heavily loss-making. On the face of it, it was a non-starter but Crathorne would eventually manage to transform the company into an upmarket producer, tripling its sales and making it very profitable. A business acquired for £10 million would float for £40 million six years later.[46] It was a showcase portraying MBOs as rejuvenating platforms that could now and again inject new life into lame ducks.

Confident that Britain was on the right track and that its industrial makeup offered many more buyout opportunities, as the Electra Candover fund was close to being fully invested Brooke, Curran and Fairservice embarked on another fundraising, the fourth in just six years! Given that the Electra Candover fund had been easier to invest than it had originally appeared, the team again decided to target the large-scale LBO segment. As of 31 December 1988, the company had reported a net asset value of almost £35 million,[47] three times CIP's valuation on the day of its IPO, and it had executed over fifty transactions since its inception. Its clout was now unquestionable. With an original target set conservatively at £200 million in late 1988, within eight months the fundraising process for the Candover 1989 Fund was completed. At closing, Candover Partners Limited (CPL), the fund manager or general partner (GP) of the Candover Group, had attracted £319 million of commitments, including £20 million from CIP. The latter was confirming its position as the cornerstone investor. Brooke and his partners had raised the largest buyout fund in Europe, and they had done so without attaching the brand of a Hoare Govett or Electra to theirs. The firm had demonstrated that it was a credible stand-alone participant in the buyout sector. It was beyond expectations but not undeserved. The second largest buyout-dedicated fund was the much smaller £200 million facility raised by Charterhouse that same year. Irrespective of the shaky economic outlook at the time, management was quietly confident that the larger end of the market was where the best deals could be made and had set a minimum equity ticket of £5 million. They had spent several months on the road and would have noticed that the larger size of some of the deals executed in partnership with Electra were of tremendous help. In a sign that the group was becoming ever more international, only just over half of the new fund's investors were British. Almost a third of the funds originated from North America.[48] More interestingly, although the firm continued to target the fast-growing UK market, it was already publicly stating its ambition to invest approximately one-third of the 1989 Fund in key European markets such as France, Germany and the Netherlands, the latter being viewed as the most active continental country for management buyouts.[49] LCB-Candover had opened an office in Frankfurt while in France the group had elected to act as an investor in Ciclad, a £31 million facility set up with local development capital organisation Institut de Développement Industriel (IDI) and French bank Crédit Lyonnais to finance small MBOs in the country.[50] Brooke and his deputy Curran were eager to have an impact outside the UK and to lead the LBO revolution on the Continent.

Between 1980 and 1989, consumer prices in Britain had risen by 89 per cent,[51] averaging only 6.5 per cent per annum, but it was about to change. Unfortunately, the fast growth environment of the second half of the decade had brought back the spectre of inflation, which dramatically increased in 1990 as the country's economy, together with the rest of the world, started to dip again. On one specific parameter, Britain still lingered behind its close European partners. Although the country's GDP per head was slowly bridging the gap, it would take another ten years before the UK would fully catch up with France and Germany on that front. Speaking to people in today's Britain, you cannot help but think that the population suffers from collective amnesia as Thatcher is more frequently remembered for being a ruthless autocratic politician rather than a courageous reformer. It is correct that many people suffered from the consequences of her high-handed economic policies, but she was trying to remodel a welfare system that had been in place for thirty years. Structurally, the country was broken. It had to be rebuilt from the ground up. Politically, her uncompromising approach made her many enemies. Economically, her neo-liberal programme brought the country back from the dead. Regardless of what one thinks of her, her legacy in the financial sector lives on. The merits of open competition across the various financial sectors are rarely disputed, even if issues about the efficacy of self-regulation and conflicts of interest are frequently raised. In an ironic twist of history, as modern Britain tries to forget the thriftless Blair and Brown era, Prime Minister David Cameron, elected in May 2010, introduced the broadest set of budget cuts – primarily to scale back down the size of the state – that the country has seen since the 1980s. Thatcherism has slowly but surely crept back into modern British politics.

Just like Thatcher had put the country's economic train back on the fast-growth, moderate-inflation track, Brooke's visionary strategy had steadily placed Candover at the forefront of the LBO industry. Less than a decade after setting up shop, he was practically crowned the 'buyout king of Britain'.[52] But he would be the first one to admit that without the financial and operational support of his institutional backers, and in particular Electra, his business would never have been able to become such a dominant force. As the firm was celebrating its tenth anniversary, it would soon be Curran's responsibility to make sure that it remained a market leader.

CURRAN'S REIGN

Chapter 4 - A Period of Transition

In the first few years of the 1990s, the world economy was attempting to digest the excess of the 'roaring eighties'. As if that was not enough of a challenge, Britain had just gone through its own political crisis. After eleven years in power, Thatcher had been forced to resign in November 1990 following a coup from within her own political party. John Major had succeeded her as Prime Minister at a time when the economy was taking a dive.

Data from the Confederation of British Industry showed that between April 1990 and April 1991, investment flows in the industrial sector had collapsed by 20 per cent. The country's GDP would sustain negative growth in 1991 and 1992. And to top it all, the rate of inflation had reached 9.3 per cent in 1990.

To add insult to injury, the buyout industry had reached adolescence and was finding the experience painful. After almost ten years of ever bigger deals, it was feeling the double blow of the economic recession and the junk bond hangover in the US. The decade had been a fantastic period of sustained development and deal-making on both sides of the Atlantic. Many US buyout firms had seen the light during the LBO boom of the 1980s: Bain Capital and Hicks Muse were both founded in 1984; Blackstone and Carlyle were created in 1985 and 1987 respectively. By 1990 though, in the face of rising interest rates, financing had dried up across the sector and several multi-billion-dollar buyouts had folded under their debt burden or were striving to stay afloat.

In a press release issued on 13 March 1990 regarding the group's preliminary results for the 1989 fiscal year, Peter Wreford had rightly explained in his Chairman's statement that the high levels of debt and excessive valuations witnessed in 1989 had helped demonstrate the superiority of Candover's business model and 'more cautious approach'. He had also emphasized that high interest rates and an unstable economy gave further backing to the idea that MBOs needed 'to be prudently financed and priced'.[53] Despite their pioneering streak, Brooke, Wreford and Curran had not failed to notice that their trade was complex and still relatively novel. It required financial prudence, thorough diligence and professional excellence, all trademarks on which the firm would establish its stature over the next decade.

They had shied away from the most aggressive methods introduced in the late 1980s although they were still expected to suffer from the backlash. In 1990, the total value of UK LBOs plummeted 60 per cent to £2.8 billion.[54] That same year, CIP's net asset value suffered its first drop since the company's flotation.[55] To confront that unexpected obstacle and position itself for the future, the firm strengthened its internal operations, beefing up its team by hiring various non-executive directors and administrative staff, including a new company secretary.[56]

It is in that bleak context that in January 1991 Curran took the helm of the still relatively young firm and became Chief Executive. Brooke took over from Wreford the role of Chairman in order to focus on promoting the firm and take on other challenges unrelated to the buyout industry. The first few years of Curran's reign would be marred by very austere market conditions. Between 1990 and 1994, deal volumes in the UK were flat. Debt finance was scarce and expensive. A period of recession, from late 1990 to early 1992, was followed by a few months of weak growth until early 1993. By the spring of 1991, the country had two million jobless workers and a rate of unemployment of 8 per cent; by the first quarter of 1993, that rate exceeded 10.5 per cent.

While the recession was raging, CPL closed seven UK deals in 1991. Through its various joint-ventures, it also completed six transactions overseas although some of its rivals were already establishing a strong leadership thanks to their permanent international offices: that same year CVC led the LBO league table on the Continent by executing eighteen MBOs worth almost £900 million via its offices in Paris, Frankfurt, Madrid, Milan and Amsterdam. Schroder Ventures had come second with fifteen acquisitions for a total of £340 million. 3i, which focused on smaller MBOs and early stage ventures, had invested in thirty businesses in France alone.[57]

Back in the UK, Candover was still investing the 1987 Fund. Its deal log included a £2 million funding for the husband-and-wife-managed underwear store chain Knickerbox and £13 million for electronic component maker Cambridge Capacitors.[58] But Candover was also looking at larger targets for its 1989 Fund. In allocating that bigger fund, Fairservice was proving very active. After acquiring food mixer manufacturer Kenwood Limited from Thorn EMI (proof if needed that Brooke's corporate connections still served their purpose!) for £54.6 million in September 1989,[59] he was also involved in the £17 million takeover of lawnmower manufacturer Atco Qualcast from Blue Circle in December 1992.[60]

The economic slump was fast becoming the industry's first major test since its inception a decade earlier. Two very large UK transactions, both in the retail sector, would send a warning to all the buyout actors that handling high levels of financial gearing could be extremely damaging. In 1989, the £630 million delisting of 200-outlet kitchen and bathroom retailer Magnet, valuing the business at 13 times earnings before tax[61] in the notoriously volatile retail sector, and the aforementioned hostile acquisition of 670-store food supermarket chain Gateway, had been financed with significant leverage.

With its Finance Director having departed within months of the MBO amid claims of deficient accounting systems and with sales cut in half between 1988 and 1992, Magnet had ended up in receivership in December 1992 and its key lenders, led by Bankers Trust, had taken control of the business after almost £700 million of loan write-offs, including the backlog of unpaid interest.[62] For the original equity backers, the company's chairman and chief executive Tom Duxbury among them, it was an ordeal worth forgetting.

The Gateway story would be even more extravagant. Faced with stiff competition from its key rivals Sainsbury's and Tesco and unable to service the £1.4 billion worth of borrowings sitting in Isosceles (the investment vehicle set up for tax structuring purposes), the business would go through several CEOs, thousands of lay-offs, a break-up strategy with the disposals of its Northern Irish and US assets, and three refinancings in as many years, but would still be a crushing wipeout for its investors after the banks had taken control in April 1993. New York-based investment firm Wasserstein Perella, for which it was the very first LBO in Europe, owned approximately 40 per cent of the company and lost over $300 million.[63] 3i had to write down its equity stake and mezzanine holding, and other players like minority buyout specialists Mercury Asset Management and Globe Investment Trust had no choice but to recognise the loss in their books.

Because of these troubled LBOs and the continuing economic paralysis, by the fall of 1992 the Candover 1989 Fund still had one-third of its commitments to be invested and it was struggling to find suitable companies to back, as Brooke stated in his half-year-results announcement. The level of activity in buyout market was in decline, but the Candover team was demonstrating its resilience by making several acquisitions like those of recruitment service provider Blue Arrow for £34 million in June 1991 and of book publisher Orion for £4.25 million in June 1992. The 1989 Fund helped the firm carry out several prestigious deals, but as for the 1985 Electra Candover fund, they were generally executed in partnership with other investors. The firm closed two LBOs beside CINVen: oilfield service specialist Expro International in July 1992 and, six months later, the £400 million acquisition of contract catering service provider Gardner Merchant from hospitality group Forte. The latter was Britain's largest buyout that year and the first with a transaction value exceeding £300 million since the beaming days of 1989. Via its 1991 vintage, CPL also took part with L&G Ventures in the country's largest buyout of 1993: the £282 million acquisition of UK private label manufacturer of household and personal care products McBride from its parent British Petroleum.[64] In March 1994, as he was announcing somewhat disappointing annual results for 1993, Brooke rightly predicted that many companies would be rationalising their interests and disposing of businesses that did not fit with their core activities. He could see that more opportunities were coming Candover's way. The firm had closed five deals in 1993; it would execute four in 1994. The harvest was fabulous and it owed a lot to the UK's brightening economy. Thanks to so much activity, the firm's NAV kept rising, reaching £60 million in December 1992 and almost £70 million by

December 1993. In the nine years since its IPO, CIP had procured a 22 per cent compound annual growth rate in net assets.

In many instances, the buyout industry was able to take advantage of the stock market recovery. Because the context remained unpredictable, the intention of LBO groups was primarily to improve efficiency and margins swiftly and to exit as soon as practicable. In July 1992, Candover had introduced Kenwood and window manufacturer Anglian Group, a business it had co-owned with Legal & General Ventures since late 1990, to the LSE. Both had generated substantial capital gains for the firm,[65] even if due to the uncertain economic and stock market situation prevailing at the time they had received a derisory response from individual investors, leaving most shares with the City underwriters. Many PE fund managers had bought underachieving assets in the middle of the recession and were benefitting as the economy was showing signs of recovery. Best friends CINVen and Candover executed numerous IPOs including those of Midland Independent Newspapers in March 1994 and Expro in March 1995, both after less than three years in portfolio. CPL would even act faster in its buyout of mobile telecom equipment maker Vero, another one of Fairservice's deals completed in collaboration with Mercury Development Capital: acquired from cables and construction group BICC for £33 million in April 1994,[66] it was floated for more than £100 million in September 1995 thanks to solid revenue growth and operating margin increase in the interval.[67] Not bad for an eighteen-month holding period! And Candover was not unique in following that approach. For instance, in July 1987 CINVen had acquired contract catering service provider Compass and had listed the business in December 1988.

Several of these rushed floats occurring in an uncertain climate, the post-IPO performance was not always a great marketing statement in support of MBOs. The shares of both Midland Independent Newspapers and furniture specialist MFI would show poor returns for several years after their financial sponsors had sold out. The newspaper group, acquired originally in 1991 for £125 million from American publisher Ralph Ingersoll, had been tightly managed ahead of its £200 million float thirty months later, but there was simply little operational upside left to support the share price.[68] As for the kitchen-to-bathroom furniture retailer, it was heavily indebted. Although it had survived the recession thanks to a refinancing, a deferral of debt repayments and strong management,[69] its July 1992 listing had occurred in the most inhospitable of economic environments, leaving no room to manoeuvre for its executive team.

The buyout experts were taking advantage of the booming stock markets and the growing interest from the public in owning shares: Candover had floated four companies on the LSE in 1994 and six listings would also take place the following year.[70] One noteworthy exit was the £100 million flotation of chemical company Inspec in March 1994: acquired from BP eighteen months earlier for £40 million, it enabled 85 per cent of the workforce, those who owned shares in the business, to also benefit from Inspec's improved trading.[71] Nowadays such 'quick flips', as they are called, raise questions about the value-added contribution of the private equity backer, but the prosperous economy had been of great assistance for CPL, helping the fund manager create significant value for its investors in a fairly short time. But it would be wrong to assume that that kind of expeditious portfolio management process was the privilege of the public market. The firm had realised fast trade exits too, for example by turning around loss-maker Atco Qualcast and selling it to German power tool maker Robert Bosch in September 1995 after less than three years in ownership, or by riding the economic recovery with motorway service company Pavilion and disposing of it after a forty-month holding period in April 1995 thanks to a £125 million bid from TV-to-leisure conglomerate Granada.

Candover occasionally played a different role from the usual operational improvement and cash management expert. Because the early 1990s recession was so prolonged, it proved an ideal time to put in place consolidation strategies. The UK hotel industry was very fragmented and was suffering throughout the down cycle. CPL partnered with John Jarvis, former Chairman and Chief Executive of hotel chain Hilton International, to back a roll-up strategy. Between 1990 and 1996, the firm and its co-investors funded Jarvis Hotels's acquisitions of ailing competitors, including those of the Embassy hotels from Allied Lyons and of the Resort Hotels group. It would be one of Candover's biggest capital development activities at the time, funded by the 1989 Fund alongside Electra, Charterhouse and Kleinwort Benson Development Capital, and a high profile build-up.[72]

Confident that it had learned a new trick, Candover's management would later back another executive in a similar build-up strategy. In July 1996, the firm would acquire £30 million worth of assets from engineering group Wellman, subsequently renamed Cork Industries, to support Nigel McCorkell, former Deputy Chairman of aerospace and electronics group Meggitt. That one would not go as smoothly, with the company spending the first year without a CEO for instance, but it would nevertheless prove that the buyout firm was able to play a consolidator role when given the chance.

Across the industry, the performance of portfolio companies was negatively impacted by the subdued economic growth between 1989 and early 1993, which affected the rate of returns for the vintage buyout funds of the late 1980s. As a consequence, the early 1990s observed the development of a more professional and systematic due diligence process to evaluate investment opportunities. Accountancy firms set up separate internal Transaction Services departments to help buyout decision-makers carry out thorough examinations of several years of management accounts and business plan projections. That move did not just benefit financial sponsors; the audit firms applied the same method when servicing their corporate clients. Similarly, law firms extended the scope of their due diligence work, adapting it to specific sectors, covering everything from the terms of commercial agreements to intellectual property rights and employment contracts. By the mid-1990s, LBO shops would have a vast team of advisers supporting them in their analysis of acquisition opportunities.

Gradually, management assessments were also outsourced to specialist firms. And after an eventful fifteen-year history, the UK buyout industry had developed a club of serial entrepreneurs, meaning individuals whose operational competence the Candovers and CVCs of this world could call upon when they looked at specific sectors. Ex-Hanson Trust or William Holdings for instance, those experienced operating executives would be brought in as CEOs, COOs or more rarely as non-executive directors. Management buy-ins had become more prevalent, management buyouts more carefully evaluated. Almost on a systematic basis, Finance Directors were replaced by a seasoned cash flow manager and cost-cutter while the rest of the senior executive team was regularly supplemented. Going forward, transactions would almost invariably be a hybrid between MBIs and MBOs, tastefully termed BIMBOs.* Operational expertise was important, but so was the intimate knowledge of the business.

The buyout industry had reached maturity. That standardisation of the due diligence procedure had two benefits for the likes of Candover: it helped them reduce the risk of making poor investments; it also speeded up the time necessary to evaluate an investment opportunity, and even helped prepare for the transition post-completion with the implementation of an integration plan. Where buyout funds used to take up to six months to diligence a target, they were now able to deliver a bid in half the time. It was becoming a competitive advantage in an industry that was more aggressive and cut-throat by the day. Every so often Candover, CINVen and Charterhouse were bidding against each other in competitive auctions as they each had fund commitments of £300 million or more to put to work. The days of co-operation and syndication between them were fast disappearing.

Even though Brooke and his team had taken a more prudent approach to buyout investing than the one adopted by many of their rivals, in particular those who had backed the Magnet and Gateway take-privates, the firm's portfolio was still shaken by the recession. Following some unfortunate investment decisions like the failure of bridal and women's clothing retailer Berkertex, acquired for £21.6 million in mid-1986 alongside Electra and Globe but gone bust in September 1992, the equally disastrous debt-laden MBO of the British Printing Corporation from dodgy media mogul Robert Maxwell in early 1989, which had eventually required additional equity injections from the Candover 1989 Fund and from co-investor Electra,[73] or the underperforming £140 million buyout of cider-maker Gaymer executed in early 1992, CPL would be a strong user of due diligence services in the years ahead. Gaymer had been acquired from beverage group Allied Lyons by Candover, CINVen and Legal & General. The close bond that Curran had built with Allied Lyons when buying off them their hotel assets together with John Jarvis had helped the firm win the battle for Gaymer.

---

* BIMBO = Buy-In Management Buy-Out

Despite that privileged relationship, because of years of underinvestment, a weak 12 per cent share of the UK cider market far behind its rivals Bulmer's 47 per cent and Taunton's 36 per cent, and the poor marketing and strategic skills of Gaymer's management team, the performance of the company post-buyout had been lacklustre. Sold for £109 million to drinks distributor Matthew Clark in October 1994, the consortium had only just scraped a profit thanks to the redemption of their loans and dividend payouts.[74]

In parallel to making big buyouts, the firm had also decided to continue to participate at the small end of the market. In order to take advantage of such opportunities, CPL had taken over twelve months to raise its 1991 Fund, with final commitments of £37.5 million, by September 1992. Whereas the 1989 Fund had a stated minimum equity ticket of £5 million, the 1991 vintage was prepared to go as low as £1 million. Brooke openly stated that the fund could well invest in the western region of Germany.[75] Faithful to his word, in January 1995, the fund would take a 40 per cent stake in German logistic service provider Wohlfarth.[76] In 1994, the firm had also taken a stake beside CINVen and BC Partners in Dutch animal nutrition company Nutreco, Europe's largest buyout that year. After a prosperous holding period, the company would be listed on the Amsterdam Stock Exchange in the summer of 1997.

Only a year after closing the 1991 vintage, Candover was back on the fundraising trail once again. As Brooke had announced in his Chairman's statement to the 1993 half-year results, the 1989 vintage was over 75 per cent invested and they had therefore embarked on a successor fund.[77] The underlying prospects of the existing portfolio looked strong, but it was a somewhat risky move. The firm had exited very few of its 1989 Fund's investments at that stage and many investee companies were finding it hard to improve profitability due to the anaemic economic growth. Brooke and Curran were being cautious, though, and the target had been set at £200 million to £300 million, with a proposed CIP contribution of £30 million to £40 million.[78]

Working with managers to implement cost-cutting and productivity enhancements in order for the investment portfolio to provide maximum support to the fundraising initiative, the Candover team's patience would be put through the mill. Despite the tangible economic recovery in the second half of 1993 and in 1994, the fund would not see a final closing until February 1995. It had taken twenty-one months for Candover to raise its sixth fund, testing Brooke's determination, and no doubt putting to contribution the intensive military training that Curran had gained during his days at Sandhurst. The fickle marketplace had forced the duo to go round a wearisome assault course, leading to several postponements of the final closing. With commitments of £307.5 million, the fundraising had for sure occurred in very painful circumstances but had nonetheless exceeded its original target. However, when looking at it more closely, it was apparent that with a £70 million commitment from CIP, the firm had been compelled to increase its own equity pledge.[79] The lack of traction from the investment community had led Brooke and Curran to call upon CIP to make up for the difference. A similar approach would be used many years later for the launch of the firm's tenth fund, with devastating consequences.

Brooke and Curran had probably hoped that the 1994 Fund would exceed the size of the 1989 vintage. But the recession was still fresh in people's minds. Also, it was the first fundraising since Brooke had left the CEO position to Curran. In the end Candover's management had to settle for a more modest but still very respectable amount. The 1994 Fund brought the firm to the level achieved by its competitors Morgan Grenfell and Charterhouse, each managing a £300 million fund at the time, and only marginally less than the £350 million being managed by British bank Baring.[80]

According to the Private Placement Memorandum (PPM), the main marketing document of any new fundraising process, Candover could in principle invest its 1994 Fund over the next five years. In reality, because the British economy went through a period of strong revival from 1994 onwards, commitments were drawn down in half the time between January 1995 and the summer of 1997. The firm was still investing principally in the lower end of the mid-market segment, meaning in companies with an enterprise value (EV) comprised between £10 million and £100 million, but it was frequently taking aim at much larger entities. Its takeover of Newmond, William Holdings's building product activities, in December 1996 and of transmission tower operator Crown Castle International, led by Fairservice in February 1997,[81] were forays into the £200 million-plus segment of the market. Obviously, because of the equity tickets involved CPL was forced to carry out these deals in collaboration with other investors. Candover's investment partners, Alpinvest and Electra had contributed to the £360 million Newmond buyout,[82] and Crown Castle had been acquired for £230 million from the BBC in collaboration with US-based Castle Tower Corporation and French transmission tower operator TDF.[83] While so far they had been exceptions, these large deals were about to become the norm.

Just because it was evolving into an influential investment firm does not imply that Candover did not take part in more exciting and quirky ventures. In January 1995, it invested £7 million in the buyout of successful British firm studios Shepperton Studios, which had just produced the big hit *Four Weddings and a Funeral*. In that £12 million deal, the LBO firm was backing two British film producers and directors who over the years had become hot property in Hollywood. The two brothers, Ridley and Tony Scott, directors of *Alien* and *Top Gun* respectively, invested £1 million alongside Candover.[84] For the first transaction of its 1994 Fund,[85] one of the country's most renowned buyout specialists had partnered with two of the most acknowledged British film producers.

Although the firm continued to invest in conjunction with other PE houses, it was now taking a more senior role in most of the transactions it completed. It was common back then for a buyout investor, including Candover, not to hold any representation on the target's board of directors, especially in the case of syndicated deals where it had only been brought in as a co-investor. With the 1994 Fund, CPL was keen to act as lead investor and to have board representation. That would be the norm for all subsequent funds.

The fast expansion of the buyout industry in the UK during that time owes a lot to the share-ownership culture that Thatcher had elicited via her privatisation process a decade earlier. LBO shops took enormous advantage of the stock markets' increasing liquidity. In 1995 alone, Candover invested £55 million in eight transactions and sold ten investee businesses, four to a trade buyer but more interestingly six had taken place through a flotation. The firm's net asset value had risen annually by an astonishing 21.5 per cent between 1985 and 1995; over the same period, the FTSE All-Share Index had risen at less than half that pace. Between 1980 and 1995, Candover had organised deals worth an aggregate value of approximately £3 billion.[86] The firm, and the whole buyout industry by the same token, could no longer be ignored or considered an irrelevant segment of the financial world. In 1996 alone, an estimated 40 per cent of IPOs in the UK would come from firms backed by PE investors. Private equity was now part of the financial establishment.

Famed deal-making sometimes brought controversy. In June 1996, Jarvis Hotels was floated on the LSE for close to £140 million. Within two weeks, Candover had chosen to sell its 25 per cent stake to sponsors UBS and SBC Warburg.[87] Of course there was nothing improper with the move, but it had caused a drop in the company's stock price from 180 pence to 156 pence, negatively affecting small individual shareholders who had bought shares at the introductory price of 175 pence. Luckily for the fund manager, in that instance underwriters UBS and Warburg were the ones taking all the heat for supposedly having misled small investors. It did not look good. After the Hays incident seven years earlier, it was the second time that individual shareholders were getting burnt on a Candover-backed IPO.

Only a year later though, the group would come under pressure once more for the highly controversial quick flip it had realised on the Eversholt deal. Eversholt was a rolling stock business – leasing equipment to the train operating companies – that had been acquired in early 1996 as part of the government's rationalisation of British Rail. Through that privatisation process, Candover and its consortium, including Electra Fleming, Alpinvest and Advent among others, had paid £580 million for a business that was rumoured to be making over £100 million in Earnings Before Interest and Tax (EBIT).[88] In what would become one of John Major's biggest business scandals, his government was accused of selling businesses on the cheap in order to finance tax cuts ahead of the upcoming elections. It was also pointed out in the press that Candover Investments plc had been a donor to the Tory Party on several occasions in the past.[89] Rubbing salt in the wound, in February 1997, one year after its privatisation, Eversholt was sold for £726 million, netting the PE firm approximately £110 million and Eversholt directors over £40 million. Individual executives of Candover were also rumoured to have made between £800,000 and £1.2 million out of it.[90] That deal alone would account for half of CIP's growth in net assets that year.[91] A parliamentary inquiry was requested and the National Audit Office reviewed the transaction once the Labour Party took power in 1997. Considering that rolling stock leasing companies like Eversholt had revenues guaranteed by eight-to-ten-year contracts with the train operators and that they were insured and covered by the Treasury for up to 80 per cent of any revenue loss, they did not represent much of an investment risk for buyout investors. The general view at the time was that John Major's government had behaved recklessly in a rush to finalise its privatisation programme ahead of the 1997 general elections. What helped Candover was that two other train-leasing companies had been privatised at the same time and they had also gone through a quick-flip scenario, making the firm no different, but certainly no better, than its peers. If the public had even suspected that British Rail's Pension Fund was also one of Candover's original seed investors,[92] who knows what proportions the scandal would have reached. Success was coming at a price; from now on, Brooke and his team needed to tread carefully.

Chapter 5 - Shifting Gear

By the mid-1990s, Britain's economy was back on track and experiencing a period of steady growth, turning into an economic model that many European governments were trying to emulate. In 1994, the country's GDP had already expanded by 4.7 per cent and the following five years would each rise between 2.5 and 4 per cent.

Supported by a government that saw free-market principles and deregulation as the drivers of growth, the PE industry was experiencing the ideal environment for its development. Again, size-wise the Candover 1994 Fund had not represented much of a progression from the 1989 Fund since the latter managed commitments of £319 million. Actually, with the £37.5 million raised in 1991, the 1989–91 equity pot had been much greater than for the 1994 vintage even though that capital had been invested during the recession. Candover had missed the opportunity to build up a bigger equity base and take advantage of the recovery, but as mentioned earlier it was due to the fact that, at the time, the UK buyout market outlook remained hazy. Total LBO deal values in the UK had gone from over £7 billion in 1989 to just £3 billion in 1990, and had stayed around that level until 1994. In 1996, the market had finally hit the £7 billion mark again and the size of deals being executed kept rising. If Candover was to take advantage of that bullish situation and of the subsequent years of economic growth that Britain would display, it needed to strike a decisive blow. The Candover 1997 Fund was going to change the firm's positioning in a meaningful way.

For the firm's seventh investment vehicle, Brooke and Curran had set the bar very high indeed. The target size had been specified at £650 million, or twice the amount of the previous fund's commitments. Hopeful, the objectives of the new fund were also opening the door to non-British markets as the PPM indicated that the firm would invest in large buyouts in Western Europe. CPL was benefiting from a positive economic outlook. By the mid-1990s, it had imposed itself as one of the most active buyout houses in the UK. After completing seven transactions in 1995, it had executed five of them in 1996. And the value of those deals put the company regularly in the top three buyout fund managers in the UK league tables. As it turns out, senior management was still too pessimistic in its expectations.

The Candover 1997 Fund gathered £850 million of capital commitments from fifty-six investors, including £100 million from listed trust CIP, and closed in December 1997, after only six months on the road. It was a master stroke. The firm's efforts had been helped by the strong returns achieved on the only exit it had realised from the 1994 Fund: the hugely profitable quick flip of the controversial Eversholt deal. Interestingly, slightly more than 50 per cent of the 1997 Fund commitments originated from investors - also called limited partners (LPs) - based in the US, including the mighty California Public Employees' Retirement System (CalPERS) and California Teachers' Retirement System (CalSTRS), and only 27 per cent were made by British institutions.[93] The firm's profile was undoubtedly becoming international. Candover had moved up a gear and so had its most ambitious challengers: CVC, Doughty Hanson and Cinven (rebranded from CINVen after gaining its independence from British Coal in 1995) also raised large funds in 1997 and the following year.

In 1997 alone, £9 billion were raised by private equity outfits in Europe, which was more than had been collected in the previous nine years. It led several pundits already concerned by the high multiples being paid by LBO firms correctly to predict that valuations of target companies could only keep on rising. The buyout specialists risked having to pay over the odds for their acquisitions, but in the meantime deal opportunities in continental Europe had pushed the value of that market to £11 billion in 1997 compared to £6 billion a year earlier. The UK market totalled £10 billion worth of transactions, but the rest of Europe was now more active. For a long time, the issue in continental Europe had been that stock markets did not offer a serious exit opportunity due to their poor liquidity, the limited interest in share ownership from individual but also institutional investors, and the antiquated and oppressive administrative burden that a listing represented for small enterprises. At the beginning of the decade, the combined market capitalisation of all the continental European exchanges had been little more than half that of London. That was no longer the case. Thanks to the Soviet Union's implosion and the fall of the Berlin Wall eight years earlier, the European bourses were very much open for business and embracing deregulation and the idea of a single European capital market.

Losing interest in the relatively smaller deals that the 1994 Fund targeted, the team would stop investing it in August 1997 with the £103 million delisting of insurance broker CE Heath. That was actually Candover's hundredth buyout since inception and it was celebrated accordingly, including with articles in the press.[94] At the time of exiting that investment many years later, the firm would however show less boasting. Oddly, Candover would only ever call down £176 million of the £307.5 million available from its 1994 Fund, or just shy of 58 per cent of total commitments.[95] It is normal for GPs not to invest all the available pledged equity in direct investments as it needs a capital reserve to support follow-on capital injections in its portfolio companies. But usually the remaining amount does not account for more than 25 per cent of total funds. The firm was either concerned that the 1994 portfolio would require further capital or more interested in putting the bigger 1997 Fund to work. Either way, over £130 million of the 1994 Fund would never be invested and would therefore be left in the limited partners' coffers.

Anticipating that the larger 1997 Fund would be more demanding on their time, Brooke and Curran promoted Buffin and Gumienny to the rank of Joint Managing Director (MD) in March 1998.[96] Also acknowledging that executing bigger deals would require a strong knowledge and training in debt lending activities, they set the firm on a hiring spree to bring in individuals with the relevant background. That year, CPL recruited Ian Gray (aged 37), a Managing Director of Bank of Scotland's structured finance division, and Charlie Green (aged 34), previously a Director of structured finance at Deutsche Morgan Grenfell.[97]

The rationale behind setting a considerably bigger fund size was to take advantage of the corporate restructurings that had become all the rage since the late 1980s, not just in the UK, but also to a growing extent in some European countries. Curran and his Deputy Chief Executive Fairservice wanted the firm to be a major actor in acquiring carved-out businesses. With the 1994 Fund CPL had already bought sizeable businesses like Eversholt, Leyland DAF (Albion Automotive) and some of William Holdings's building products activities. The 1997 Fund would follow that trend and push it even further.

Finally, the new vintage had another unstated objective: to reduce the number of syndicated transactions and restrict the number of co-led deals to the bare minimum. As Curran confirmed at the time, Candover could now underwrite £200 million of equity in a single deal on its own.[98] The company wanted to impose itself as a lead investor of recognised standing and, as stated, it was by then regularly confronted with rival bids by CVC, 3i and Charterhouse. In February 1997, for instance, Candover had lost to Cinven in the £500 million buyout of private hospitals owner BMI. From that point on, if it needed third parties to back the firm in supplementing its equity tickets, CPL would give priority to its regular trusted investors or bankers, such as Alpinvest, Goldman Sachs and Legal & General. The firm had already started acting that way when investing the 1994 Fund, but its investment strategy had not been as systematic as it would be going forward. That approach would allow Candover to build a strong independent operation without having to share the glory.

As a nice side effect of the bigger fund, Candover would naturally generate higher commissions. The firm reported a near doubling of profits in the first half of 1998 and Curran acknowledged that it 'mainly reflected higher fee income after the establishment of the £850 million Candover 1997 Fund'.[99] The economics of a buyout firm are quite straightforward indeed.

In January 1998, the firm completed its first transaction out of the 1997 Fund.[100] It acquired Fairey Hydraulics, the aerospace engineering service division of listed company Fairey Group plc, for £55 million. As you might recall, the PLC had been one of Candover's investments in the

1980s; to execute that buyout, Gumienny had taken advantage of the firm's past relationship with the parent company in a manner that would become his trademark as the years went by. Many of the subsequent transactions backed by the 1997 Fund would be spin-offs of large corporations. Among others, Candover's portfolio company Regional Independent Media (RIM), a group of forty-four titles, was originally the regional newspaper publishing division of United News & Media and was acquired for £360 million in February 1998. In what was by now a common affair, CPL had brought in business partners, in that instance Alpinvest and Goldman Sachs, on the deal and the US bank had actually structured and underwritten a £115 million high-yield bond to help the consortium outbid rivals.[101] Similarly, the Earls Court & Olympia exhibition centres were sold to Candover by Peninsular & Oriental (P&O) in October 1999.[102] Many of these businesses required senior management changes and, as explained, Candover often worked with buy-in teams – as was the case for the Earls Court and RIM acquisitions - to get a better understanding of the business and its upside potential, and to be ready from day one post-completion. In most cases, those large carve-out deals required a lot more involvement from the investment executives than the smaller buyouts the firm was used to, hence the resolution to bring in sector experts and operational managers. Still, because the UK economy was expanding at a brisk pace, CPL's portfolio companies were generally recording strong trading performances.

For the first time in the firm's history, several mid-to-large MBO deals funded by the 1997 Fund would take place outside the UK with CPL as lead investor. The €136 million buyout of Diamant Boart from Union Minière in Belgium in July 1999 had been led by Christopher Spencer, a Director who had been recruited in late 1998 to market the firm on the Continent. The Diamant Boart deal and the c. €480 million delisting of Irish packaging company Clondalkin in October 1999 were successful international incursions and would encourage the firm's senior executives to be bolder when investing the group's subsequent funds.

Besides these foreign inroads, in the late 1990s the firm oozed Britishness. Its head office, at 20 Old Bailey, was in one of London's most traditional business districts. Opposite the historical, neo-Baroque building of the Central Criminal Court, commonly known as the Old Bailey, it was located a stone's throw from St Paul's cathedral. The firm had moved there in 1990 as it had grown out of its previous premises. The office had its own cook and frequently entertained guests over lunch. The board of directors of Candover Investments plc held its meetings there and was occasionally treated to a sumptuous meal with access to a wine cellar to match. CPL's employees also had lunch in-house unless they were out entertaining clients or being entertained. Corporate schmoozing was not just encouraged; it was expected and considered the best way to originate deal opportunities. Outings included pheasant shootings, attendance at Ascot's horse races or a visit to London's fanciest restaurants. Until 2005, the firm also had its own corporate box at Twickenham's rugby stadium. I fondly remember hosting a few lunches there before watching the French team usually get trounced by England. Employees were treated well during the Curran era. The firm was thoughtful in the way it considered its employees; it was a nice touch coming straight from the top. To some extent, it is that conservative corporate culture centred round a proven and tested business model that explains why at a time when many of its peers were throwing money at what was frequently being dubbed the Internet revolution, Candover remained focused on the fundamentals and continued to invest in traditional, non-technology-driven sectors of the economy.

Curran had correctly identified that PE activity in several countries of continental Europe was finally reaching meaningful volumes. So in October 1997, he had set up a joint venture in France with Chevrillon Philippe, a French investment boutique run by its founder Cyrille Chevrillon, to look at deals with a value in excess of £50 million.[103] The French fund Ciclad that Candover had helped establish almost a decade earlier had been productive, but it was only participating in small LBOs, a segment that CPL had stopped focusing on after its 1991 vintage. It was important for the group to chalk out a consistent plan of action across all geographies. Already at the time, many of the firm's rivals had put people on the ground. A key driver of success in this industry is the ability to establish close relationships with senior management teams, M&A specialists, and senior advisers and consultants at the local level. The Candover brand was revered in Britain, but its various overseas initiatives targeting smaller transactions via joint-ventures or third-party funds meant that, in the late 1990s, the UK buyout firm was still relatively unknown to senior executives and decision-makers in France, Germany and other major foreign markets. The German joint venture set up in 1995 with Legal & General had supplied only a few small deals.[104] The firm's extensive list of contacts in London's financial district was not proving sufficient to establish it as a credible investor in other European markets. By taking the JV route, Candover had also chosen a different path from that of its major challengers who had set up permanent offices to support their international development. 3i, for instance, had opened Paris and Frankfurt offices in 1983 and 1986 respectively; continental Europe accounted for 10 per cent of its portfolio by the mid-1990s and represented almost 100 transactions in 1997 alone.[105] Similarly, CVC had established its Frankfurt presence in 1985 and its Paris and Milan outposts in 1986 and 1987 respectively. Schroder Ventures, Permira's predecessor, had launched its German operations in 1986 and was in Italy since 1988 and in France since 1989.

Not only was Candover falling behind its UK counterparts, but the competitive landscape had recently become even more crowded when US private equity giants had opened European outposts: Carlyle had set up shop in Paris in 1997, KKR and Clayton Dubilier in London in 1998. By the late 1990s, most senior talent had been poached by the likes of 3i, Bridgepoint, BC Partners and their US equivalents.

And just like they had during the float of Jarvis Hotels and the Eversholt quick flip, Candover's business practices were again being questioned in October 1998 because of the firm's restructuring strategy at RIM, just months after the newspaper publisher's acquisition. A leaked internal memo had shown that Chris Oakley, the buy-in executive that Candover had backed to lead the transaction, was suggesting a 'well-planned, big bang approach' to staff cuts at the *Yorkshire Post*, one of RIM's titles.[106] The buyout firm was believed to have bid over 11 times EBIT[107] for the newspaper group. Valuing the business at 2.6 times its 1997 sales when comparable companies were reported to be worth 2 times, in Buffin's own words the fund manager had paid a full price[108] with the help of the expensive Goldman Sachs-underwritten high-yield bond[109] and was now putting the company's CEO under pressure to come up with actions on cost-cutting. The firm was not winning friends in the media community.

As the 1990s were coming to a close, Candover's management team could nevertheless remain confident that it had finally struck gold. The strong economic environment across Europe was very promising and the buyout sector was benefitting from the increasing allocation of institutional money towards the private investment segment, even if it was not taking the extravagant dimensions witnessed by the Internet-obsessed VC space. The next CPL fund had every chance of making a bundle and, as had been the case for the 1997 Fund, Curran, Fairservice, Buffin and Gumienny would be the key beneficiaries to reap the rewards. To prepare for that next phase of development well in advance, in May 1999 Curran and Fairservice respectively stepped down as Chief Executive and Deputy Chief Executive and into the Executive Chairman and Deputy Chairman positions. Curran was replacing Brooke as Chairman.

On 11 May 1999, during Candover Investments plc's Annual General Meeting (AGM) and in his last address to the firm's shareholders, Brooke looked back on the long road that Candover and the British PE industry had travelled since 1980. While the firm had closed over 100 transactions in eighteen years, the progress made by the whole industry was truly remarkable. The British Venture Capital Association (BVCA) now had 116 members, up from 34 when it had been launched in 1983. In 1981, a total of £200m had been invested in 150 buyouts and buy-ins, with an average size of £1.4 million. In 1998 £13.4 billion was committed to 644 transactions, with an average size of £21m. Brooke had pointed out that the larger funds, such as Candover's, had in part replaced investment banks in fuelling the growth of British enterprises.[110] The group's founder could be proud of his achievement and he was leaving on a high. In 1998, Candover's net asset value had jumped 25 per cent, reaching almost £200 million[111] and representing an incredible 22 per cent compound annual growth rate since CIP's IPO in December 1984. The ten-year compound net asset increase had been 18.6 per cent per annum compared to the FTSE All-Share's 11.2 per cent. The firm would complete nine transactions worth a total of £1.5 billion in 1999, by far its most active year ever.

But the first clouds were looming on the horizon. Several large deals had escaped Candover in 1999 and US buyout specialists were showing strong interest in UK and continental European assets. Seeking to follow a roll-up strategy with its portfolio company RIM, the LBO expert had spent the whole year chasing newspaper publisher Mirror Group, but the process had dragged on due to countless counterbids by competitor Trinity and because of the significant push-back from Mirror's management.

In June, Texas-headquartered buyout shop Hicks Muse had beaten Candover in the £822 million takeover of biscuit-maker Hillsdown Holdings. After an uninvited bid in early May, Hicks Muse had gradually built a stake in the publicly listed company. Hillsdown's CEO, hoping to keep his job, had preferred to partner with the trusted London-based Candover. Hicks Muse had built its stake up to 29.9 per cent,[112] making it impossible for the CPL bid to get a 75 per cent approval from Hillsdown's shareholders. The UK fund manager had behaved in the traditional polished way that the City had grown accustomed to over the years. The Texans had thrown the rule book out of the window and paid an 84 per cent premium over the share price before news of the talks had emerged. Candover's friendly, CEO-supported MBO approach had lost to the hostile takeover method. That really took the biscuit! For good measure, Hicks Muse had even partnered with Nabisco later in the year to go after a bigger prize: United Biscuits.* The US firm had boldly pursued Hillsdown to help market a $1.5-to-$2 billion European fund that it was trying to raise.[113] After a short-lived invasion during the Gateway skirmish of 1989, the Americans were back in town. This time, they were here to stay, ready to change the rules of the game. From now on, bidding would become more warlike, deals bigger and financial gearing more audacious. Unqualified to compete with indigenous firms like Candover when it came to building close ties with local European business managers over a long period of time, US funds would often revert to paying huge multiples and structuring their deals more aggressively to compensate. And as an indication that US practices were gaining ground, in September 1999 the UK Takeover Panel had allowed the insertion of break fees, also called inducement fees, into acquisition contracts. These penalties were a way for the potential acquirer to cover the cost of mounting a bid and to make sure that the target was genuinely interested in considering an offer. Until

---

* The deal would be won by Cinven and PAI in April 2000

then, they had been deemed illegal, as a form of financial assistance, even if in practice they had often been tolerated. The game was on!

The year had also observed a real surge in jumbo corporate mergers and acquisitions, including British mobile telecom operator Vodafone's $60 billion purchase of US-based AirTouch in January followed by its defiant £80 billion offer for German engineering and telecom group Mannesmann ten months later. The technology, telecom and Internet sectors were certainly not the only ones to overheat: US retailer Wal-Mart's unfriendly £6.7 billion bid for UK supermarket chain Asda in June and several tie-ups between European banking giants, including those of Banque Nationale de Paris (BNP) and Paribas, and between Royal Bank of Scotland (RBS) and Natwest, showed that the whole M&A landscape was simmering with excitement. European buyout firms, however, were still primarily targeting deals below the £1 billion mark. With the exception of the unusual Eversholt privatisation, Candover was yet to lead a single deal valued above £500 million. Recognising that they could not underwrite big tickets on their own, some PE groups had decided to bury the hatchet and partner like in the old days. In 1999, CVC and Cinven had joined forces for the £825 million buyout of betting shop manager William Hill. Similar club deals were happening on the Continent. They would all need to shape up now that the Americans had set up shop.

In a strange coincidence that was a telling sign that the Old Bailey-based firm increasingly risked being confronted to a more inimical scenery, the day before Hicks Muse had successfully clinched Hillsdown from the firm's claws, Candover had acted as a 'white knight' to partner with the CEO of underperforming LSE-listed Hall Engineering, a small steel-based engineering company, to fend off the unwelcome approach of TT Group, a trade competitor. The £125 million public-to-private (PTP) was no comparison to the conspicuous Hillsdown take-private. As we will see, it would also prove to be an unfortunate investment decision, leading Candover to return the weakly performing business, renamed Acertec, to the stock market many years later. It was an ominous sign that just when Brooke was moving on and Curran was taking the less hands-on Chairman position, maybe Candover was facing the difficult choice of having to change its well-mannered ways.

Nonetheless, throughout the year, as related above, the firm had been very active. It was still showing that its influence in the UK's sub-£500 million segment was unparalleled. As mentioned, in October it had backed the Morris brothers in their £155 million acquisition of the Earls Court and Olympia exhibition centres in West London. And a month later, it was making its first investment in the healthcare research sector with the £55 million buyout of Scottish clinical testing company Inveresk. Candover had finished the year with the £194 million purchase of the specialised engineered systems division of troubled engineering group Charter. A very busy year indeed!

In the 1990s, Candover had been part of all the major investment trends. The decade had been a tale of two halves.

During the recessionary years, many PE groups had played a consolidating role; Candover for instance had tested the waters of build-up strategies, doing well in the case of Jarvis Hotels and returning a respectable profit from Cork's engineering roll-up.[114] That approach had been one of the firm's major developments, as echoed by Brooke in the 1998 annual report. The purpose was to develop investee companies into substantial businesses and into sector leaders.[115]

They had also benefited from the increasing focus of large companies on their core competences. It was the end of the conglomerate business model. Both Thorn EMI and the Hanson Trust had been demerged into several entities in 1996. Thorn had even been acquired by Japanese bank Nomura's private equity outfit in 1998. Other mini-conglomerates like Rank, William Holdings and Wassall would soon be deconstructed piecemeal and often fall into PE hands. Over the period, carve-outs like the 1991 acquisition of Pavilion from Rank had been Candover's main source of deals, often because the parent company was in trouble or under pressure from its shareholders to re-align the business around core activities. Opportunities had also arisen from the Conservative government's privatisation programme, but it was almost completed by the mid-1990s: Candover's European Rail Catering and Eversholt acquisitions had both come out of the late privatisation of British Rail. And although they were not the firm's bread and butter, turnaround opportunities had multiplied during the recession. The restructuring of Stoves had been a success, but Brooke and Curran knew that CPL did not have the internal capabilities to get so hands-on. The firm would generally shy away from such transactions in the future.

The second half, and markedly the end, of the 1990s had witnessed the growing frequency of public-to-privates (accounting for a quarter of total UK buyout deal value in 1999) as PE firms were taking advantage of the relatively low valuations in traditional sectors, especially when compared to the ludicrous price tags enjoyed by technology companies in those days. With Clondalkin and Hall Engineering, and even during the failed Hillsdown process, Candover had demonstrated that it was no stranger to that practice. The UK market was also becoming far more competitive and club deals between financial sponsors, which had been the norm during the early 1990s, were now few and far between. Candover, Cinven and 3i were more frequently rivals than partners.

But what characterises the late 1990s was the sudden demand for LBOs in continental Europe. A market that had seen €3 billion worth of buyout deals in 1993 was more than ten times larger six years later. Its size had even exceeded that of the UK market in 1997 and 1999. Whereas it had taken minority or secondary roles in non-UK buyouts in the early 1990s, with the Wohlfarth and Nutreco deals in particular, CPL had recently been more adventurous by taking controlling stakes in Diamant Boart and German company Vestolit. Candover was late in the game, but it was doing its best to catch up.

Finally, as discussed, the UK buyout industry greatly benefited from the rise in individual share-ownership. Thanks to the resounding success of the USM – replaced by the Alternative Investment Market (AIM) in 1995 – and the liquidity of the main section of the LSE, a substantial proportion of floats in the 1990s were of PE-backed companies.[116]

CIP's 1999 annual report was issued in late March 2000. In his first statement as Chairman, Curran acknowledged Brooke's contribution, highlighting the latter's 'vision and enthusiasm' and thanking him for the guidance he had offered the rest of the team over the years.[117] It was time to prepare for a smooth transition. Just as Brooke had passed on the baton to Curran back in 1991, it was now Buffin and Gumienny's turn to take on operating duties. The conquest of Europe was about to start.

Chapter 6 - Into the Big League

Stephen Curran had already spent more than eighteen years at Candover. Many of his past executive decisions had helped shape the company into one of the predominant players in the British PE industry. Because of his vast experience and integrity, he was deeply respected and the power of his character was never questioned. He was a man of principles even if his military background could make him appear at times somewhat aloof and hidebound. He had an organised, well-thought-out way of guiding the business. To many people inside and outside the firm, Curran was Candover. In 1999, the firm remained a top-tier LBO investor that inspired respect and envy throughout the London financial community.

Once Curran had stepped down as CEO – retaining responsibility for the strategic direction of the firm - Buffin and Gumienny were handed over joint day-to-day operational leadership.[118] Since they had joined the firm in the mid-1980s, the two of them had primarily held investment duties. Gumienny had always felt very comfortable with deal execution. His commercial skills were extremely well honed and he was excellent at negotiating with vendors or at entertaining bankers and entrepreneurs, or even at selling the firm to the various intermediaries on which deal-sourcing depended. Frequently in the office by 7 a.m., he was a hard-working and passionate deal originator, a dedicated and instinctive investor. For several years, he had been very successful at building himself a strong origination and execution tally, including the Shepperton Studios, Cork, Newmond, Fairey Hydraulics and Clondalkin transactions mentioned before. During the very prolific 1990s, Buffin had equally led a large number of acquisitions. His deal log included the likes of Midland Independent Newspapers, Eversholt and RIM.[119] Both men would now need to balance their primary investment functions with their new operational and back-office mandate.

The years 2000 and 2001 were brutal for the world economy. The Internet bubble had at long last, and after years of inaccurate predictions, burst in March 2000. Stock markets across the world, specifically the ones with a strong technology bias like the NASDAQ and its equivalents in Europe, were experiencing the biggest correction in a generation. Between March 2000 and March 2001, the NASDAQ Composite Index fell by 57 per cent. Large, established technology firms were hammered, the shares of telecom equipment manufacturer Cisco and online media company Yahoo losing more than 70 per cent and close to 90 per cent of their value respectively over the same period. Between 1995 and 2000, venture capitalists and stockbrokers in North America and Europe had sunk a fortune or two in telecom start-ups with questionable business models, technology concepts without revenues, Internet companies yet-to-be profitable and fraudulent corporations like telecom operator Worldcom. The vast majority of these losses would never be recouped. Traditional sectors did not suffer a similar blow, but the entire economy faced a serious slowdown which risked making investors more conservative in their commitments.

With the bursting of the technology bubble as background, Candover played the card of the conventional fund manager. Even though the company was not a participant in the Internet sector, most companies being simply too small and CPL's investment focus being in established industrial and service sectors, it was still a laborious market to invest in. But the British economy was healthy and since Candover, in the main, invested at the time in the UK, the firm was not significantly affected by the dramatic ending of the dotcom mania. Sellers and buyers were uncertain about the likely impact of the crash, but CPL still managed to close deals. In October 2000, it completed the buyout of Rank's holiday division in partnership with Bourne Leisure, a caravan park operator based in the UK. That transaction helped the firm get closer to the 75-per-cent-invested threshold for the 1997 Fund[120] that would allow Curran, Buffin and Gumienny to start the fund-marketing process for a new vintage.

The Rank deal had been a well-run but drawn-out affair. Candover had known Bourne Leisure's founder Peter Harris for a while and had developed a strong relationship with him. The fact that the firm's long-time partner Legal & General was an investor in Bourne since 1997 had helped. Presumably so had Gumienny's passion for horseracing: Harris was a multimillionaire racehorse trainer. Independently, the two of them had set their sight on Rank's caravan park division for some time. In fact, back in November 1998, Candover had approached the group with an offer. At the time, Gumienny was working with John Garrett, former head of Rank's leisure division, a unit which comprised many assets including the holiday activities.[121] As for Harris, he knew extremely well some of the parks run by Rank, having sold them to the conglomerate back in 1979.

Armed with that inside knowledge and after sketching out a strategy for the combined entity, Bourne Leisure had put a £700 million price tag on the business thanks to the support of Candover, L&G Ventures and debt finance from UK bank Barclays. Combining Rank's £419 million turnover to Bourne's £150 million[122] had created Britain's largest caravan park operator in a fragmented, stable but growing sector benefiting from high barriers to entry due to the regulatory requirements behind new site openings. Although CPL and L&G together only held a 28.5 per cent stake in the combined entity, the investment would be a strong performer for the 1997 Fund.[123]

With the scepticism surrounding the public stock markets and the economy, it was an uphill battle to source and complete deals. It was even more strenuous to raise a new fund as investors were particularly hedgy throughout 2000 and 2001. Notwithstanding, in early 2001 the firm's senior executives decided to launch the campaign for their next vintage. The target size range, set at €2.5 billion to €3 billion, was 100 per cent larger than the 1997 Fund. It was meant to be Curran's last fundraise at the helm of the company and an audacious move since it aimed at transforming the firm from a bellwether British investor into one of Europe's foremost buyout funds. It was about time. Continental Europe was fast becoming the most sought-after market.

Few recognised it at the time but this new fund would represent a significant strategic change. Until the 1997 vintage, CPL had invested the vast majority of its equity in the UK – with some noteworthy exceptions like the very rewarding investment made out of the 1994 Fund in MC International, a FF300 million French manufacturer of refrigeration systems, in January 1997.[124] Candover had launched the 2001 Fund with the stated aim of investing a large portion in France, Germany and the Benelux,[125] but its management was still maintaining a general bias towards the UK market, probably thinking that the latter would continue to generate the majority of their deal flow. In reality, the industry was about to witness a tremendous rise in LBOs across Europe while the number of UK transactions would remain relatively flat for the next five years.

Again, after almost twenty years of doing buyouts, the CPL senior management team had achieved mixed results in continental European markets. Because of the complex regulatory context and the recession of 1989 to 1992, many British venture capitalists had originally showed an understanding of France and Germany that was more or less limited to eating croissants for breakfast on the Champs-Élysées or drinking beer at the Oktoberfest. With the notable exception of Brooke who had worked on several international assignments, including in Bonn with Her Majesty's Diplomatic Service in the mid-1950s, many buyout practitioners had initially found it hard to build international credentials. CIP had had its share of mishaps. In 1987, LCB-Candover – subsequently renamed Deutsche Candover after CIP's stake increase in the venture from 40 to 90 per cent in 1990 -[126] had been set up as the firm's first meaningful foray outside the UK. The German activities had not produced the intended results and had more or less stopped in the early 1990s when the British fund manager had publicly acknowledged its spasmodic achievements.[127] From 1995, as already discussed, CPL had tried actively to look at the German market via a joint venture with British insurer Legal & General; this was also a disappointment and the partnership had dissolved within three years with LGV-Candover changing its name to Legal & General Ventures GmbH.[128] Since 1986, the group had been present in the Netherlands via a joint venture with local specialist Venture Capital Investors (VCI), but very few transactions had come from it.[129] The Cambrian Fund, Candover's Italian initiative launched in 1991, had not fared much better.

By the early 2000s however, the best established firms, including Permira and 3i, were active investors in France, Germany and many other foreign markets. With its 1997 Fund, CPL had only closed four deals outside its home market, three of them in 1999 alone, in a late spur of activity that could not hide its flimsy track record. That compared unfavourably to the eight foreign LBOs carried out by British outfit Doughty Hanson's 1998 fund and an astonishing thirty non-UK transactions by CVC from the same vintage.

The UK was a much more developed and professional market from a private equity point of view and CPL's capabilities should have logically given the firm the edge in deal execution in foreign markets. But because of its lack of steady, long-term experience in those countries, Candover urgently needed to place non-British individuals in a position to originate transactions and impose the brand locally. In an environment that had seen the continental market's share of total European buyouts go from one-third in 1995 to approximately 50 per cent by 2001, it was the only viable strategy to win deals.

Fortunately, the company's joint venture partner in Paris sourced and completed a transaction as Candover was launching its new fund. On 20 March 2001, the London-based firm and its French partner Cyrille Chevrillon closed the €920 million acquisition of frozen food retailer Picard Surgelés from French retail behemoth Carrefour. It was a real coup, not just for Chevrillon, but also for Candover and its European Director Christopher Spencer. Previously a non-entity outside the UK, CPL was stating its intentions. It showed that it was serious about investing on the Continent and was able to win prized assets in very offensive auctions, having beaten Apax, CVC and even local actor PAI to the post.[130] Frozen food was traditionally low-quality in the UK; not in France. Picard was a premium retailer and a strongly performing business. The fact that Candover was in the middle of a fundraising initiative for an investment vehicle claiming to be serious about investing outside Britain made that acquisition compelling. The group would commit €138 million of equity to the transaction.[131] It represented 16 per cent of the 1997 Fund's total equity commitments and was, according to the firm's publicly disclosed information, its biggest ever ticket in a single transaction. Candover was making a strong statement.

The Picard purchase, CPL's last transaction out of its 1997 Fund, unquestionably helped convince prospective investors that the firm was on the right track and led some to commit money to the 2001 Fund. The timing of Candover's first sizeable deal outside the UK could not have been better as the environment immediately after the Internet crash remained challenging to raise money. When he had publicly launched the fund-marketing campaign in March 2001, Curran had acknowledged that it was not going to be easy due to the recent stock markets' plunge. The firm was unfortunate in its timing; 2000 had seen a record in fundraising for European buyout houses, with €48 billion collected across the region, an 89 per cent increase on prior year.

The first half of 2001 would still record a *c.* 60 per cent increase in PE activity compared to the first half of 2000, but the collapse of the tech bubble was making everyone nervous and the morose economy had forced many buyout fund managers to put some of their portfolio companies into receivership. In Britain, over two-fifths of exits during the two years following the dotcom blow-up were estimated to come from bankruptcy filings or involuntary loss of ownership such as repossession by the lenders.[132] Throughout the year, partly because of the confused context, Candover had unsuccessfully bid for many businesses in the UK and on the Continent. By the end of the year, it had failed to acquire Whitbread's pub activities and Dutch bank ING's brokerage business Williams de Broë in competitive auctions. But it had also avoided a potentially disastrous transaction.

In August 2001, the firm had entered into an exclusivity period with Swissair, Switzerland's national airline, in order to complete its due diligence ahead of a final bid for the company's ground handling service subsidiary Swissport.[133] The national carrier was a desperate seller, being on the verge of bankruptcy because of its CHF15 billion* debt load. To make things worse, two weeks later the airline industry was thrown into chaos following the September 11 terrorist attacks in the US. Swissair was forced into administration. The value of Swissport was suddenly much lower than what Candover had proposed to pay, but Gumienny was

---

* CHF = Swiss franc

leading the charge and could see a golden opportunity: how about buying the business on the cheap from a forced seller? He had known Swissair for many years, having sold portfolio company European Rail Catering to them back in 1997,[134] so he was in their good books. The two sides certainly could work something out.

The year 2001 had been trying for all. Market data showed that the number of mergers and acquisitions in the UK had tumbled by almost 60 per cent over the prior year. The dotcom crash and geopolitical tensions had shaken investors, even if the total deal value of the European LBO market itself was down a more tolerable 12 per cent. Candover had shown determination by closing a sizeable deal on the Continent and was still in discussions over Swissport. Opportunities could be found for those who remained calm. The 2001 fundraising process had been gruelling, but over €1.5 billion of commitments had already been received.[135] The following year's prospects appeared gloomy and few people knew what was in store.

On 8 February 2002, Swissair and Candover at long last reached an agreement on the Swissport transaction. A business with a CHF1 billion price tag before 9/11 had been sold by its ailing parent company for a measly CHF580 million or 5.8 times EBITDA (Earnings Before Interest, Tax, Depreciation and Amortisation).[136] Candover had got away with it. Had it bought the company in the summer of 2001, the deal would have been an instant write-off by mid-September.

Four months later, CPL finally closed its eighth fund with commitments of €2.7 billion, in the middle of its original target range. Due to the unsettled economic conditions affecting the technology market, a skilful investor with a devotion to traditional sectors had reassured LPs, but it had taken fifteen months for the process to complete. Curran's strong selling point was that the firm had stuck to its proven business model, its activities in conventional industries like engineering, leisure and publishing. It had not invested in high-tech or new media companies despite the external pressure and the hype surrounding that part of the economy in the late 1990s, recognising that its deal team did not have the technical and operational proficiency to assess such opportunities. That had helped convince hesitant US investors, still reeling from the stock market correction and the horror of 9/11, to come on board. At the time, the firm had also widely publicised the 55 per cent gross IRR it had achieved on its 1994 Fund.[137] And that fund's performance was truly exceptional: the firm had recouped 5.7 times its outlay on Eversholt, returned 7.5 times its investment in transmission tower operator Crown Castle, and multiplied its equity five-fold on IT consulting firm Detica.[138]

Recognising that it had limited credibility in many of the continental European markets, the firm decided to bring in Cyrille Chevrillon as Managing Director.[139] Candover had opened a Paris office in October 2001 and proceeded in staffing it with local investment executives. Chevrillon joined as head of the French business in December 2002, having already helped the firm close its acquisitions of MC International in 1997 and more recently of Picard Surgelés. Curran and the Frenchman had known each other for many years, since the days when Chevrillon worked in the London office of US investment bank Salomon Brothers in the late 1980s. Both had a similar nonchalant style to investment management based on long-term relationship-building and judicious deal selection. The appointment of a close and trusted business partner was a way to limit the risk usually associated with international expansion. Thanks to his strong credentials in France, over the following few years Chevrillon would actively introduce deals to Candover and attempt to satisfy the UK fund manager's aspirations to become a credible buyout actor in the French market. It is also in 2002 that CPL decided to take a closer look at the Spanish market. The firm chose to retain a local financier as adviser to introduce transactions that would meet its investment criteria.[140]

While Curran had found a straightforward solution for CPL's French strategy, things were not going as smoothly for the firm's foray in Germany, a market that the City firm had failed to grasp ever since its inception. Candover had backed one of HgCapital's portfolio companies Pipeline Integrity International in its takeover of German competitor Pipetronix in 1999, and the small buyout of German PVC producer Vestolit executed by Buffin that same year[141] had also demonstrated that the firm was serious about investing in that country. However, as was the case for other LBO houses, Germany remained a tough nut to crack.

Senior management would have found solace in the fact that the weak deal origination had arisen from a combination of factors that could be handled better in the future: the 1990s joint venture with L&G, a UK entity, was clearly a *faux pas* and a local partner would have been a more judicious approach. Politically, Germany had spent most of the 1990s integrating the eastern region of the country, forcing local entrepreneurs to focus on reunification and national consolidation rather than calling external capitals for international expansion; the next ten years promised to be more rewarding for foreign investors. Finally, the disintegration of the technology bubble was expected to benefit traditional investors like Candover in a country known for its dominant position in manufacturing and industrial sectors.

Even though many PE groups had prefered to withdraw from the country due to the frustratingly sluggish dealflow, Candover took the decision to recruit a German team and to open a local office in the summer of 2003. Based in Düsseldorf, the office was led by Dr Kurt Kinzius, an experienced deal doer hired in May 2002 who had been Head of Corporate Development and M&A for German telecom operator Mannesmann Group.[142] His local network was expected to bring credibility to an investment firm that had a limited track record in the largest European economy.

Weeks before opening the Düsseldorf office, CPL had actually signed a very prestigious German transaction. In May 2003, the firm had acquired the scientific, technical and medical publishing arm of German media group Bertelsmann Springer for €1.05 billion. Although that deal had been sourced and completed by Director Simon Leefe[143] out of the London office, it helped the firm draw attention to its pan-European credentials. Candover would nonetheless struggle to complete other transactions in Germany and Kinzius would even leave in late 2004.[144]

Besides these efforts to build a foreign presence, it was important for CPL's strategy to be coherent with its identity, its established management model, its prudent and composed corporate culture. It seemed crucial for the existing leadership style and reporting procedures to be preserved. As is common in the industry, the firm's investment approach outside its home market was defined by its headquarters. The real danger for CPL as it was trying to expand abroad was that strong local personalities would dilute or even damage its brand, or worse, undermine the authority of the Executive Committee. Some of the company's competitors had experienced how painful such internationalisation process could be and had, in some cases, seen local teams take the independent route. In Europe for instance, Apax France operated separately from the rest of the Apax Group while by early 2005, because of ill-judged investment decisions made by its US colleagues during the Internet and technology euphoria of the 1990s, Hicks Muse's European team would resolve to spin itself out and form Lion Capital. Candover was doing its best to control its expansion and limit the risk of brand erosion.

Inevitably though, the effect of haphazardly opening offices on the Continent was to dilute the firm's DNA. Until 2000, Candover had been openly labelled one of a handful of tremendously successful PE investors in the UK. Until that date, any M&A adviser based in London knew that the City-based buyout pioneer was a serious contender in any mid-market auction in the country. But following its entry into continental Europe, the group was now one of many pretenders for the pan-European crown.

Private equity investing clearly requires the ability to strike the right balance between risks and rewards and, unsurprisingly, local deal-making was at times proving difficult. In the first half of 2002, for example, when working on the acquisition of French electrical product manufacturer Legrand, Candover partnered with Paris-based investment firm CGIP. As the deal represented a multi-billion-euro ticket, US buyout giant KKR was also part of their consortium.[145] In the end CPL would not go ahead with it, missing the opportunity to participate in a €3.6 billion buyout,[146] Europe's largest LBO transaction that year. Disappointingly, the firm had failed to take advantage of a situation somewhat similar to the Swissport deal. Like Swissair a few months earlier, French electrical equipment group Schneider, the owner of Legrand, was a forced seller. In this case, the European Commission had disallowed Schneider's acquisition of Legrand back in October 2001 on competition grounds. Schneider had to dispose of the business before the end of 2002 and was therefore selling it at a loss. It was and remained the largest LBO transaction ever considered by Candover on the Continent.

Admittedly, given its size it was probably outside CPL's investment remit at the time.

Again, once the firm had decided that its identity was no longer that of a British investor but of a western European player, its image imperceptibly changed. With continental Europe regularly representing a bigger market than the UK – in both 2002 and 2003, over 63 per cent of European PE transactions had occurred on the Continent[147] – notwithstanding its strong British heritage, Candover saw no alternative but to accelerate its push overseas in an attempt to take advantage of these opportunities. Executing deals in foreign markets naturally remained unnerving, but it offered promising prospects in spite of the occasional doubts expressed by some observers regarding the implementation risks associated with such a strategy.[148]

Chapter 7 - Identity Crisis

Throughout its history, Candover had consistently been a star performer of the buyout industry in the UK, but in 2004 its deal-origination out of foreign offices was still nascent and somewhat erratic. When peers such as Advent and Bridgepoint had successfully built a local franchise in various European markets and were often considered well-integrated local actors, understandably Candover was perceived as a British outfit. Its market positioning was tricky to place in the PE landscape. To understand this point of view, it is important to explain how limited partners go about allocating their funds across the GP spectrum.

They look at the PE world according to a three-dimensional matrix-like model. General partners are either generalists or sector-focused, either national or transnational or even global, and they can be low-cap, mid-market or large buyout investors, depending on the size of the funds they manage. In the mid and late 1990s, CPL had been comfortably labelled a British mid-market generalist fund manager similar to Charterhouse or HgCapital. It was now attempting to mutate into a pan-European large cap fund comparable to its brethren Permira and BC Partners. But the large buyout segment of the industry was already very crowded. In addition to the traditional big UK-originated pan-European private equity houses, the European market had seen the recent emergence of US players like Blackstone and KKR. Non-British European funds such as France-based PAI and Swedish EQT were also endeavouring to make some room for themselves in the large-end segment, no doubt attracted by the lucrative management and transaction fees chargeable annually.

To most investors, this rush for size was becoming indecent, and it meant that the European mid-market segment, investing in enterprises with a valuation of €100 million to €500 million, was no longer adequately served. In the case of Candover, there was also the risk that the deal team did not have sufficient credentials in international M&A activities. For LPs that had participated in CPL funds for the last ten years and had, in some cases, co-invested with the firm on transactions, Candover's move away from its core competence (UK mid-market) and into an unfamiliar but promising competitive segment (large pan-European) represented a significant change in strategy. There was a real possibility that the firm would increasingly pit itself against more sizeable opponents that had been implementing a European action plan for ten years or more. Whereas out of its 1997 Fund the firm had closed just one transaction with an EV above €1 billion (by taking a minority stake in British caravan park operator Bourne Leisure), it would participate in five of them out of the 2001 Fund (three of them outside its home market). The risk profile of the fund's portfolio was changing.

In essence, CPL's partnership with Cinven on several large transactions – UK bingo and casino operator Gala, and Dutch and German publishers Kluwer Academic Publishing and Springer, all completed in 2003 - had partly alleviated the danger associated with that fundamental conversion. Their close collaboration had even led certain City observers jokingly to call the alliance 'Cindover'. It was curious that that nickname had come about in 2003 as the firms' investment activities and strategies had been far more intertwined and aligned during the 1990s. You will recall that Candover and Cinven had worked jointly on many buyouts back then. In those days, LPs accepted that cooperation as a market practice whereby buyout houses syndicated deals among themselves. I have already mentioned that the acquisitions of Gardner Merchant and Expro International had been executed alongside Cinven, and the two houses had teamed up on the Pavilion deal in 1991 and the Nutreco transaction in 1994. Cinven had also inherited the portfolio of Globe Investment Trust, one of Candover's seed investors, after British Coal Pension Fund had taken Globe private in a £1 billion hostile bid in 1990.[149] It is that milestone that had led Candover and Cinven to become close associates. Throughout the 1990s the two GPs had backed the IPOs of many jointly owned businesses including those of Motor World Group, Midland Independent Newspapers and two of Fairservice's home runs: building services company Keller Group and cooker manufacturer

Stoves.[150] Although it was one of its most regular bedfellows, Cinven was not the only peer with which Candover executed deals. Since the firm's early years, Legal & General, Electra, Montagu Private Equity and Advent International had been frequent investment partners.

In the early 2000s, however, LPs did not look at such club deals in the same positive light. Since limited partners were often investors in the funds of several GPs, especially when firms operated in a similar size-bracket of the industry, they did not appreciate having multiple exposures to the same deal. The LPs' policy was to diversify and hedge their investment risk by choosing fund managers with different investment strategies. Seeing them work together on too many transactions heightened the risk profile of their positions by reducing their diversification without increasing returns. It was tolerable if an investment went well but disastrous if it tanked.

Portfolio performance was also becoming an area of concern. The Candover house was still proudly standing tall in the PE landscape, but cracks were emerging in the foundations. Some of the firm's investee businesses were facing some headwind, partly due to the market context, but also because of the pressing debt amount they operated under.

By the second half of 2004 Ontex, a Belgium-based private-label hygiene product manufacturer acquired from its founders in late 2002 and delisted from the Euronext stock exchange in February of the following year, had started to suffer from intense price competition from its key US rival, Procter & Gamble. P&G was the manufacturer and fierce marketer of the star baby diaper brand Pampers. Probably recognising that the Belgian company was heavily leveraged under CPL's ownership, P&G had launched a price war in some of Ontex's key geographies. At the same time, increases in the oil price rendered part of Ontex's main raw materials, absorbing powder, more expensive. Finally, as is common in the mass distribution sector, the company's clients, supermarket chains like Carrefour and discounters like Aldi, were piling on the pressure by requesting regular price reductions.[151] Things looked bad but it would get worse for both the portfolio company and its owner.

It was a disappointing state of affairs. Ontex had represented a ground-breaking transaction for the firm. With an EV exceeding €1 billion, at the time it was the largest take-private ever orchestrated by a PE firm in Belgium. Working with the son of the original founder, Candover was confident that it could back the target in its purposeful expansion strategy and was enthusiastic about the prospects of developing the business into new geographies. It had been a much contested auction, but in the end CPL had outbid French buyout fund manager PAI Partners. A value of €92 per share[152] represented a very generous premium over the €59 the stock had been valued at before rumours of a sale process had become public in the summer of 2002.[153] In hindsight, it is evident that CPL's bid of 8 times EBITDA[154] and the debt leverage at 5 times EBITDA[155] had put a strain on the business. It is unclear whether paying a lower multiple for the business would have enabled CPL to make a decent return on the investment, but it would have helped it weather the storm that was coming its way. Above all, Candover would have avoided the negative press coverage it got regarding that deal over the following years.

The acquisition of the founder's 78 per cent stake had been executed in law firm Linklater's Brussels offices in the early morning hours of a cold day of November 2002.[156] The two sides of the transaction had spent the entire night with their respective lawyers, going through the various equity and debt documents and agreeing the steps necessary to carry out the PTP over the following months. Straight after signing, exhausted from a 24-hour-marathon negotiation, the Candover deal team, namely Gumienny, Directors Ian Gray and Jens Tonn, and I, had hit the first opened bar we could find and started celebrating. It was seven in the morning and the lack of sleep coupled with the chilling temperature outside should probably have called for a warm coffee. But we had other ideas. The bar's owner was soon lost for words and, sadly for us, fast running out of booze. She could not bring the drinks fast enough. The four of us downed wine, beer and the only bottle of champagne the bartender could ferret out of her cellar (I did mention that it was the first bar we could find!). After several years in London, I had from time to time experienced what the Brits commonly call a liquid lunch; that was my very first liquid breakfast. After a sleepless night aiming to tie the remaining loose ends of the transaction, I could feel the combination of an empty stomach and the diverse mix of alcoholic drinks have an immediate effect on me. After my second Irish coffee, I stopped making sense of our conversations. We were celebrating, that's all I could make out. A few hours later, as I was dozing off in the Eurostar train bringing me back to London, I was quietly satisfied about having closed my first transaction at Candover. Little did I know that this deal was the beginning of the firm's sorrows.

Meanwhile, CPL kept piling on the deals as the buyout market was entering a period of euphoric activity. In 2003, private equity had accounted for over 20 per cent of the UK's M&A activity by value, up from 5 per cent three years earlier. Between 1998 and 2003, the value of British companies owned by financial sponsors had risen from £23 billion to £83 billion.[157] PE investors were getting so active and aggressive in their pricing that stock market listings were regularly shelved in favour of a management buyout. LBO firms seeking to exit an investee company would frequently run a dual-track process for good measure, but invariably the complexity and costly undertaking of beauty parades to convince equity analysts that the high valuation they placed on the IPO candidate was justified would pale into insignificance beside the generally unconditional and generous bids received from other PE houses. Stock markets were still recovering from the Internet indigestion and buyout groups were sitting on a vast amount of undeployed capital that they had not been able to invest in 2000 and 2001. As a result, the UK had seen fewer than 130 PE-backed IPOs in 2003 compared to more than 200 in 1997. As for trade bidders, many were in recovery mode after gorging themselves during the late 1990s or were simply unable to access the kinds of cash piles the banks were offering to the buyout specialists.

After doing only five deals in the previous three years, in 2003 Candover had been one of the most active amongst large financial buyers in Europe, closing six transactions worth a total of €6.6 billion. In addition to the Ontex acquisition, the firm had pursued UK bingo hall and casino operator Gala in a tertiary buyout (meaning that Candover was the third successive financial sponsor to own it) from CSFB Private Equity. Completed at an EV of £1.24 billion, or 11.8 times EBITA (Earnings before Interest, Tax and goodwill Amortisation),[158] the transaction raised questions about what value Candover and its co-investor Cinven could possibly bring on board that the two previous management buyouts had not already delivered. Operational efficiency enhancements, product rationalisation and organic growth had probably been maximised by now so extracting any further improvement would be laborious. On the positive front, there was plenty of upside to be derived from the UK government's upcoming gambling liberalisation.

With that acquisition, the two investment firms were simply taking their peers as models. In 1999 Europe had recorded €6 billion worth of sponsor-to-sponsor transactions; their value had reached €11 billion in 2002. The surging trend in secondary buyouts, as they were termed, was in its infancy. CPL had just completed its first ever secondary, the type of deal it would soon take a liking to. More on that later.

As the year 2004 progressed, Candover's investor relationship team had been preparing for the launch of the firm's next investment vehicle. It would be Candover's ninth fund and the target size had been set at €3 billion. But before the fundraising process could start, the firm had to reach one of the industry's sacred milestones: typically, a new fund cannot be raised until at least 75 per cent of the previous funds' commitments have been called down, i.e. invested. As already observed, the investments in Bourne Leisure in the second half of 2000 and Picard Surgelés in early 2001 had been that trigger point for the launch of the 2001 vintage.[159] In mid-2004, CPL had some way to go before reaching that stage and being able to initiate the next campaign.

But thanks to bullish corporate activity across Europe, it was moving fast towards that target. In July 2004, it had completed the $925 million carve-out of parts of Swiss company ABB's oil and gas activities under the Vetco brand; in September it had bought the specialist polypropylene and cellulose films division of Belgian chemicals group UCB for €320 million (later renamed Innovia Films), and in November it had executed the €370 million MBO of Belgian financial information publisher Bureau van Dijk. While Candover looked very well positioned to close another transaction, namely the secondary buyout of the Swedish manufacturer of car racks and boxes Thule, it needed to execute another deal successfully in order to reach the coveted 75 per cent threshold.

ALcontrol was a portfolio company of mid-market PE house Bridgepoint. It was a well-run Dutch business that operated environmental and food-testing laboratories across Europe and the seller's bankers BNP Paribas were running a tight ship since the launch of the auction in October. Facing a long list of rival bidders, CPL threw its resources behind the acquisition process and offered €340 million for the asset, helping Bridgepoint earn a five-time investment return and pushing the Candover 2001 Fund beyond the 75 per cent drawn-down limit.[160] By December, the firm had completed the deal and was ready to launch its 2005 vintage.

Taking advantage of a reinvigorated economy, the year 2004 had seen the LBO market rise by 25 per cent to exceed €80 billion. As a sign that the rest of Europe was gaining in stature, for the third year running the Continent was almost twice as large as the UK market. The year had also witnessed the vast promotion of an innovative banking product that would upend the LBO industry over the next few years. Businesses increasingly started being auctioned by their PE-backers with the help of 'stapled financing', meaning that the terms (pricing, maturity and amount) of the debt structure were pre-approved by the lending institutions in order to speed up the sale process. It is worth commenting that the procedure became a standard way to push and accelerate buyout transactions between 2004 and 2008. It would be a core feature of the bubble expanding over that period as it was virtually taking away the risk of the deal collapsing because of financing issues. Before the advent of stapled finance, the prospect that the financial sponsor would fail to secure the necessary debt package, or even the delay involved in obtaining it, could convince a vendor to sell to a trade buyer or to float the business instead. By eliminating the financing unpredictability, that mechanism was giving an edge to financial buyers. As buyout funds grew in size, the available commitments would enable LBO groups to sign bigger equity tickets and subscribe more liberal, often very low-margin, pre-arranged debt packages in order to outbid competing offers from strategic buyers. At first sight, everybody was a winner. The seller was getting a better price; the lender was making decent profits thanks to the greater quantum of debt; and the financial buyer was able to invest its funds by paying more or at least acting faster than its trade rivals. We will see later that it was not so simple. Stapled financing would lead to a wave of secondary transactions that greatly affected the corporate landscape. Similarly, due diligence reports, traditionally mandated to lawyers, accountants and other consultants by the prospective buyer in order to assess the risk profile and value-creation potential of a target, were now frequently being prepared by the vendor's advisers in order to accelerate but also, let's not beat around the bush, to draw as favourable a picture of the 'bride' as one could get away with. The practice was soon to spread and would be known as vendor due diligence (VDD).

Together with the increasing use of online data rooms where interested buyers and their advisers could access electronically a vast quantity of more or less relevant legal, financial and administrative documents to carry out their assessment, these were the symptoms of a seething market. Investors, bankers, buyout fund managers and external advisers were all trying to get a piece of the endlessly expanding pie. And in this mad push forward, with all the excitement nobody outside the firm really noticed that, because of a sector decline in the late night entertainment industry,[161] night club operator First Leisure, one of the Candover 1997 Fund's investments following its £210 million acquisition back in January 2000,[162] had gone into administration. At the time of its downfall in May 2004, First Leisure was the fourth largest UK buyout failure ever.[163] But the market was decidedly looking ahead for bigger, quicker, riskier deals.

With an as-yet-untested international expansion strategy and some of their portfolio companies like First Leisure and Ontex (by then the latter had been written down by 75 per cent)[164] experiencing structural hardship, Candover's leaders decided to launch a new fund in the spring of 2005. Several successful realisations like the secondary buyout exit of French retailer Picard Surgelés in October 2004, on which Candover had made 2.7 times cash-on-cash,[165] and the disposal of Swissport in August 2005 for a 2.6 times return,[166] promised to be of great assistance to market the next fund. The hyperactive M&A market would also help. The year 2004 had already shown a strong upsurge in the total value of buyouts across Europe and 2005 would be another record-breaking year for PE, ultimately rising by 45 per cent over the prior year to reach €120 billion.

Candover obviously took part in that frenzy and executed in particular the £150 million buyout of Wood Mackenzie, a research and consulting service provider for the energy and life sciences industries, in the summer of 2005. The business was owned by Scottish bank Halifax-Bank of Scotland (HBOS) and was a strongly performing company run very smoothly and efficiently by a straight-talking leadership team. It was what I could only describe as a classic Candover investment target. Management was very resourceful and its expertise had helped build a respected brand in a market with high barriers to entry due to Wood Mackenzie's highly valued proprietary research. Revenues were subscription-based and recurrent. Surely, it would be a no-brainer decision internally. All we had to do was convince the consulting firm's directors that we were the best financial partner they would come across that side of the English Channel.

In a mild Scottish afternoon of July 2005, after a three-month auction process run by the local office of accountancy firm Deloitte, the deal was signed. I still hold a vivid – well, I might be overstating it – memory of the closing day. That morning, while the seller's and Candover's lawyers were toiling away to prepare the various completion documents, CPL Director Ian Gray, some of our advisers and I went to the pub to down a couple of pints of the local brew. Receiving a call that parts of the documentation were ready to be executed, we popped back into the office to sign them. And as we were told by our lawyers to go take some 'refreshment' as the rest of the papers were being drawn up, we went back out for a swift one. By the time the last transaction forms were initialled mid-afternoon, champagne was available to toast the deal. The evening was spent crawling from one boozer to the next. To this day, I still cannot recall whether we stopped for a bite or even if there is such a thing as a restaurant in Edinburgh's city centre. The fact that Gray was originally from Edinburgh had been a key contributor to our winning the deal in a hotly contested battle. We had seen off competing bids from British PE houses 3i and HgCapital[167] and it is fair to suggest that the investment crew's drinking ability and advanced state of inebriety that evening had convinced the target's senior management team that we meant business. As we will see later, Wood Mackenzie would go on to be one of Candover's best investments in recent times.

By mid-2005, an exit for bingo hall and casino operator Gala was being considered. The company had disposed of its loss-making, high-end Maxims casino the previous year and was now a much more focused high-volume, low-stake gaming business.[168] The UK government's original plans to create one or even several super-casinos kept being pushed back though - they would eventually be scrapped entirely in the face of fierce anti-gambling lobbying - and the upcoming smoking ban in public places promised to be a disaster for a company whose client demographics included many smokers. Still, the ban was two years away so the business continued to grow, even if at a moderate pace. The casino activities appeared the most affected by the unpredictable environment, increasing sales by 5 per cent but suffering a fall in operating profit of 13.6 per cent in the 2005 fiscal year.[169] The challenge was that the Gala transaction was a tertiary buyout. The deal team had partly pinned their hope on the government's industry liberalisation plans and super-casino project to create the necessary upside and generate adequate returns on the investment. Having considered an IPO, Candover and Cinven had to admit that without a promising growth story, there was limited appetite from the public markets much beyond a £1.8 billion valuation. The upswing would have to be found somewhere else, most logically through an add-on acquisition. By bringing in mega-buyout firm Permira in August to take a 30 per cent stake in Gala that valued the business at £1.9 billion,[170] the duo had gathered the necessary equity ammunition to go on a shopping spree. And it did not take long for it to take place. In October, Gala was ready to acquire bookmaker and Internet gaming operator Coral Eurobet in another tertiary buyout for £2.2 billion, representing slightly more than 10 times EBITDA,[171] or 13 times EBITA.[172] That was a mega-deal, paid at a big price, and would represent the largest UK management buyout that year[173] and the third largest ever in the country.[174]

Usually, add-on acquisitions are meant to represent an incremental build-up on the original investment. Coral Eurobet was bigger than the original £1.2 billion Gala transaction. Maybe Gumienny had promised himself that he would not lose the Coral deal a third time. Back in late 1998, he had partnered with the Tote, the government-owned betting group, to acquire Coral from its then owner Ladbroke.[175] With the benefit of hindsight, he had certainly realised that his choice of partner had not enabled the firm to table the most attractive bid. In mid-

2002, CPL had been frustratingly outbid once again, this time by rival buyout shop Charterhouse.[176] Like Candover, Permira was a determined bidder. Coral Eurobet was never going to get away this time. With a combined enterprise value of £4.2 billion (or €6.1 billion) funded with £2.8 billion of loan facilities,[177] Gala Coral would be the UK's biggest PE-owned business in 2005.

Working in private equity during those boom years was captivating. Deal opportunities came in droves and there seemed no end to it. Between 2002 and 2005, the value of buyout transactions in Europe had practically doubled to reach €120 billion. And to take advantage of this golden age, Candover's ninth fund would play its part. Throughout the year, thanks to the positive economic climate CPL had marketed its 2005 Fund with relative ease. Closing €500 million above its original target size of €3.0 billion, it represented a 31 per cent increment on the 2001 Fund's €2.7 billion ticket. Eighty per cent of the commitments had come from existing investors.[178] More interestingly, only a quarter of the funds originated from UK investors compared to 60 per cent for Candover's 1985 Fund, showing that the firm, but also the industry as a whole, had become a global affair.

Candover had changed its market positioning once and for all, but the firm's newly appointed adversaries Cinven, Apax, CVC and BC Partners would raise funds well above the €4 billion mark during the same vintage period. It is a shame, as due to the hard cap it had set on its 2005 vintage, the firm had reportedly turned away investors towards the end of its fundraising process.[179] At the peak of the economic cycle, capital was galore.

By the end of 2005, the 2001 vintage had completed its last transaction by acquiring the high-tech optics division of French firm Thales, later renamed Qioptiq. And to prove that the market was positively bullish, the 2005 Fund's very first investment was closed as early as January 2006, only two months after the closing of the fund-marketing initiative. Starting with the €445 million acquisition of cable TV operator UPC Norway from its parent Liberty Global, 2006 would be another fabulous year for CPL.

Importantly, the new fund was the first in the firm's history in which a member of the original management team – meaning Brooke, Curran, Fairservice and Symonds – would not take part. Curran and Fairservice had chosen to bow out as the new fund-marketing campaign was taking shape. It meant that a new generation would now implement the European expansion strategy started almost five years earlier. Since both men had led the 2001 fundraising and were among the main beneficiaries of capital gains achieved by the fund,[180] they were considered 'keymen' by Candover's investors. In PE parlance, a keyman is an executive who is considered one of the most valuable contributors to a fund manager's investment strategy and performance. For that reason, GPs always take great care at managing a leadership transition in order to prepare their investors for the retirement of these central figures. Importantly, such linchpins are so important that their departure gives LPs the right to call back their money if they wish to do so. In recent years, a second layer of directors, namely John Arney, Ian Gray, Charlie Green and Simon Leefe had been groomed and were soon to join Buffin, Gumienny and Chevrillon at the top,[181] hoping to gain the investors' trust and become the new keymen. By mid-2006, Candover's succession process would be finalised and would dramatically change the fund manager's corporate culture and destiny.

BOOM AND BUST

Chapter 8 - Bubble Trouble

In the early months of 2006, the private equity world, not just in Europe but globally, was showing signs that it was operating in a bubble. Deal sizes were taking monumental proportions, volumes were growing in an exponential manner, and public statements from the industry's key figures were becoming more outlandish.

One commented that the industry could see a $100 billion fund being raised within ten years. Another added that we could witness the first $100 billion management buyout transaction within months. The few dissenting voices, singularly the ones questioning the sustainability of the LBO-related debt levels,[182] were lost in all the noise. As we ponder these bullish statements five years down the line, we cannot be surprised at the way things eventually panned out. The largest fund ever raised at that time had a $15 billion sticker on it and no LBO had yet exceeded the $35 billion mark. It is fair to say that we will not see a $100 billion fundraising process or deal for a while.

Flush with cash, PE firms had moved to the top of the food chain and turned into the ultimate predator. Throughout the year, several senior industry professionals confirmed that, in their view, no company was now too big for buyout groups, implying that any corporation could be a target. Mobile telecom giant Vodafone, one of Britain's largest publicly listed companies at the time, and one of its most profitable, was the top prize. The only question was to know which fund would snap it first. Today, such comments appear fanciful. Back then, they were taken very seriously.

People could be forgiven for such candid behaviour, but we must not forget that only six years earlier the world of equity markets, venture capital and investment banking had suffered an existential Armageddon following the end of the equally extravagant and excessive technology craze. Some of the senior personalities getting carried away in 2006 had already lived through the hangover of a telecom transaction gone sour in 2001 or an IT service portfolio company gone belly up in 2002.

In a last gasp before a deep dive, the 2006 buyout whale would see the value of total European transactions increase by a further 45 per cent over the previous year to exceed €170 billion. Surveys also show that enterprise valuations were at an all-time high. In the UK, in 1990 average EBIT multiples of large buyouts, described almost cutely as being above £100 million, stood at 9 times; they had reached 11 times in 2000 but 16 times by 2006.[183] As we have seen, steeper valuations had been encouraged by ever more generous debt packages. Total debt multiples that had been below 6 times throughout most of the 1990s had by now reached an average of 9 times EBIT. Borrowing money was cheaper than at any time in the history of the LBO industry. From 15 per cent in 1990 the Bank of England's interest rates had gone below 5 per cent by 2005. And PE groups kept taking advantage of these attractive offers by regularly refinancing the debt structure of their existing portfolio companies, using the proceeds to pay themselves a dividend. It was a modern gold rush that could only end like any of them before it.

Curran resigned from his Executive Chairman position on 8 May 2006. The pace of activity was getting swifter so it was time for the next generation, full of energy and ambition, to deal with the dizzying speed. Curran was 62. He had worked at Candover for the last twenty-five years, turning it into a revered mid-to-large-cap buyout player and helping it take a first step on the European continent. He had left his own mark on the firm's corporate culture, but it was for Buffin, Gumienny and the next layer of executives to ensure CPL's future success. Curran himself knew that running a pan-European organisation required people with a more international background than his. He had always been proud of his English heritage. I remember several conversations that I had with him over the years about his property in the English countryside and the various problems related to the staff running his farming estate. He was old school and that was his strength. After the departures of Finance Director Philip Symonds and Deputy Chairman Doug Fairservice in 2004, Candover Partners Limited had just lost the remaining link to the management team of its early days. It was emotional stuff.

With a brilliant career spanning thirty years in the world of LBOs - twenty of them at Candover - Fairservice had been a masterful investor and a prolific originator. Many of his deals had been solid performers. Of course they were executed at a time when collaboration between buyout houses was more prevalent than competition, but that performance meant that Fairservice, aged 58 by the time of his retirement as a director of CIP in May 2006, had been one of the firm's best value generators.

Curran was replaced by Gerry Grimstone, an accomplished financial services professional who had been a non-executive director on the board of CIP since July 1999, and the group's Deputy Chairman since May 2004 as a replacement for Fairservice. Interestingly, whereas Curran had been Executive Chairman, Grimstone was taking on the role in a non-executive capacity. It was a very important nuance as it implied that CIP was taking a more hands-off observatory and advisory function similar to other CPL investors. It would presumably grant Gumienny and Buffin more freedom to set the company's strategic direction. Curran stayed on the board of CIP as a non-executive director until December of the following year, but from mid-2006 he stopped being involved in the day-to-day administration of the firm.

As the sector was showing signs of excess, some LPs were starting to question the investment profile of the most sizeable LBO transactions. Investors were getting seriously upset by the number of secondaries that had been carried out between 2002 and 2005. They considered deals like Gala a symptom of the large buyout funds losing their traditional ways of proprietary deal sourcing.

My analysis would suggest that, in the first half of the 2000s, Candover had not closed a higher proportion of sponsor-to-sponsor transactions than many of its rivals. In truth, these investments were a major trend of a resurgent market. Without providing an exhaustive list, between 2002 and 2005 Candover had executed four secondary buyouts across Europe (Gala, ALcontrol, Thule and Wood Mackenzie)[*], but so had US financial sponsor Warburg Pincus, pan-European giant BC Partners, and mid-market operator ABN AMRO Capital. Several funds had closed three secondaries during that period, including Paris-based LBO France and UK mid-market fund Montagu Private Equity. It was the symptom of an industry running short of options in an overheated, overcrowded market. Candover had completed no secondaries out of its 1994 and 1997 Funds, but had closed several of them out of the 2001 vehicle. We will see that the company would up the ante for its 2005 vintage.

The frustration of many limited partners towards secondary buyouts originated from the fact that the majority of them were investors in several of the large PE outfits. If Candover bought one of Bridgepoint's portfolio companies, and if an LP was investor in both funds, the proceeds that it would collect back from Bridgepoint on the realisation of the portfolio would simply be drawn into commitment to pay for Candover's purchase. When such occurrence was rare, it did not raise many questions, but by 2005 and 2006 it was becoming common practice, even turning into a viral infection.

LPs consider that GPs earn significantly higher management fees than asset managers and are therefore expected to demonstrate superior investment ingenuity. Where mutual funds like Fidelity earn annual commissions of 0.5 per cent to 0.8 per cent of assets under management, PE firms charge 1 to 2 per cent of committed funds depending on the size of the funds. Such commitments do not even need to be drawn down as the fee is levied on the amounts pledged by LPs. If fund managers simply contented themselves to pass on investee businesses among themselves, limited partners estimated that GPs could not honestly justify exhorting commissions twice as high as those earned by traditional asset managers. General partners had also got into the habit of charging monitoring and directors' fees to compensate them for the time spent working on portfolio companies – even though it is clearly part of their duties – and away from deal origination activities. Something needed to give. Especially if you consider that some GPs, primarily the large US firms, were also charging transaction commissions – although in most cases a large portion of those was offset against management fees. LPs and some

---

* Technically the tertiary buyout of Coral Eurobet in October 2005 could also be included, but because it was an add-on acquisition it has been left out

industry researchers believed that returns from secondaries would logically be lower than those of primary buyouts as most operational improvements would in principle have been achieved during the life of the first buyout. Consequently, they should warrant lower management fees. It is true that many of CPL's distressed assets in 2008, 2009 and 2010 would end up being companies purchased from other financial sponsors. Maybe investors did have a point after all.

The manner in which the secondaries' due diligence process was executed during the heyday of the buyout bubble actually made them riskier. It seems counterintuitive since the argument brought forward by PE professionals is that these companies have already put in place a strict cost and cash control policy so their performance should be easier to predict. But it assumes that the purchaser carries out the usual conscientious due diligence. What happened from 2004 on is that the buyout fund managers selling their portfolio companies in a secondary process considered that because such disciplined policies had been implemented, the interested bidders didn't need to carry out as much analysis as would be required for a primary buyout. As already referred to above, VDD reports started being concocted by the seller in return for the commitment made by interested purchasers to respect a very tight bidding schedule, often reduced to a few weeks rather than the traditional two to three months. During those weeks, access to the target's senior leadership would be limited, sometimes just for a two-hour management presentation overseen by the seller's advisers or one of its employees to make sure that the Q&A sessions remained 'civilised', that is without too many tricky questions that might upset the management team and make them decide to go with a suitor less regarding and demanding. Several transactions, some very large, were even executed within days following a somewhat cursory examination. When you look at the dreary performance of those secondary LBOs five years down the line, the word 'executed' truly has several connotations!

The PE market was in overdrive, but the Candover deal team still needed to invest its newly raised fund. Many transactions, principally sponsor-to-sponsor buyouts, were being run via highly pugnacious auctions, with fixed deadlines being set by sellers. Sell-side due diligence was taken for granted without the possibility for buyers to undertake their own review.

Bidders had to provide guarantees of deliverability by a certain date. Reverse break fees, payable by the interested purchaser in case it failed to stand by its indicative bid, were being offered or accepted by financial buyers desperate to clinch the deal and to put their equity to work. Candover was doing its best to stay involved and pursued aggressively auctioned businesses. Secondaries like those of automotive information service provider EurotaxGlass's in May 2006 and Swedish mattress manufacturer Hilding Anders in October 2006 would be won at 'top-of-the-range valuations', a view that would soon be shared by many of the companies' lenders. Because of their hefty multiples in excess of 10 times EBITDA, both would eventually require some serious debt restructuring.

The Hilding Anders transaction was the firm's third Scandinavian deal in two years. The three of them had been sourced and executed by Director John Arney. The latter had joined CPL in late 2002 and was on a roll. His successful deal-making since joining the firm had won him a promotion to Managing Director in May 2006. Not bad for a 38-year-old, but that was only a first step in the right direction.

As an aside, it is interesting to note that it is in the midst of that brisk environment that the firm's co-heads chose to go through a major refurbishment of their 20 Old Bailey head office. Called the 'fish tank' by some employees due to its glass-walled design, the revamped two-storey office was a significant departure from Candover's traditional, individual-office layout. A modern, twenty-first-century pop art style was a drastic change from the partnership's modest, unassuming beginnings. The new office had more the appearance of the Tate Modern museum than that of the head office of a blue-chip investment firm. Years later, Brooke himself would not hide his contempt that they had made a hash of it, arguing that they had 'tarted the whole place up'.[184] Looking at some of the photos in CIP's annual reports of 2006 and 2007, it seems that Candover had given itself a new identity.

From the new bosses' point of view, the office's bright open plan arrangement was sending the unambiguous message internally that the Curran era was behind them; Buffin and Gumienny were now in charge. At the same time, Candover was taking on more space on the sixth floor as it needed to accommodate the growing staff intake. In early 2002, the firm employed thirty six people; by December 2005 it had close to sixty employees, over forty-five of them at 20 Old Bailey. At the end of 2008, the headcount would have mushroomed to 100, approximately three-quarters of them based in London. Despite the fact that personal offices had been turned into spacious open plan to make additional room available, the extra floor capacity would be occupied in no time.

Candover's decision to redesign its offices reminded me of what is sometimes referred to as the 'curse of the new head office'. As a firm expands to adapt to booming market demand, it often requires additional space and takes the opportunity to modernise its headquarters, often lavishly. By the time the offices are brought up to the appropriate scale, the economy has already started to cave in. It is all the more dramatic in a bubble climate as the eventual market correction makes the new office extension look even more extravagant. For now, the new headquarters were standing proud.

Over the years, to avoid having to waste too much time in auctions where it had no particular competitive advantage, CPL had evinced a real talent for establishing unique angles during a transaction or forming a solid relationship with vendors early on, ahead of a sale process. In mid-2006, Permira was preparing its Italian portfolio company Ferretti for an IPO, although for good measure it had also decided to run a sale process. It was public knowledge that Ferretti was a quality asset, so it was promising to be a heated auction. But CPL had an inside track. In the summer of 2005, Gumienny had sold a 30 per cent stake in portfolio company Gala to Permira. The casino group was an asset that Permira had coveted for years; Candover and co-investor Cinven had done them a favour, or so they thought, by giving them a share of the juicy pie. A year later, Gumienny, Gray and Italian Director Aldo Maccari were in a strong position to negotiate with their peer and take a majority stake in a secondary buyout of the Italian yacht manufacturer. On 27 October 2006, after what appears to have been a short due diligence process,[185] the deal had been sealed and the firm was taking control of Ferretti for an eye-catching €1.76 billion valuation while Permira remained a 10-per-cent-minority shareholder.

That transaction was prestigious: it was in the luxury yachting sector and it was very visible in the Italian market. But it had been won at a high price, for more than 14 times the EBITDA reported during the financial year ended 31 August 2006.[186] From the point of view of CPL's investors, it must also have raised more eyebrows. Having spent years telling GPs that they were not thrilled by the recurrent secondary buyouts, suddenly Permira and Candover were getting involved in some sort of deal-swapping merry-go-round. And as if to prove the point, both PE firms would end up having their hands full with the Gala Coral and Ferretti investments.

For Candover, the ship builder was not only a world-class asset to include in the 2005 Fund; it also enabled the fund manager to complete its first transaction in Italy, a year after hiring its first Italian executive and only one month after the opening of its Milan office.[187] With that transaction, the firm had just closed its seventh buyout in a year and its fifth for 2006 alone, showing that it was actively participating in the LBO boom.

Italian deals were being led out of London and the Spanish market was getting the same treatment. Via one of the firm's most trusted and enduring investors, Gumienny was taking charge in the auction of theme park operator Parques Reunidos. Standard Life Capital, the PE arm of Edinburgh-based insurance company Standard Life, a long-standing limited partner in many of Candover's successive funds and a co-investor beside CPL on several large transactions like Springer, Hilding Anders and the freshly completed Ferretti,[188] had been an investor in Parques Reunidos alongside Advent International since 2003. Additionally, it is interesting to note that the Scottish insurer and the Candover Group shared a particularity that no other bidder could claim: they had the same Chairman, Gerry Grimstone.[189] In a tightly-run auction managed with expert precision by Advent, thanks to the contribution of the executive team of Bourne Leisure, one of its previous portfolio companies, Candover scooped the prize, outbidding Apax and CVC, two of Standard Life's other GPs, in the process. Though that was again achieved at a high cost, the target was a steady and strong performer and offered great consolidation opportunities across its sector. Two-thirds financed with debt,[190] the transaction was closed in January 2007 and reported to be worth €935 million or 12.6 times EBITDA.[191] Standard Life had provided an invaluable angle, enabling CPL to table an attractive offer, and even chose to remain a co-investor in the Spanish attraction park operator. As always, Candover had relied on an element that had served it well in the past: its unrivalled network of UK business contacts.

That deal was the firm's first buyout in Spain, ignoring the tiny syndicated ticket it held since 2005 in cable operator ONO.[192] Just like Springer in Germany four years earlier and Ferretti in Italy in 2006, the Parques Reunidos acquisition could have given the impression that the Europeanised British buyout group's expansion strategy on the Continent was bearing fruit. In reality, because these LBOs had been, at least in part, run from the firm's headquarters, Candover remained somewhat London-centric. The opening of the Madrid office in the summer of 2007 would never enable CPL to close another deal in the country. The timing of that opening had occurred only a few months before the PE industry would run out of steam. In addition, the Spanish economy was about to enter its biggest adjustment in thirty years, killing the group's hope of building a sustainable presence in that market.

In the first half of 2007, the world economy was already showing signs of vulnerability. In the spring, the US real-estate boom, encouraged for many years by the ballooning mortgage-backed securities market and loose regulatory oversight, had suddenly hit the wall. Increasingly, questions were being asked about the low quality of such huge property-related borrowing and the impact it could have on risk and returns for the institutional market, including pension funds.[193] The European buyout industry was starting to feel the effects of that debt crisis and there was a sense that PE had reached a climax even if fund managers continued actively to pursue investment opportunities. As he had announced the group's interim results for the first six months of 2007, Grimstone had rightly pointed out that the maturing 2001 portfolio had enabled Candover to make some significant realisations, but that the sector's immediate future was getting harder to predict due to the volatility in the banking markets. He had nonetheless confidently noted that the same market uncertainty could prove a good period for investing at lower valuations.[194]

As the year progressed Candover was in fact pursuing several opportunities, including the buyout of French tax recovery and cost-saving service provider Alma Consulting.

Once again the €800 million[195] buyout of Paris-based Alma had a London flavour even if the French investment team was clearly managing the process locally. Simon Marc, a French national based in Candover's London office, had joined the firm in June 2006 from Apax France. He knew the Alma subject well. Apax's Paris office was indeed the owner of the advisory business since November 2005 and Marc had worked on that deal during his stint at Apax.[196] That surely made the due diligence process easier to apprehend, helping the CPL team focus on the key issues and expedite its internal administrative procedures. More importantly, Marc knew Alma's management personally, which could prove crucial in winning the deal. In a secondary transaction, or tertiary in that particular case, the target's senior management is very much the ultimate decision-maker. There comes a time in the sale process when the target's executives realise that they are no longer sellers of the business, as they would if they were disposing of the business to a trade competitor who would then have the desire to make changes at the top. Once a secondary is seen as the most predictable exit route, the company's CEO, CFO and other key executives put their buyer's hat on and pick the financial sponsor they feel most comfortable dealing with. The fact that they had come across Marc from his days at Apax certainly reassured them that he was an individual they knew they could work with.

By December 2007, Alma was bought out for an estimated 11 times EBITDA,[197] helping CPL bring the draw-down level of the 2005 Fund to 57 per cent and already inviting speculations about the timing of the fund manager's next vintage.[198] After EurotaxGlass's, Ferretti, Hilding Anders, Parques Reunidos and Capital Safety Group, CPL had just closed its sixth secondary buyout in a little more than eighteen months and was boldly advancing towards the launch of its tenth fund.

And by then the firm was operating in an exceedingly hostile marketplace. As a side effect of the subprime mortgage crisis that had recently emerged, since the early summer several mega-LBOs had struggled to gain support from banks or be distributed to the secondary market. In the UK, two sizable transactions had seen the syndication of their debt fail. The buyout of retailer Alliance Boots by KKR and the £4.2 billion takeover of music publishing and recording group EMI by British buyout specialist Terra Firma in May 2007 had cost their lenders dearly. The £11.1 billion Alliance Boots deal, financed with £8.2 billion of debt or the equivalent of 8.5 to 9 times projected EBITDA,[199] was the first delisting of a FTSE 100 company arranged by a private equity house and the largest LBO in European history. Not quite a $100 billion-transaction yet but getting there!

Across the Atlantic, it looked like the entire sector was embroiled in what could be described as a family feud, though brothers and sisters were fast turning into distant relatives. Several jumbo transactions, such as the $7.4 billion buyout of wretched car manufacturer Chrysler by Cerberus, had been completed, but their underwriters had been unsuccessful in shifting the debt. Some of the very large LBOs that had been signed in the first six months of 2007, including the Apollo-backed $6.5 billion buyout of chemical maker Huntsman, had proven impossible to finance, forcing their financial sponsors to walk away from the deal, sometimes by paying a gigantic reverse break fee for the privilege. Unable to syndicate their loans as the hedge fund and collateralisation industry had run out of liquidity, lending banks were reneging on their commitments to finance transactions that they had previously agreed to back. Buyout houses were suing or threatening to sue their lenders, but were themselves going through some very public and acrimonious legal battles with the vendors with which they had originally agreed a deal. To get out of their contractual obligations, some would be lucky enough to be able to call upon a material adverse change (MAC) clause.* Others less fortunate, like Apollo in its withdrawn bid for Huntsman, would end up with hefty bills in termination penalties and out-of-court settlements.

Back in Europe, the mood remained far more civilised. Nevertheless, in the case of the EMI transaction, after several months on the road Citi had proved incapable of syndicating its fully underwritten

---

* See Appendix A: Glossary

multi-billion-pound debt. It would eventually be considered the poster child of the European buyout mania. Adapting its investment approach to the prevailing conditions and to ensure the smooth and speedy completion of the deal, Candover had rolled over Alma Consulting's existing senior debt package in exchange for granting the lenders higher margins and had topped it up with mezzanine, thereby taking away most of the financing risk.[200]

Given the context, the second half of the year had been so weak that the total value of buyout transactions in Europe for the whole of 2007 was practically flat on the previous year. Because of the challenging debt environment, in the last six months of 2007 the size of the European LBO market had shrunk by more than 40 per cent over the first half of the year. Worldwide, stock markets had reacted angrily to the uncertain climate by dumping shares across the banking and property sectors. All major stock indices had seen a sharp fall in value since the summer months, and with gloomy words like 'inflation' and 'recession' making front-page news, the year ended on a sombre note.

Unsure about what the current volatility meant for Europe and for themselves, as the year drew to a close Candover's decision-makers were pushing ahead, ready to execute the delisting of Dutch industrial group Stork. The fundraising team, led by Buffin, would soon be able to launch CPL's mammoth 2008 Fund. The buyout industry's steam-liner was coming to a standstill, but the Candover raft was picking up speed, set to lead the way.

Chapter 9 - All Bets are Off!

Heartened by a very fruitful investment campaign over the previous two years, senior management had resolved for the next fund's target size to be noticeably larger than its predecessor's. But the timing was far from ideal.

At a macro level, because of the debt syndication issues already discussed, monthly values of buyouts globally had plunged from approximately $165 billion in May 2007 to less than $25 billion in August of the same year.[201] Britain had also just witnessed its first bank run in over 140 years. In September 2007, following its request for a liquidity-support facility from the Bank of England, Newcastle-based Northern Rock had seen queues of customers form outside its branches as rumours of its imminent collapse spread. The bank's senior executives even had to face the humiliation of undergoing a parliamentary investigation to explain how it had got it so wrong. Details surfaced that that small independent local bank from the north-east of England had in reality become the country's third largest mortgage provider in 2006.[202] During the first six months of 2007, in a final dash to the summit, it had arranged almost one in every five new home loans in the country. In a classic case of overtrading, Northern Rock's messy balance sheet and the inability to securitise its mortgage book as the credit squeeze set in would scare all likely commercial and financial rescuers away. Running out of cash, it was taken over by the state in February 2008, in Britain's first nationalisation since that of the shipbuilding and aerospace sectors in 1977.

In the US, the subprime tsunami was taking such proportions that, in view of multi-billion-dollar losses suffered by their bank, the CEOs of Merrill Lynch and Citigroup had resigned on 30 October and 4

November 2007 respectively. By the end of the year, the panic was global. European banks like Deutsche Bank and Credit Suisse had all revealed phenomenal losses due to their exposure to the US mortgage market. Switzerland-headquartered UBS alone had recorded a $10 billion loss in December 2007. In the UK, Barclays and HSBC had also disclosed the extent of the damage with their own subprime-related losses, prompting the Bank of England to set up, days before Christmas, a £10 billion-facility to provide liquidity to the country's banking system.

All these banks were regular lenders Candover used to call upon to finance its buyouts. In preparing to launch a new fund, the firm's senior directors must have known that the ride promised to be bumpy. Gumienny himself had publicly acknowledged in the summer of 2007 that the absence of a strong syndication market together with a significant worsening of credit terms meant that funding for transactions could only get trickier for a while.[203] Despite such liquidity problems, the firm's investment team had pushed for deals to complete in late 2007 and early 2008. The 2005 Fund would soon be sufficiently invested and get ever closer to the all-too-familiar trigger point of 75 per cent, thereby allowing CPL to get on the fundraising trail once more. In CIP's 2007 Report and accounts released in March 2008, Buffin and Gumienny stated that the Stork acquisition had brought the invested amount of the 2005 vintage to 72 per cent and they had therefore resolved to start marketing a €5 billion successor fund.[204]

In the middle of a worldwide banking crisis and what was already been dubbed the 'credit crunch', the firm's senior leadership wanted to raise a fund that was 43 per cent larger than its predecessor. Instead of waiting for that 75 per cent drawdown level to be reached and see how the crisis evolved, CPL had chosen to accelerate the fund-marketing process in a very speculative environment. However, the firm had been so efficient at investing its 2005 Fund that it was tempting to launch a new marketing process, to build a war chest capable of taking advantage of what would surely be lower enterprise valuations during the widely anticipated financial crisis and economic slowdown.

It is worth going through the Stork bidding process in more detail, as it also shows that the challenging context required Candover to be bolder in order to get closer to the almighty 75 per cent tipping point. Back in June 2007, Gumienny had tabled a bid for the publicly listed company. It was no secret that the Dutch target was in play. Since the summer of 2006, hedge fund managers Centaurus and Paulson had built up a 33 per cent stake in the company and requested the dismemberment of the conglomerate, explaining that the various activities of the group, including aerospace services, food processing technology and technical services, would be better managed and create more value if run separately. Stork's management had opposed such a suggestion, but after several months of open tactical aggression from the two hedge fund managers, the company's shareholders had finally 'welcomed' the idea. Attempting to offer a way out for all parties, Candover had made an offer at €47 a share in June 2007, valuing the business at 7.6 times its 2006 EBITDA.[205]

Unfortunately for the LBO firm, such a 'low-ball offer' had expectedly been perceived as wholly inadequate by some shareholders, and Icelandic food equipment maker Marel, one of Stork's business partners, had taken advantage of the situation by gradually building a stake in the target. Marel's aim was to prevent Candover from getting board approval for its takeover bid, in a cunning move reminiscent of the 1999 Hillsdown battle between the City firm and its US rival Hicks Muse. In September 2007, Marel stated that it was determined to bid €415 million for the Dutch group's food technology activities, thereby helping Stork's management retain its independence while realising significant value for the conglomerate's shareholders. It appeared a more attractive offer than if management sold the whole group to the UK buyout specialist. For good measure, by that time Marel and its co-investors had even managed to build a 43 per cent stake in the listed company. After months of negotiations, Candover had reluctantly agreed to raise its bid to €48.40 a share and to sell the strongly performing food technology division to the Icelandic trade bidder in the process, despite having spent six months categorically rejecting any call for a carve-out. At some stage, CPL had even considered going through with the deal even if it only received 51 per cent of the target's shares.[206] In the end, the take-private was sealed on 15 January 2008, with acceptances from

98 per cent of the shareholders. An underperforming asset like Stork offered significant upside potential, so to counteract the credit market volatility, CPL had obtained from its supporting banks Barclays and Goldman Sachs that they fully underwrite the debt.[207] Nothing could stop Candover in its track. If only the firm's senior executives had known where that track was leading them...

When Paulson and Centaurus had demanded the slicing up of the company, it had a market capitalisation of €1.3 billion. Eighteen months later, because Marel's intrusion had almost scuppered the public-to-private, Candover was paying €1.64 billion for Stork, even though the company's performance had seriously worsened – in particular that of its aerospace component division where EBITDA had tumbled by almost 75 per cent in 2007.[208] During the year, the Dutch group's total operating cash flows had dropped by almost 30 per cent to €149 million,[209] translating CPL's final offer into an EBITDA multiple of 11 times as profit margins had declined from 10.5 per cent to 6.9 per cent. And because of the credit crunch, and to some extent Stork's unimpressive trading, the lenders had reduced their debt package from 6.5 times to 5 times EBITDA, forcing CPL to make up for the difference by increasing its equity ticket.[210] For that reason, the Candover Group had poured over €450 million of equity,[211] or 13 per cent of its 2005 Fund, into the target. If it was not evident to some that delisting processes often lead bidders to pay a full price, Stork's complex, protracted and antagonistic takeover battle should help clear any doubt.

During the second half of 2007, CPL's fundraising team had prepared for that big moment. They would have tested the water, spoken to several LPs, and would certainly have received indications that many of them were prepared to back the firm, maybe even up their commitments on the previous fund. At €5 billion, Candover would enter a new segment of the private equity arena. When allocating their money, limited partners had established three different categories for large buyout funds. Firms managing between €2 billion and €5 billion were simply called large (3i, Bridgepoint and Candover's 2001 and 2005 funds participated in that segment). Firms with €5 billion-plus were termed very large, with BC Partners and Cinven being the main actors in Europe. Finally those managing commitments greater than €10 billion were labelled mega-funds and included European representatives Apax and Permira, and US giants Blackstone and Texas Pacific Group (TPG). If successful, the new vintage would bring Candover into the 'very large' category.

As stated, the context was shaky. It was one thing to come to market earlier than usual in such a forbidding financial environment – CPL had raised funds in 1997, 2001 and 2005 so should have logically waited till 2009 to start fundraising – but it was even more audacious to set the bar so high: as commented, at €5 billion the 2008 Fund's target size was more than 40 per cent above that of the 2005 vintage. In spite of unsettled conditions, as the banking system was freezing up, the new fund marketing campaign had been launched in February 2008. It would prove a terrible mistake.

Remarkably, in CIP's 2007 annual report, while still trying to grasp the meaning of recent events, Buffin and Gumienny asserted that large deals aside, the market and Candover's deal flow continued to display resilience.[212] That statement, made on 31 March 2008, does not appear to take into account the quickly deteriorating market circumstances. While it is impossible to comment on the strength of the firm's own log of deal opportunities at the time, by March 2008 it was apparent that the entire industry was going through a serious correction, and not just at the high end. Senior bankers were refusing to take on new lending mandates; many could already buy debt positions in existing LBOs on the secondary market at a significant discount. The volume of deals had gone backward in the previous six months for one simple reason: there was little appetite for more buyout debt.

Why the sudden gloom? The way the debt markets worked at the time could be best described as a game of 'hot potato'. The senior bankers and mezzanine lenders financing heavily leveraged transactions knew that they were harmful instruments. Those debt providers are not naïve; they are highly sophisticated credit specialists that had seen it all before. Some had lived through the junk bond mania of the 1980s or the Magnet and Gateway blow-ups of the early 1990s. Others had seen overvalued acquisitions of Internet, IT and telecom corporations fail during the fallout of the technology boom of the late 1990s. The last thing the buyout lenders wanted to do was to hold these new time bombs on their books. So they simply syndicated the loans to institutional investors called credit hedge funds or collateralised loan obligation (CLO) funds. By the summer of 2007, however, those institutions had run out of capital and stopped purchasing LBO loans as the subprime crisis was taking hold. Just like the oversupply of mortgage-backed securities had led to the housing debt crisis, the glut of PE-sponsored loans was creating a serious issue in the buyout segment. Not that it should have surprised anyone: during the last few years of the credit bubble, through the formation of Special Investment Vehicles (SIVs), the major banks had themselves been involved in some form of self-dealing practice of 'I'll buy your hot potato if you buy mine' (don't ask!) in an attempt to prop up liquidity in a market that was already finding it difficult to absorb the large volumes of PE-related debt. Suddenly, CLO investors had smelled a rat and were not taking any more positions. Unable to find a patsy to pass on the parcel to, leveraged bankers were stuck with it. In Europe, Alliance Boots and EMI had seen such syndication process fail, but they had since been joined by countless relatives. As long as the syndication markets were shut, the large buyout transactions could not occur. An imposing debt overhang was forming. Already buried under a vast amount of subprime debt, the last thing investors needed was to be left with freshly produced, aggressively priced, sometimes unsecured buyout loans.

In a Candover-sponsored quarterly barometer published in April, it was stated that the number of PE transactions had sunk by 21 per cent between the fourth quarter of 2007 and the first three months of 2008. Deal values were also down 34 per cent, a third consecutive quarterly drop. The Barometer revealed that the buyout sector had been particularly affected by the market downturn, reporting its lowest quarterly total in almost four years and a 33 per cent decline on the previous quarter. While it went on to claim that the mid-market value range, where Candover operated, was more resilient, it is a rather rosy view of the world since total deal value and volume in that range (EV of €160 million to €1.65 billion) were down 36.5 per cent and 13 per cent respectively on the previous quarter. On closer inspection, in that same mid-market segment, the last three months of 2007 had already suffered declines in both value and volume of more than 30 per cent over the previous quarter.[213] After recording such gigantic market corrections during the previous six months, many might well have concluded that the situation required a timing reassessment of any fundraising initiative. In fact, as the Q4 2007 Barometer was being published in early 2008, Gumienny himself had commented: 'The wheels have well and truly come off the debt market'.[214] In their eagerness to raise a new fund, Candover's directors seem to have underestimated the impact that the financial crisis was likely to have on their strategic plan. If we had to date the exact juncture when the group's destiny changed for the worse, the first quarter of 2008 would be that defining moment.

There is one further piece of evidence that the first quarter of 2008 would actually have sustained a much more pronounced correction in the UK if it was not for a very unique 'tax incentive' for businessmen to close deals during that period. The UK government had decided to increase the rate of capital gain tax by 80 per cent from 6 April 2008 on. Obviously keen to pay 10 per cent rather than 18 per cent on the capital gains arising from the sale of their business, many entrepreneurs were attempting to sell part or all of it before that fateful deadline, as specified in the aforementioned Candover-sponsored barometer. A dip in activity for the rest of 2008 was therefore widely anticipated and reported in the press. Gumienny himself must have known that several of the conversations he had held in the first three months of the year, including those with the owners of Towergate and Bourne Leisure, were connected with that exceptional circumstance.

Failing to recognise that we were not just in the early months of an economic correction, but that the world was also entering a major financial crisis, Grimstone added in his Chairman's Statement to the 2007 annual report that a downturn in the markets had often proven to be a good time to invest. We were then at the end of March 2008, only weeks after the collapse of US investment bank Bear Stearns, suffering from its exposure to the by then world-famous subprime mortgage market, had impelled the Federal Reserve to organise a rescue and to push the bank into the arms of JPMorgan Chase for a pittance. Since the beginning of the year, several global banks including UBS and Lehman Brothers had announced new equity and debt issues, acknowledging that their subprime positions were creating monumental liquidity issues. There could therefore be no doubt by that time that a global banking crisis was taking hold.

Grimstone's comment is absolutely correct, but the extent of the credit slowdown over the previous nine months invited veteran investment professionals to prudence. It is in that environment that CPL was attempting to raise a new fund with a minimum target size of €5 billion. Yes, 3i had raised a €5 billion fund in 2006; indeed EQT, traditionally a much smaller player than Candover, had closed its latest vintage at €4.25 billion in November 2006; and PAI Europe was about to complete a €5.4 billion fundraising in May 2008. All these funds had been launched when the market was going strong and investors were still optimistic. Regrettably, the wind had turned.

It could be tempting to think that the Candover leadership had wrongly assumed that the liquidity crisis would only affect the property sector and not so much the buyout market. In reality, the firm had already sampled first-hand a few months earlier the effects of credit drying up. In July 2007, it had planned to refinance scientific publisher Springer by replacing the mezzanine portion of the financing structure with cheaper senior and second lien tranches but had had to withdraw that process completely due to market volatility.[215] And as we saw the Alma Consulting transaction later that year had called for some ingenuity to be financed successfully. With these unsettling incidents, the tricky Alliance Boots and EMI transactions, and the fact that by early October 2007 already $300 billion worth of LBO loans had been rumoured to remain un-syndicated worldwide,[216] Candover's management team must have suspected that the immediate future would increasingly become hazy. A statement made by Buffin the previous summer, as he was commenting on Candover's results for the first half of 2007, confirms that he was aware of the implications that the new state of affairs could ultimately have on the business, even if he believed that sub-€1 billion transactions would be less affected[217]: 'The situation in the debt markets will stop the kind of very large deals we tend to do from happening'.[218]

Brushing such concerns aside, as mentioned the firm's investor relations team had sounded out the market in the later part of 2007 and was confident that several key investors would make commitments towards the new fund. Conversations would naturally have included Standard Life, a trusted party thanks to the Grimstone connection, an investor in previous funds, including the 1997, 2001 and 2005 vintages,[219] and a co-investor with the firm on many past transactions. Other long-standing LPs like HarbourVest, a very influential institutional investor and one of Candover's existing participants in the 2001 and 2005 funds,[220] would certainly have been approached. However, because of the slowing economy and the fact that many of CPL's investee companies had been structured with significant debt and were therefore likely to suffer from the challenging credit context, questions remained regarding the fund manager's ability to return cash to investors from its existing portfolio. Something would have to be done to instil trust in the fundraising initiative.

By early April 2008, Candover could no longer ignore the fact that the markets were worsening. Having previously considered the introduction of portfolio company Gala Coral to the London Stock Exchange, the firm was forced to call the IPO off as stock markets remained shut and Gala's trading was flagging. As expected, the introduction of the smoking ban in the UK in 2007 had negatively affected attendance in bingo halls: in the fiscal year ended 29 September 2007, the bingo operations had sustained a 13 per cent drop in operating profit.[221] In January 2008, the business had disclosed that it was shutting five of its bingo venues, maintaining at the time that it was part of a regular portfolio review.[222] But the truth had finally come out that due to significant underperformance against the management business plan (EBITDA had only risen by 1.8 per cent in the fiscal year of 2007), the company's leverage sat at a demanding 7 times EBITDA.[223] Threatening to take control of the company, Gala Coral's lenders had requested new funding from the three equity houses Cinven, Permira and Candover. After months of squabble with the banks, on 4 April the three of them were dragooned into injecting £125 million of new money to keep control of the gambling company. It was revealed that the performance had deteriorated further due to the introduction of new regulation in the second half of 2007 forcing the group to remove jackpot machines from bingo halls. Neil Goulden, Gala Coral's CEO, showed that he was more in touch with reality than his shareholders by declaring that the company's flotation was unlikely to take place before the end of 2010.[224] As it turns out, that prognostic would still prove too optimistic.

By now, data regarding the economic performance of many European and North American countries were starting to trickle in and were not painting a pretty picture. It was undeniable that the credit squeeze was having an impact not just on the mortgage or LBO sectors but on the whole economy. GDP growth had turned negative in the first quarter of 2008 for several of Britain's trading partners, including Ireland and Scandinavian countries. Alarmingly, both the Canadian and US economies had also declined during that period.[225]

In spite of the weak environment, Candover continued to support the fundraising effort. Striving to encourage investors to commit to the 2008 Fund, the CPL team had appointed Italian powerhouse Mediobanca and US bank Merrill Lynch as book runners to prepare the introduction of Ferretti on the Milan stock market.[226] As a definite side effect of the press exposure gained through the secondary buyout of the luxury yacht maker, Candover had built itself a name in Italy. Thanks to that notoriety, by June 2008 the firm had found another Italian target to get its teeth into and announced the acquisition of a 40 per cent stake in fitness equipment manufacturer Technogym. There must have been concerns about the prospects of a business that was so dependent on a positive economic outlook. Increase in gym memberships and new venue openings are key drivers of demand for Technogym products, but they imply steady economic growth. The financial and banking markets remained jittery and warnings of an impending world recession were growing louder, so purchasing a minority stake in a business run by a strong-minded entrepreneur came across as risky. Still, the transaction gave the opportunity for Candover to call down about €180 million of its 2005 Fund commitments,[227] thereby exceeding the 75 per cent threshold, and to market the 2008 vintage to the most reluctant, irresolute LPs. The firm's top brass gave it their seal of approval.

And a few weeks later, after several months of a merciless battle against US-based energy group Halliburton, including a stop by the

Royal Courts of Justice, Candover and its most trusted co-investors Goldman Sachs and AlpInvest announced that their bid for UK oilfield service provider Expro International had been signed. Funded by both the 2005 and 2008 Funds, it would be CPL's last ever acquisition. At £16.15 a share, the firm had raised its bid twice, and at some point even outbid itself in a pre-emptive strike against Halliburton.[228] CPL had paid a mind-boggling 74 per cent premium over the pre-bid share price, valuing the company at close to £2.0 billion, or above 11 times EBITDA.[229] By raising their price from the initial £14.35 a share[230] to their final offer, they thought the deal had become too dilutive for the US group's shareholders. But for the senior management of Halliburton, early estimates of the potential synergies possibly made the acquisition of Expro value-accretive, implying that it would immediately improve the group's profitability. Halliburton had indicated that it could bid £16.25 per share; undoubtedly it could have extracted millions of dollars in cost savings. Still, Candover managed to win approval from Expro's board of directors. After a shareholders' revolt and several days of court hearings where the complexity of Britain's Takeover Code became apparent to the judge himself, Expro was handed over to Candover's consortium.

The consortium had somewhat underestimated Halliburton's willingness to pursue the transaction aggressively. The Candover boys knew the US oilfield services giant well, having bought Wellstream, a small manufacturer of flexible pipe systems, from it back in 2003. For all that, they had not anticipated that the fight for Expro would be so brutal. Arney, who was leading the deal, had strong credentials in the oil sector. Gumienny and he were behind the July 2004 acquisition of oil and gas equipment maker Vetco. But the Expro deal had been driven down to the wire at a time when the oil price was at a recent peak: the barrel of crude oil had reached $144 on 3 July 2008. The price of oil is indeed a key factor to determine the spending power of Expro's customers. The higher the price, the more money oil majors Exxon, BP and Shell make, and the more they can invest in well equipment and services. Accordingly, Expro's management had been able to report a strong set of results in the twelve-month period to March 2008, with revenues up 18 per cent and underlying operating profits up 29 per cent on prior year.[231] The higher the oil price, the more profitable drilling is. It was one of the reasons behind the solid returns obtained by Candover on the Vetco deal, the price having risen from \$45 to \$75 per barrel during the period of ownership. With Goldman Sachs's energy sector analysts predicting in the spring of 2008 that the oil price could only go up, precisely to \$200 a barrel within two years,[232] the Expro investment looked set to become a home-run.

It was a very combative move supported by Candover's Investment Committee, one destined to close the 2005 Fund's investment period with a €195 million-plus equity call. Importantly, it also helped put more than €305 million of the 2008 Fund's money to work[233] before the new vintage had even seen its first closing. Although sector analysts had pointed out that Candover had had prior experience in the oilfield service industry,[234] the entry multiple paid on Expro was higher than that of the Vetco deal. The latter had partly benefited from the fact that, at the time of the transaction, its owner Swiss engineering conglomerate ABB had been afflicted by a heavy debt burden and asbestos-related claims in the US.[235] There was no such reason to attempt to buy Expro for a reasonable multiple.[236] In addition, and as further evidence of the firm's intent to maximise its chances of winning the deal, Candover and its co-investors had used some obscure but increasingly popular scheme of arrangement allowing it not to have to file a registration statement with the US regulator, and making it easier to orchestrate a delisting of Expro, therefore speeding up the acquisition process.

Time will tell whether it was a battle worth winning, but in view of the pugnacious manner with which the Expro PTP was conducted, only a year and a half later a recapitalisation would be carried out, replacing the senior debt with a high-yield bond to allow the company more breathing space to manage its debt burden. With Expro, Candover had completed a hat trick in just seven months. The firm was doing its best to remain active in a sullen market. If it wasn't for Goldman Sachs and AlpInvest, the firm would have found it difficult to execute that take-private. In all likelihood, it would have failed to attract other co-investors and would clearly have been unable to fund the €1 billion-plus equity ticket on its own.

By now the environment was crumbling fast, but Candover was still optimistic about the market opportunities for the rest of the year. In the second quarter of 2008, market data indicated that the number of buyouts in the lower end of the large-cap segment, CPL's area of focus, were down a further 18 per cent, and the total value of such transactions had dropped 28 per cent. Still, in Candover's activity barometer Buffin opined that because five large LBOs had taken place in the previous four months, there were reasons to remain optimistic. He added that, despite the difficult conditions, the PE industry had often proven resilient in a downturn.[237] The group's target segment had suffered a 62 per cent decrease in value terms between mid-2007 and the three months to June 2008, plummeting from a total value of €26.5 billion in the third quarter of 2007 to €10 billion in the second quarter of 2008 across Europe, but the firm nonetheless remained bullish.

Sure, CPL had closed three deals in 2008, but they had all summoned the astute negotiating talent of expert dealmakers. Stork had taken seven months of trials and tribulations dealing with unpredictable hedge fund managers and a carve-out strategy for the benefit of Marel. In the end, CPL had ended up with a trimmed-down prize. The owner of Technogym had only considered the sale of a minority stake; the investment team, in contrast to a general inclination to hold a controlling stake in portfolio companies, had accepted the purchase of 40 per cent of the business. As for Expro, the acrimonious battle with Halliburton had driven the fund manager and its co-investors to pay a lot more than originally intended. Expro was also above the top end of the equity house's target range, so it had required CPL's close relationship with a premier investment bank like Goldman to pull it through. Candover would need that kind of support if it wanted to remain an active investor despite the slowing deal flow.

Yet, the firm's senior partners could no longer ignore or deny the impact that slowing demand had had on the Gala Coral investment. The drop in attendance at the investee company's bingo venues had been amplified by the stalling economy. Candover had cut Gala Coral's book value by half as noted in CIP's June 2008 interim report. The firm had had little choice in the matter. Back in March SVG (Schroder Ventures Group), one of Permira's main LPs, had publicly reported that it had reduced the carrying value of the business by almost 50 per cent to reflect lower market comparable earnings multiples.[238] Already at the time CIP had showed a more sanguine view by only writing Gala Coral down 15 per cent in its own 2007 annual report.* Six months later, since the gambling and betting group's performance had failed to improve, Candover could not possibly have recorded the investee company at a higher valuation than that of SVG without losing face.

The senior executives at both CPL and CIP were nonetheless ready to send a positive signal regarding their fundraising initiative. They knew that they could not realistically announce a first closing of the 2008 Fund at less than half the originally stated target size of €5 billion. Unfortunately, by July 2008 CPL had only received firm commitments worth €1.8 billion from LPs, including Sacramento-based pension fund manager CalPERS and loyal investment partner AlpInvest.[239] At that stage, it was still unclear how secure Standard Life's commitment to that new fund was.[240] Due to a lack of appetite from several prospective limited partners, CPL needed a commitment of €1 billion from CIP in order to have a first closing exceeding the €2.5 billion mark.

Amazingly, Grimstone supported the idea. Of course he had agreed to it when the new fund had been launched earlier in the year,[241] but the circumstances had changed dramatically. The fact that it represented twice the LP's commitment to the Candover 2005 Fund did not seem to concern CIP's board of directors either, even though CPL was finding it exacting to make realisations, that is to dispose of its investee companies. Other than the sale of residual stakes in a couple of already partially realised investments, Candover had failed to make any portfolio exit since the beginning of the year. In order to commit €1 billion, the group's Chairman needed to be confident that sufficient cash would flow from CPL back to CIP; that was the listed company's principal source of funds in order to make good such a colossal pledge. With financial markets falling apart, and a buyout sector showing worrying signs of fatigue, it looked like portfolio disposals would be a delicate affair for the foreseeable future. Grimstone himself had raised that point repeatedly, first during the interim results announcement in September of the previous year, and again in the group's 2007 annual report released in March 2008.

---

* Although an element of that difference can be attributed to the fact that the entry book value was lower for Candover than for Permira, the latter having acquired its 30 per cent stake in Gala in 2005 at a higher EV than the one paid by Candover and Cinven in 2003

News that the national economy was being affected by the financial crisis, like some North American and European countries had been in the first quarter, was now official. Various sources announced that the UK's GDP growth had been flat or slightly negative in the second quarter of the year. And other major European nations, including France, Germany, Italy, the Netherlands and Spain, had joined the list of shrinking economies.[242] Irrespective of the heightened prospects of an economic recession and the risk of infection from the credit crunch, the firm was still confident about the success of its upcoming fundraising and had in parallel started to expand its deal origination capabilities. In recent months, CPL had gone on a hiring spree, assembling an investment team to cover Eastern Europe. In mid-August, Candover publicly announced the formation of Candover Eastern European Partners (CEEP). Complete with a team of five practised professionals, these activities were to be financed initially by CIP and would be independent from CPL's main operations, even if Buffin and Gumienny were named board members.[243] In addition, the group had opened and locally staffed offices in Mumbai and Hong Kong to support its existing portfolio companies in that part of the world, but also to start building an operational structure in the fastest growing region of the global economy. In view of the group's still fairly thin experience in foreign markets and the laborious economic situation, the CEEP move and CIP's Asian office openings seemed risky. Even in a prosperous financial environment, developing the business further away from home would have been a stretch. In the conditions prevailing at the time, it was ominous. But the new initiatives certainly formed part of a grand vision. Expanding in Asia was the best way to prepare Candover's eventual entry into the next LP category: the highly coveted 'global mega-large' €10 billion-plus segment.

Seeing AlpInvest and Goldman Sachs co-invest alongside CPL to acquire Expro International might have contributed to give the impression that all was well in the best of all possible worlds. No doubt Grimstone would have been reassured that these well-versed investors were disposed to back the firm in that transaction. However, because the US investment bank was a frequent M&A adviser and debt provider to CPL and AlpInvest had been an LP in recent funds (including as far back as the 1997 vintage)[244] and a co-investor in previous Candover deals (it had participated in the delisting of Ontex as revealed in its 2008 annual review,[245] but also in the Newmond, Eversholt and RIM buyouts in the 1990s as discussed earlier), they were both finding it natural to look after a long-time investment partner. Goldman Sachs knew they could count on Candover and its portfolio companies to generate fees in the future – the US bank would for instance co-lead the refinancing of Expro's senior debt a year later. Netherlands-based AlpInvest was a very powerful pension fund manager, and the participation in the delisting was simply part of its diversification strategy. An equity ticket in the oil services and systems group was a drop in the ocean for Goldman, arguably the largest private equity co-investor in the world, and for the Dutch LP which administered €30 billion of capital; by contrast, Expro was CPL's second largest LBO ever.

Looking closely at Candover Investments plc's annual reports in 2006 and 2007, one also gets confirmation that the group's identity had become more modern and dynamic. In line with the newly renovated 20 Old Bailey offices, the 2006-07 reports are flashier and jazzier than their 2005 equivalent. The graphs and tables in bright green colours are evocative of those verdant plate-glass panels at the refurbished head office. The power within the organisation also seems shared more equally by CIP's non-executive Chairman and CPL's two co-heads. The photos of Grimstone, Buffin and Gumienny feature prominently with the very contemporary Candover offices in the background. Further, the operational section reserved for CPL has been expanded. By the time the 2008 annual report was published in the spring of 2009, we can conclude that CIP had gone back to its roots: the bright office images have been removed and Grimstone's photo is included in the traditional low-key black and white version used by Curran back in 2005. For someone picking up the 2005 and 2008 reports, nothing would seem out of place in the good old British investment firm. In the interval though, major changes had occurred and tarnished the hard-earned reputation of the 25-year-old institution. Here is how.

As it turns out, CIP's commitment was announced with much excitement on 27 August 2008.[246] And rightly so. Candover Investments plc's share price was close to its all-time high set back in February that same year,[247] reaching 2,280 pence on 29 August. It reflected the recent Expro acquisition, the promising expansion strategy in emerging markets, and the shareholders' confidence in the fundraising process. Shareholders knew that a larger fund would automatically increase management fee income and proceeds from realised assets. The group had reached a market valuation of approximately £500 million and controlled or co-managed the equivalent of €15 billion of debt and equity positions. Grimstone reiterated his view that it was 'a good time to invest, with company valuations and debt multiples back to more sensible levels',[248] prudently adding that realisations would be 'harder to achieve'.[249] Since the beginning of the year, notwithstanding the seriously worsening financial landscape, the group's senior management had remained bullish as demonstrated by their deal activity. No one suspected that the shattering collapse of US investment bank Lehman Brothers was only days away.

With CPL reporting its new fund's first closing of €2.8 billion, the fundraising team went back on the road to market the 2008 vintage to those investors who had refused to come in for the first round. Unfortunately, Lehman's fall on 15 September had startled many of them. In the hours that followed the US bank's bankruptcy filing, HBOS, one of Britain's leading property lenders, had to admit that its mortgage portfolio was in dire straits. Two days later, in a forced bail-out overseen by the Bank of England and the Treasury, it was acquired for £12 billion by its competitor Lloyds TSB. The events of the second half of September had plunged the PE sector into complete disarray. Because of the strong interconnections between banks worldwide, the Lehman and HBOS episodes were deeply affecting Candover's prospective investors. It was clear that that new phase of the credit crunch would slow the 2008 Fund's marketing efforts further, and that CPL would have to wait till the dust settled before many institutional investors could contemplate underwriting firm commitments. Worse still, stock exchanges across the globe were tumbling once again and the debt markets remained shut, making any sale of investee businesses all but impossible.

Within weeks, the situation of the banking and financial sectors had become hopeless. On 7 October, the UK government had announced a £50 billion rescue package for the banking industry, only to be forced to part-nationalise the two largest retail banks RBS and Lloyds TSB/HBOS three days later. It was Britain's turn to either let the mortgage lenders repossess houses of defaulting borrowers or organise a large-scale bail-out financed by the taxpayers. Gordon Brown's government would choose the second option, thereby instantly replacing hundreds of billions of pounds of private sector liability into sovereign debt.

It was also evident that the buyout loans had been stuck on the banks' balance sheets for the last twelve months. The previously mentioned SIVs that had been designed to help banks keep the toxic debt off their books had been folding at a rapid pace in the US. As explained, third parties such as credit hedge funds and CLO funds had endured a considerable withdrawal of capital. The banks had built up liabilities without being able to amass corresponding assets in equivalent amounts. Since a vast portion of banks' assets usually originate from individual savers, many desperate lenders in the UK and other overexposed regions had tried to attract new customers by hiking their savings accounts' interest rates. As could be expected, this practice would fall short of the vast quantity of capital necessary to maintain the banks' liquidity ratios, eventually forcing many national governments to rescue them.

With the storm gathering momentum, many GPs frantically rushed the final closing of their latest fundraise. Pan-European mid-market investor Bridgepoint, which had launched its fourth fund in the wake of the debt syndication crisis twelve months earlier, disclosed in late October that it had raised a whopping €4.8 billion, exceeding its target by 20 per cent and only marginally missing its hard cap of €5 billion. But it had taken the company six months to raise the last €800 million, proving that the market had recently tightened up.[250] North European LBO specialist Nordic Capital's seventh fund was also closed in November, exceeding its target by €600 million and reaching its hard cap of €4.3 billion.[251] Both had been lucky in their timing; the fundraising doors were being shut behind them.

The decision by the Candover senior management team to launch a new fund eight months earlier was now seen as a life-threatening sentence for the firm. It seems that they had underestimated the impact that the events of the second half of 2007 would have on their business, the LBO sector and the whole economy. Having lived through the endless but ultimately successful 2001 fundraising, they had presumably assumed that the world was entering a similar correction. They believed that the 2008 fundraising would be drawn out – the 2001 process had taken fifteen months – but that it would eventually happen. The context was different however.

Back in 2001, CPL's fundraising had been successful because investors were looking for a haven away from the information technology and telecom catastrophe. A traditional, shrewd investor like Candover had rightly been interpreted as the ideal solution to sort the wheat from the chaff. In 2008, spooked investors were retreating into state-guaranteed savings accounts or government bonds, and more poignantly away from the over-leveraged alternative investment world of property, hedge funds and private equity. Large funds like Candover's, and in particular mega-funds, were partly seen as the culprits behind the present messy situation the way Internet start-ups and the overinflated NASDAQ had been perceived seven years earlier.

At the time the firm had been aided by the magical returns of the 1994 Fund, which had benefited as we have seen from the generously underpriced Eversholt privatisation and other stellar realisations. The 1997 Fund's performance was far less flattering and coupled with a fragile-looking 2001 vintage would have made edgy investors hesitant to take the plunge, especially post-Lehman. Back in September 2001, as he was announcing CIP's half year results in an uncertain climate following the end of the dotcom bubble, Curran had stated: 'Of course prices have fallen and purchasers want tomorrow's prices while vendors want yesterday's, but it is possible to buy and it is possible to sell'.[252] In the months following the Lehman debacle, buyers and sellers had disappeared. There was no market. Because it was coupled with the credit crunch, the 2008 downturn was more akin to the fallout of the late 1980s LBO bubble, when deal values had dropped 60 per cent due to debt shortage, than to the post-NASDAQ crash era, which had primarily affected early-stage investing.

It is in those last few weeks of 2008 that Managing Director Charlie Green took the decision to quit the firm.[253] There was no press release to explain the reasons behind the move, but we can speculate that he had taken the view that Candover's future was sealed. Sure, Green's portfolio companies Equity Trust and EurotaxGlass's were probably reeling in the severe economic downturn, but they were in no way the only ones. All of the firm's senior executives were now humbled by some of the investment decisions they had made in the previous five years. After going through three different CEOs and Finance Directors over a four-year period, suffered a significant deterioration in trading since its 2003 delisting and failed to carve out its incontinence and healthcare division in a last attempt to solve its cash-strapped position,[254] Gumienny's Ontex had been refinanced favourably in the early months of 2007 in what could be termed 'perfect timing' ahead of a sudden change in market conditions.[255] The credit markets had been shut ever since that recapitalisation. In any case, Candover had already written off a large chunk of equity on that deal. Gambling group Gala Coral and yacht maker Ferretti, together with ALcontrol, the soil and food testing service provider sponsored by Simon Leefe in late 2004, were the ones facing the least enviable position. Profitability at Gala Coral had slipped by 10 per cent over the preceding twelve-month period, pushing the company's already stretched financial gearing ratio to 7.8 times EBITDA.[256] Facing sharply weakening prospects, portfolio company Ferretti, which had prepared for an IPO since April, had been forced to operate a strategic review. Its CEO Vincenzo Cannatelli, brought in by Candover in early 2007, was on the way out.[257]

Green had been with the firm for ten years and was very well respected in the financial community. He had led and executed many deals for CPL and worked with Gumienny on several transactions including the Swissport and EurotaxGlass's LBOs. Whatever the personal or political circumstances, his departure was a major blow for the business. It was the first time in the firm's 28-year history that a member of its senior leadership team had quit. Even Chevrillon's resolution to take a back seat from Candover in 2007 had seen him assume the transitional non-executive position of Vice Chairman of CPL.[258] Given his MD title and his seat on the Executive Committee, Green was presumably a keyman for the 2008 Fund, so his leaving was a sign that the latest fundraising initiative was in jeopardy. It was the precursor of a major reorganisation that was to take place in the first half of 2009, the first of a series of events from which Candover would never recover.

In the meantime, as the economy continued to deteriorate – in the third quarter, the UK's GDP had fallen by 0.6 per cent and the eurozone had officially entered a recession after two successive quarters of negative economic growth - and the financial markets were consumed by panic, the European PE sector had recorded a drop of more than 50 per cent over the previous year. In the whole of 2008, less than €85 billion worth of transactions had been completed, taking the industry back to its 2004 level. The volume of transactions was only down 18 per cent on prior year, indicating that it was essentially the large LBOs, heavily dependent on debt financing, that were feeling the impact of the credit crunch. By the end of 2008, the sector's new challenges had more to do with bail-outs than buyouts. As the year drew to an end, US carmaker Chrysler, acquired as you may recall by hedge-fund-manager-turned-buyout-specialist-extraordinaire Cerberus at the peak of the debt extravaganza, started going through a nationalisation procedure with the help of a government protection scheme. In the UK alone, almost 150 PE-backed companies had gone into receivership or were taken over by their debt-holders, representing over 40 per cent of the industry's realisations that year.[259]

Candover had chosen to remain extremely active during the year. While the group had invested £400 million in equity throughout 2007, including follow-on contributions to its existing portfolio, it had almost tripled its capital commitment during 2008 by putting over £1.1 billion to work.[260] Meanwhile, the entire sector had experienced a severe correction with industry data showing equity amounts being invested in UK MBOs plunging 59 per cent between 2007 and 2008, with the large segment of the market (defined as transactions worth more than £100 million) experiencing an even bigger drop of 72 per cent.[261] Falling in line with the market, other large and mega-buyout funds had elected to massively scale back their deal-doing: the amounts invested by Apax during the year had declined by 40 per cent compared to their 2007 level and Bridgepoint's were down 60 per cent to €395 million.[262]

Comparing CPL's deal volumes against its peers' makes the countercyclical nature of the group's investment activity as glaring. In the first twelve months of the financial crisis - that is from September 2007 to August 2008 - Candover had completed four transactions, the same number as during the twelve-month-span leading to the credit crunch (between September 2006 and August 2007), a period soon to be acknowledged as the peak of the buyout hysteria. In contrast, the vast majority of the group's competitors had adapted to the new market environment and slowed down, in some instances very significantly, their investing pace. Mid-market and upper mid-market participants were cooling down: Bridgepoint had closed six buyouts in the year preceding the credit drought but only two in the twelve months leading up to the collapse of Lehman Brothers while Charterhouse's number of investments was down by half over the same period and Cinven's by a third. Similarly, across Europe the industry's giants were adopting a more subdued attitude: KKR's tally had plummeted from six to only one transaction, CVC's from five to two, and Permira's adjustment had been even more drastic, plunging from nine pre-financial crisis to a single acquisition between September 2007 and the summer of 2008. As the storm was taking hold, the most dominant LBO managers were shortening the sail.

Had Curran still been Executive Chairman of CIP in 2008, it is likely that, faced with such dire conditions, he would have pushed back on CPL's request and proposed a much lower contribution amount from CIP. He might even have asked CPL to reduce the overall target of the 2008 Fund. In November 2010, he would assert to have been opposed to such a large commitment which he 'considered too big compared to the firm's assets and therefore too risky'.[263] Unfortunately, having stepped down from his position as a non-executive director of CIP's board in December 2007, by the time the new vintage had been launched he had no further connection with the group other than as a shareholder of the listed entity.

That Grimstone was unable to recognise the likely impact of the financial crisis on the business is difficult to reconcile with his background as a very knowledgeable senior executive of the financial industry, including as a former corporate financier at British investment bank Schroder. It is possible that he had relied on assurances from CPL that portfolio realisations were only momentarily delayed. The IPO of

Italian boat manufacturer Ferretti had been postponed because of unfavourable conditions, but in their mind it had simply being pushed back and it was only a matter of time before the exit would happen. Energy information service provider Wood Mackenzie was performing strongly and was certainly also a sale candidate. Assuredly, Grimstone's inside knowledge of Standard Life's investment activities would have reassured him that if the Edinburgh-headquartered insurer had chosen to co-invest alongside CPL in the recent Stork takeover[264] and was going through its due diligence to participate in the Candover 2008 Fund, there was no reason why he should withhold or cut back CIP's commitment.

Regardless, even in a strong economic climate, the €1 billion undertaking would have required perfectly timed exits from CPL's portfolio in order for CIP to have any hope of gathering the necessary funds to participate in future capital calls. Since almost all of the limited partner's cash resources were derived from the realisation of its subsidiary's past investments from the 2001 and 2005 funds, the €1 billion pledge was essentially dependent on CPL's ability to dispose of recently acquired portfolio companies. However, with a typical investment period of five years for the new fund and assuming 20 per cent of its commitment being drawn annually, CIP needed at least €200 million to be returned from CPL every year between 2008 and 2013 in order to invest that much annually towards the 2008 vintage. The listed trust had only once before received such a large cash up-flow from its subsidiary; it was in 2007, at the peak of the bubble. To hope for a similar annual performance in the years ahead was a big ask. Another way of demonstrating how challenging CIP's undertaking was is from analogy with the property market. The typical loan-to-annual salary ratio that a bank is usually willing to grant an individual borrower is about 3 times, with a peak of 5 to 6 times recorded during the recent real estate bull market. A €1 billion ticket represented 6 to 8 times CIP's average annual realisation proceeds over the previous three years.

The year 2008 had witnessed the buyout industry's perfect storm and Candover's problems had gone from bad to worse. By the end of the year, as the firm was still marketing its new vintage, it had only exited one portfolio company from its 2005 fund, the Norwegian cable operator Get (formerly UPC Norway). It had made no exit for the previous twelve months other than the disposal of its residual stakes in publicly listed Aspen Insurance and Wellstream in what was its smallest number of realisations in any given year since 1985. Prospects for the following few months were gruesome and the Candover 2005 Fund did not look set to record any exit in 2009 either. Painful decisions needed to be made internally. Only a miracle could now save the fundraising campaign.

Chapter 10 - Annus Horribilis

Unfortunately the year 2009 started the way 2008 had ended. Worldwide, as stock markets continued their free fall, central banks and governments were trying every trick in the book to avoid a repeat of the Great Depression of the 1930s. Britain was embroiled in a bitter political crisis as Prime Minister Gordon Brown stood accused of having made things worse for the taxpayer by building gargantuan public deficits that risked plunging the country back to the 1970s.

In the middle of that financial and economic meltdown, it was apparent that the private equity industry would not escape unscathed. Many PE firms were experiencing pressure from their LPs or from within. French financial sponsor PAI was going through its own internal coup when its two most senior partners - the original executives behind the funds' own management buyout from French bank BNP Paribas in 2002 - were forced out. PAI ended up having to halve the size of its latest fund and scale down its investment team. Following its hairy buyout of EMI, which had valued the music publisher at a towering 15 to 18.5 times EBITDA according to various sources,[265] and the decision to book a €1.37 billion provision for permanent impairment of investments in its 2008 Annual Review,[266] Terra Firma was also implementing a reorganisation. Seven years after setting up the business, in March 2009 its founder Guy Hands abandoned his CEO title to solely retain the chairmanship.[267] Having to cope with over £2 billion of financial gearing, 3i had replaced its CEO in January[268] and was rationalising its operations by discontinuing and selling on the secondary market its early-stage investment portfolio. Under pressure from its LPs following the liquidity issues of listed investment trust SVG, one of its key investors, mega-firm

Permira had also reduced the size of its latest fund, a €11.1 billion investment vehicle, and given the opportunity for all its investors to cut their commitments.

In the last three months of 2008, obtaining firm commitments for additional capital had been a challenge for all PE fund managers. But Buffin, Gumienny and Grimstone knew that they had bigger problems. The fall of Lehman Brothers had not only led to financial indecision from a macroeconomic standpoint. Down to the level of microcredit and the buyout market, there was no financing available. Individuals were not alone in being turned away by their local banks whenever they requested a consumer loan or a mortgage. Buyout transactions had all but disappeared. Most mezzanine lenders had either gone out of business or run out of money. As had been the case for over twelve months now, senior bankers were attempting to work off their existing portfolio of stressed loans and were not in the mood to add any new positions. Some existing credit lines on the secondary market were often quoted at 20 or 30 pence on the pound so there was little appetite for new products offered at par.

Crumbling under its €1 billion debt load, investee company Ferretti was not showing signs of improvements. The Italian yacht builder had suffered a serious trading adjustment in the last quarter of 2008: its order books had shrunk in the weeks following the liquidation of Lehman Brothers as its wealthy clients had progressively realised that their fortune had sunk in line with the stock markets. In mid-January 2009, Candover was rumoured to be in the process of appointing debt advisers Rothschild to support them on a possible financial restructuring exercise,[269] and only weeks later a covenant breach[270] had shown that trading at Ferretti was going downhill at a very fast pace indeed.

In that environment, CPL had been incapable of achieving exits from its portfolio. In late 2008 and early 2009, even great quality assets like Springer and Wood Mackenzie could not find a buyer; not because of their intrinsic performance, but because their acquisition could not be financed. Since CIP depended heavily on the fund manager's portfolio realisations, it was becoming patent that it would not be able to make good its €1 billion promise to the 2008 vintage. Not now, and not in the foreseeable future.

And the inevitability of the sentence was delivered in the early part of 2009. The group's finance team had to bow to the fact that, because of its €1 billion liability and a significant drop in net asset value, CIP was at risk of not being a going concern, an accounting term used to indicate that the business faced significant solvency issues and was exposed to the probability of folding within the next twelve months. The 2008 annual report shows that discussions between the group and its external auditors Grant Thornton were serious enough to warrant a detailed explanation and justification by CIP's directors about the adoption of the going concern basis in their preparation of the group's accounts. A nine-line section in the previous year's accounts had turned into a multi-paragraph seventy-four-line component in the 2008 version. With the benefit of taking a step forward and looking at CIP's 2009 annual report, the group's accounts give a very scary picture of the situation the company was in when the auditors had carried out their traditional annual review in the early days of 2009: including the pledge made by CIP towards the Candover 2008 Fund, the ratio of outstanding commitments (i.e. CIP's liabilities) to net assets was a shocking 393 per cent as at 31 December 2009. Since CPL had executed several successful realisations during the year and the group's portfolio had shown an improvement in book value between December 2008 and December 2009,[271] we can only assume that the net asset position in early 2009, during the annual audit when Grant Thornton and Candover's internal finance department were desperately trying to make sense of it all, would have been even lower, and the aforementioned ratio inversely higher. A company that needed €200 million to flow upstream from its subsidiary on an annual basis had only received *c.* €65 million from CPL's investment disposals in 2008. With 2009 looking like another challenging year, as they were going through the books the auditors must have predicted that the €135 million shortfall was likely to be the first of a long series. In their independent statement to the 2008 financial accounts, Grant Thornton had inserted an *Emphasis of matter* section to draw attention to the fact that the Group faced 'material uncertainties over future results and cash flows'.*

---

* An emphasis of matter paragraph is used by auditors to indicate that a significant or fundamental

The Candover group was actually in even more financial trouble. In anticipation of the 2008 Fund and the expansion in Eastern Europe and in Asia, CIP had issued several multi-million, multi-currency bonds in 2007. The internal review would likely have shown that there was also a risk that the firm would be unable at some stage in the near future to meet its contractual obligations in relation to the interest or capital repayment schedule for those bonds. Used to dealing with portfolio companies defaulting on their debt obligations, the group was now confronted with the possible scenario of breaching its own loan note covenants.[272] Covenants are a set of requirements that a borrower must meet in order to be in compliance with its lending agreement; they act as advanced warning signals to give enough time for borrowers and lenders to negotiate new terms and recapitalise the company if need be. Going through the annual reports of 2007 and 2008, we notice that CIP had raised a total of £150 million in three tranches of senior debt, each subscribed in a different currency. A company that had no full-time employees – since all its directors were non-executives – was piling on complex financial gearing, with one tranche listed in the US and denominated in dollars presumably to finance the firm's Asian initiative or even the occasional deal in the US,[273] one line in euros supposedly to finance the CEEP team build-up or other European plans, and the third in British pounds, issued in January 2008 and therefore having a different redemption schedule than the first two. Inevitably the firm was incurring exchange movements on the foreign-currency-issued debt, but to try and alleviate that uncertainty the US dollar-denominated term loan had been hedged so CIP was also incurring derivatives gains and losses. Once again, this was a holding company employing no full-time staff. The tortuous financing arrangement must have kept CPL's Finance Director busy and sleepless at night. It was an unfamiliar situation for the company. Since its inception and the £2 million loan that Brooke had contracted back in 1980 to help set up the company, Candover had never handled long-term debt on such a scale, and this for a very simple reason: it did not need to. If successful, buyout investing is a very, very cash-generative trade.

---

uncertainty has occurred and therefore requires disclosure to enable the user of the financial statements to have a better understanding of the company's performance

Looking at the group cash flow statements in CIP's annual reports between 2005 and 2008, there might be an equally disturbing reason behind the firm's liquidity dilemma. The 2007 and 2008 loan subscriptions had originally been completed to support the group's 2008 fundraising and its respective expansion strategy.[274] But it is very likely that confronted by commitments towards the Candover 2005 Fund and the pace of investing adopted by the CPL deal team in 2006, 2007 and 2008, CIP could have run out of money by mid-2008, thereby defaulting on part of its commitment. Going through the firm's 2005 accounts, the net cash position was £189.4 million at the year-end. By the end of 2006, it was £63.4 million due to the numerous equity calls made to invest in the Get, EurotaxGlass's, mailing company DX Services, Ferretti and Hilding Anders transactions. In 2007, we note that total cash available, ignoring the cash inflow related to the debt raised in January of that year, would have become £120.4 million at the year-end thanks to significant portfolio realisations from CPL, i.e. the disposals of Vetco, Bureau van Dijk, Get and Thule. But then we get to the 2008 accounts: again ignoring the £33 million of debt-related positive cash flow, the net cash position would have reached a negative balance of almost £20 million because of the large equity calls coming from CPL to finance the buyouts of Stork, Technogym and Expro. In fact, CIP's cash position had benefited from a positive £35 million-exchange movement. Had it not occurred, the net cash situation at the end of 2008 could have been minus £55 million. From this analysis, it appears that, without its £150 million loans, CIP would have run out of cash by the time the Expro equity call had been made. In order to eschew that situation, Grimstone would have had to request from the firm's deal doers that they slow down the pace of investments and accelerate the rate of disposals. Instead, in the summer of 2008 CIP was in effect using borrowed money in order to finance its equity share in the leveraged buyout of Expro.

At the risk of stating the obvious, liquidity in the world of private equity is of paramount importance. Back in March 1998, when reporting the firm's 1997 annual accounts, Curran had been asked why the company was hoarding so much cash on its balance sheet; its cash-to-NAV ratio was standing at 56 per cent at the end of December 1997. The group's Chief Executive had explained that it was to satisfy CIP's commitment to the 1997 Fund.[275] Ten years later, the PLC's board of directors seemed to have forgotten this golden rule.

Such a plight could altogether have been averted. In 2006, between the annual dividend distribution and a one-off payout, CIP had returned over £100 million in cash to its shareholders. It was not a contractual obligation, simply a decision by Curran to return some of the liquid assets the company was sitting on. Evidently, in his typical efficient and organised ways, he knew that it did not make sense for Candover to hold so much cash on its balance sheet that it did not have a use for.[276] In order to meet short-term needs such as capital calls from CPL, the parent company had contracted a one-year term loan of £33 million in January 2006. That in itself was unexpected. Why decide to leverage, even if only for one year, CIP's balance sheet when he could have instead reduced the cash-back to the shareholders? Only Curran could explain what his thinking was at the time. If I had to venture a guess, it is possible that holding so much liquidity was seen as a drag on the listed trust's share price due to lower returns achieved on cash assets compared to PE investments. However, while it is indeed a handicap in times of strong market performance as experienced in 2006, cash offers a valuable safety net when public markets turn bearish like they did in late 2008. In any case, Grimstone could have used some of that £100-million bounty to fund the firm's emerging markets conquest and some of its equity calls two years later. Such a bold push into new geographies had certainly not been in Curran's plans and, as he was retiring, he felt it was his duty to tidy up CIP's balance sheet before handing over the reins. In his Chairman's statement to the 2005 annual report, he had explained that after taking into consideration the group's cash flow position, CPL's realisation timetable and future capital commitments towards the 2005 Fund, CIP's board of directors had favoured a one-off £100 million cashback to shareholders.

It appears that there was a breakdown of communication and a discontinuity in the firm's strategy between the Curran era and the early months of Grimstone's chairmanship. What was the point of returning £100 million in cash to CIP's shareholders in early 2006 only for the group to raise £150 million worth of loans over the following eighteen months? It might seem hazardous for an investment firm participating in leveraged buyouts to be gearing up its own balance sheet, but it was another sign that the industry was operating in a bubble and that the day of reckoning was approaching.

By the middle of February 2009, the findings of the group's annual audit left CIP with no alternative but to acknowledge that it was not in a position to abide by its original commitment to the 2008 Fund.[277] The group admitted that it would have to reduce the size of its 2008 Fund due to CIP's inability to honour its €1 billion commitment. CPL reset the fund target down to €3 billion. Because other listed buyout funds, including 3i and Permira's limited partner and original owner SVG, had had a rough ride in recent months, few outside the firm truly understood how bad the situation was. In effect, that decision was opening Pandora's Box.

As is common for fund-marketing documentation, the Candover 2008 Fund's PPM contained an opt-out clause whereby any LP would be entitled to withdraw its commitment if one of the cornerstone investors, in this case Candover Investments plc, became insolvent or risked becoming insolvent should it be forced to continue investing. By admitting that CIP was unable to fulfil its duty,[278] CPL was in effect giving the option for all other limited partners to walk away from the new fund. At that time, the world's leading public stock indices were at a thirteen-year low. For institutional investors, liquidity was preferable to liability; receiving money now was better than risking defaulting on future financial requirements. Most LPs were likely to decide to exercise their right under the early termination clause. The structure of the Candover Group would also have made them nervous. If CIP went under, what would happen to CPL, its wholly owned subsidiary?

Earlier in the month of February, the industry's bigwigs had attended the pompously named SuperReturn Conference, private equity's main European gathering taking place in Berlin. Momentarily christened 'SuperWrite-Off' by the doomsayers, the event had as usual drawn over a thousand representatives from the best-established buyout shops together with investors, lenders, investment bankers, lawyers, consultants and various other advisers. The mood was decidedly down. Market data indicated that the deal flow had crashed in the previous year, and there was no evidence that things would improve in 2009. Several of the sector's leading figures warned that portfolio realisations would be more laborious as the credit squeeze made it complicated for interested buyers to fund acquisitions. Candover's senior executives knew all about it.

The publication of the company's 2008 financial statements had been eagerly awaited by business journalists across London. Following the release of the group's preliminary results on 2 March 2009, they analysed every comment with excruciating detail, making Candover's position almost unbearable. CIP's public humiliation would also apply to the CPL team, most outsiders not truly grasping the distinction between the fund provider and the fund manager. Newspaper articles noted that net assets per share had halved between 31 December 2007 and 31 December 2008. The value of seven portfolio companies had been chalked down partially or entirely. The loss of Ferretti, following Candover's resolution not to participate in its recapitalisation, was also related and proved, if needed, that the group's grief was not only due to CIP's over-commitment but also partially to poor investment choices by the CPL crew in the previous five years. The situation was desperate. It would soon become irreparable.

I indicated earlier that the firm had pre-empted the 2008 fundraising before it had even exceeded the coveted 75 per cent investment threshold for the previous fund. There is another piece of evidence that supports my argument that CPL had come to market too soon. Limited partners have always kept a close eye on the realisation (that is the proportion of investee companies exited) of preceding funds before subscribing to a new vehicle. Historically the CPL team had generally been efficient at making sure that a meaningful number of disposals had already occurred ahead of launching a new vintage. But the 2008 process had not followed this quintessential rule. To demonstrate my point, let us consider the most recent fund-marketing processes run by the firm.

When it had closed its 2001 fundraising in June 2002, Candover had already exited six of its fifteen investments from the 1997 Fund and nine of its thirteen investments from the 1994 Fund; that is a realisation ratio of 40 per cent and 69 per cent respectively. By the time it closed its 2005 process in November 2005, the firm had realised one full and one partial exit out of its 2001 vintage and thirteen out of fifteen from the 1997 Fund, implying realisations of 12 per cent and 87 per cent respectively. At the time, the good exit ratio of the 1997 Fund and the flourishing LBO market had assuredly convinced LPs to participate even though the 2001 vintage had achieved few disposals. But the point is even more glaring when we consider that CPL held the first closing of its latest vintage in August 2008 and it had only disposed of one company from the 2005 Fund and seven from the 2001 Fund (9 per cent and 44 per cent realised). The 2008 Fund was raised too early and the upcoming economic recession was likely to make sale processes very knotty, and a proper assessment of the unrealised portfolio next to impossible. Grimstone himself would later admit during Candover Investments plc's AGM on Wednesday 13 May 2009 that the firm's investment realisation strategy had been wrong.[279] We will never know, but LPs would perhaps have reacted differently if Candover had raised its new fund in late 2009. By that time, it had disposed of ten (63 per cent) of its 2001 portfolio companies. Instead, because of CPL's low portfolio realisation ratio, CIP's cash flow problems and the adverse economic climate, the group was forced to contemplate various strategic options.

As early as the month of March 2009, stories spread that several parties had approached the company and were considering making an offer for parts of its underlying portfolio. By then, the group's public status was becoming a serious drawback. Its listing on the stock exchange obligated CIP to disclose far more information regarding its performance than its peers did. Following some sparse details divulged in February, press reports after newspaper articles and online financial newswires helped spread a simple fact: it was no longer a rumour, Candover was in trouble.

Feeling the pain, management could nonetheless comfort itself in knowing that it was not alone. In an activity survey that Candover published in April 2009, the extent of the buyout crash could now be quantified: the total value of European PE-backed transactions in the first three months of 2009 had reached just €4 billion, the lowest quarterly level since the third quarter of 1996, representing a plunge of 94 per cent compared with the second quarter of 2007, and more than 50 per cent down on the last three months of 2008. The number of deals was also well down, with just 60 per cent of the number completed in the first quarter of 2008. No LBOs of more than €1 billion had gone through during the period, reflecting the lack of activity at the large end of the sector.[280] The extent of the market correction had a strong resemblance with the Internet crash nine years earlier.

It was not just the buyout industry but the entire economy that was in reverse. Seeking to revive the economy, the Bank of England had slashed its base rate from 5.5 per cent in December 2007 to 0.5 per cent by March 2009, its lowest point ever since the central bank's foundation in the late seventeenth century. By now, the only subject economists could not agree on was whether the country, and the rest of the world for that matter, would endure a depression or a deep recession.

No one was better placed than the banks to know that new market conditions called for new rules. Royal Bank of Scotland, 60 per cent owned by the British government since November 2008 and the original senior debt and mezzanine underwriter for the Ferretti deal back in 2006, had decided to play hard-ball with equity providers Candover and Permira. The RBS-led syndicate of lenders had rejected a proposal made by the buyout firms in early February to inject more equity in exchange for a significant debt write-off.[281] Instead, in a debt-equity swap that was to halve the yacht manufacturer's leverage, RBS, Mediobanca and the rest of the senior syndicate would take a majority stake in the business alongside founder and Chairman Norberto Ferretti and his senior management team. The second lien and mezzanine lenders would also become equity-holders in exchange for writing off their debt.[282] In a stroke that was a terrifying sign of things to come, Ferretti's creditors had taken control of the company after only a few months of relentless negotiations. A business that was still showing promising double-digit revenue growth and preparing for a stock market float in September of the previous year[283] had become a complete write-off six months later, representing an equity loss not far from €300 million for Candover.[284]

With no alternative, by early April Candover entered into a standstill agreement to suspend the fundraising process of its 2008 Fund and further investments for a period of six months.[285] The beleaguered group, advised by Merrill Lynch and Lexington Partners, confirmed that it was in discussions with various parties to discuss a range of options. Conjectures abounded about the identity of the interested bidders. British secondary fund Coller Capital, CIP's shareholder Electra, Paris-based listed investment firm Eurazeo, Italian group Bi-invest controlled by the Bonomi family, investment bank Goldman Sachs, vulture fund Harbour Capital, PE gatekeeper Hamilton Lane, global alternative asset manager Blackstone and US funds of funds like Paul Capital were all rumoured to be among the 'short-listed' third parties taking a look at CIP or at CPL's portfolio.[286] On 1 April 2009, the group's share price had reached 80 pence, a 96.5 per cent drop from its high the previous year. Its market value had nose-dived below £20 million for the first time since 1987. Such a low valuation on April Fools' Day certainly attracted the vultures, but to CIP's shareholders it was no laughing matter.

Candover's share price had gone from approximately 1,100 pence in the year 2000 to over 2,200 pence in the summer of 2008 but back down to 800 pence on 31 December 2008 and below 100 pence three months later. Institutional investors, among which original seed equity providers BP, Electra and Prudential and esteemed co-investor and strategic partner Legal & General,[287] had lost heavily on the valuation collapse. In recent years, as economic growth and cheap borrowing had boosted the profitability of CPL's portfolio, the company's shares had quoted at a significant premium to the underlying net asset value. The firm had traditionally been prudent in its book valuation, leaving some room for upside at the time of the portfolio realisation, but as the buyout bubble was gaining momentum the share premium had reached unhealthy proportions. At some point in early 2007, the stock of the investment trust would even quote 36 per cent above NAV, leading financial journalists euphemistically to consider it 'fairly priced'.[288] It obviously could not last and the market correction since the Lehman Brothers incident showed that investors were unsure what the group's net assets and CPL's investment holdings were now worth. They had punished the stock accordingly.

On Wednesday 13 May 2009, during CIP's Annual General Meeting with its shareholders, Honorary Life President Brooke was visibly affected by the turn of events. Overwhelmed, Candover's founder spoke of the group's desperate and precarious situation and of the harm done to its reputation. At the time, like many he probably secretly hoped that the damage was not beyond repair. But he knew that the coming months would be decisive. Implying that, as the banking meltdown was making front-page news, Candover's directors might have misjudged the foretelling signs of the credit crunch, Curran expressed his incredulity 'that the board was not aware there was a financial crisis'.[289] Many of CIP's non-execs were former bankers or investment managers and some still acted on the board of various financial services institutions. None of them would have failed to note the uncharacteristically downbeat Royal Bank of Scotland's half-year analyst presentation on 8 August 2008 - nineteen days before CIP had announced its €1 billion pledge to the Candover 2008 Fund – when the Scottish bank's Chief Executive Sir Fred Goodwin had announced £6 billion of write-downs due to credit market exposures, called off the interim dividend payout and stated that the world was facing the worst banking crisis for a generation.

A very apologetic Grimstone, gnawed by remorse, was universally being blamed for the company's distress. He would later admit to have offered his resignation, but shareholders had chosen to renew his mandate,[290] certainly not in a sign of unrestrained support – Curran had opposed Grimstone's re-election,[291] but because they knew that it was important to maintain some continuity at the top while the group tried to survive.

Now that the firm had publicly admitted past mistakes, conversations and negotiations needed to take place between members of CPL's Executive Committee. Given the distressed investment portfolio, the forsaken fundraise and the ongoing negotiations with potential acquirers, it was time for a change in leadership. Arney would have welcomed the idea of making room at the top. Back in late 2002, he had left the proprietary buyout division of US investment bank JP Morgan, CCMP as it was now known, to join Candover. At the time, JP Morgan Partners was not a strong player in Europe's buyout industry and was likely never to become one. The business was run from its New York headquarters and the European team was often given scant responsibilities. The odds of making it to the top were better in a British traditional outfit like Candover. Soon, his career move would be vindicated. Until then, irrespective of who was vying for the crown, a new leadership structure was needed. After ten years of joint leadership, the GP had to revert to the simpler and more coherent model that had been in operation in the past, first under Brooke, then with Curran. The solution of a single leader to run the firm going forward was the only palatable option, not just from an internal point of view but to reassure external investors as well.

It was a significant decision. By June, a new, simplified organisational design had been chosen. Buffin was stepping down from his Managing Director position and from the Executive Committee, but staying on in a senior advisory capacity to sort out the remaining loose ends of the aborted 2008 fundraise. After the best part of ten years spent heading the GP's investment strategy, Gumienny was assuming the less hands-on position of Chairman of CPL.[292]

Arney asserted his claim for the top executive role thanks to his almost immaculate investment exploits at the time. He was a highly regarded deal doer. One of his investments, Hilding Anders, was feeling the effects of the recession, and Expro had clearly been bought at a big multiple, but there was nothing exceptional in this. In such ambiguous times, all major buyout houses across Europe and America had to deal with distressed assets. Other than that, he had produced significant returns for CPL and was in a strong negotiating position to thrust his views. His achievements spoke for themselves: car equipment manufacturer Thule had extracted 2.5 times the original investment, grossing a 40 per cent IRR;[293] on Vetco the firm had made 4.1 times its money[294] and the quick flip on cable TV operator Get had yielded 2.2 times or a gross IRR of *c.* 50 per cent.[295] Six and a half years after joining the firm, Arney was taking on full operational duties and was named Managing Partner, or de facto CEO. Leefe, the 44-year old Managing Director and member of the Executive Committee who had been with CPL for the last seventeen years,[296] kept a senior partner function. The corporate upheaval that had started at the time of Green's departure six months earlier had finally ended. As a matter of fact, when it was obvious to everyone that the fund-marketing process would never run its course, the media exposure of Candover's misfortune had helped Arney impose himself to guide the firm forward. Without getting into the press comments regarding the power struggle between them,[297] Buffin and Gumienny had had little alternative but to relinquish their thrones. A new generation was now in place.

In this management shakeup, other senior executives, including star dealmaker Ian Gray, were sacrificed to the benefit of the new structure. The originator of home-runs like Inveresk, which had returned 4.6 times CPL's original investment,[298] and Wood Mackenzie, which was to generate a gross cash-on-cash multiple of 2.7 times,[299] Gray had been one of Gumienny's protégés. The two of them had collaborated on many deals, including Clondalkin, Bourne Leisure, Ontex and Ferretti. With Gray being left out of the new leadership structure, the firm was losing some of its talent, but the hard truth was that it could no longer afford it.

Before departing, Gray had in fact completed the disposal of research and consulting service provider Wood Mackenzie in a £553 million tertiary buyout by Charterhouse.[300] As just stated, that transaction would yield excellent returns for CPL, and importantly for CIP given the latter's precarious financial position at the time.[301] It had been an interesting sale process. US private equity giants Bain Capital, Hellman & Friedman and Warburg Pincus had been earnest bidders for the energy consultancy, but they had failed to read the script properly. Although Charterhouse had been a runner-up for part of the process, it had eventually won the hotly disputed auction. Wood Mackenzie was a strongly performing company run, as discussed before, by a purposeful Scottish management team. It helped that Charterhouse's investment team had a heavy Scottish flavour. Malcolm Offord, who had executed the transaction, had studied Law at Edinburgh University, which cannot hurt when you are aiming to buy a business in that city. And the individual who had led Charterhouse's own MBO from UK bank HSBC in 2001 was its Chief Executive Gordon Bonnyman, a Scot through and through. In addition, the vendor and the purchaser had known each other for many years, both professionally and personally. Thanks to his contacts in the Scottish community, Gray had delivered a fantastic deal. Wood Mackenzie's first-class management team had not disappointed, consolidating the company's position in the energy sector and enabling Candover to gross a very respectable 56 per cent IRR on the transaction.[302]

My take on that stellar performance is straightforward enough. It originates from a decision by Paul Gregory, Wood Mackenzie's CEO, and the rest of the leadership team to allocate a sizeable stake in the business to many of the company's staff members. It is rare for senior executives to offer access to such an incentive to a large number of workers. In the end, around 100 employees had participated in the buyout.[303] Without denying Gregory and his senior colleagues any of the merit they deserve, it is equally important to stress that the high returns achieved by Candover on that transaction probably owed a great deal to the staff's financial incentives and to the management's generosity. Together, they were reported to have pocketed £170 million from the transaction.[304] It was socialism meets private equity, empowerment meets wealth creation. Proof if needed that LBOs can also be beneficial to rank-and-file employees and that Candover was still capable of sharing its good fortune, like it had done via the privatisation of IT group Istel and the Hays MBO in the 1980s and with specialty chemical company Inspec's workforce in the 1990s.

By the end of the summer of 2009, Candover also had to let go its entire CEEP team, shut down its Asian operations and axe some of its British and continental European executives. The Düsseldorf and Milan offices were closed. The firm had to face the truth: its expansion strategy overseas had failed. It needed to cut back in order to have any chance of survival. The cost of sacking the investment teams and closing its activities outside Western Europe amounted to £3.8 million. But the biggest reorganisation charge would come from the reduction of staff at the head office and continental outposts: the triumvirate Arney, Gumienny and Leefe needed an additional £7.5 million to put past errors behind them.[305]

Acknowledging its own organisational shortcomings, Candover Investments plc appointed Malcolm Fallen, former CEO of IT and telecom group KCOM, as Chief Executive in September 2009. Grimstone's non-executive role had never really given him enough clout. CIP was reasserting its authority and Fallen stated so in the group's 2009 annual report by admitting that the arrangements between CIP and CPL were not sufficiently robust and needed to be formalised. The two entities had 'therefore entered into a binding agreement' to clarify the rules of engagement pertaining to their financial and administrative relationships.[306] It was too little, too late. Over the following year, Fallen's role would be to sort out the group's messy situation and prepare for an orderly funeral.

A month later, CPL decided that indebted portfolio company ALcontrol, which had previously been rumoured to be in danger of breaching its banking covenants,[307] was still facing an uncertain future and would be too risky and costly for Candover to attempt to bail it out. Following the appointment of an administrator[308] and a financial restructuring, GSO Capital Partners, a credit investment fund owned by US asset manager Blackstone, had become the majority owner. Now that its coffers were running on empty, Candover needed to be selective in choosing which portfolio positions to keep and preferred to record a *c.* €175 million[309] equity loss rather than throw good money after bad. That same month, the firm took an active role in refinancing yet another strained investment: bed and mattress manufacturer Hilding Anders. For an additional SEK 400 million equity ticket,* the buyout group would retain a 50.1 per cent stake[310] in the Swedish company that it had acquired from Investcorp in 2006, thereby acknowledging that its original €290 million[311] equity investment was virtually worthless.[312] The move had eroded Candover's original 81 per cent holding to the benefit of the mezzanine holders which were to control a third of the business in exchange for swapping their loan.

Openly pursuing its disposal programme for the 2001 Fund in order to strengthen CIP's financial footing, on 12 December 2009 the firm and co-investor Cinven successfully sold scientific and technical publisher Springer for €2.27 billion to a consortium of investors led by Swedish group EQT. Unfortunately, because Springer had approximately €2 billion of various loans on its balance sheet,[313] the disposal did not generate much additional cash for the two private investors.

It was a somewhat disheartening result. In its 2006 Report and accounts, Candover had indicated that, by the end of that year, it had already received 1.6 times its original investment in the publishing group through a series of refinancings. Because it was keen to return cash to CIP, the fund manager had reluctantly launched the sale process at a time when the publisher's trading performance was suffering from the economic downturn and public market earnings multiples had tumbled. Another reason behind the financial sponsors' decision to sell at 8.2

---

* SEK = Swedish krona

times EBITDA[314] a business they had acquired for a multiple in excess of 10.5 times six years earlier[315] was the high debt burden under which Springer was crumbling. As early as March 2009, CPL had anticipated the fall in market valuations and written the company down 20 per cent in its books.[316] Back then, the two owners had looked at several options, including an outright sale or for a third party to inject fresh equity in order to recapitalise the business[317] as it was experiencing a downgrade in credit quality in line with the market. But no one had volunteered to take the bullet. The two investors had paid themselves a €300 million dividend during the refinancing process of May 2006, leaving no cash equity in the business and at the same time stretching the portfolio company's balance sheet by bringing its debt level to almost twice the amount used to finance the original acquisitions of Kluwer Academic Publishing and Springer's scientific publishing arm back in 2003. Consequently, the banks supporting EQT's secondary buyout in late 2009 were requesting an additional equity injection of €450 million from the Swedish financial sponsor and its co-investor Singapore-headquartered GIC in order to bring debt down to a more manageable level.[318] It was a telling example of how inadequately capitalised some PE-backed assets had become during the credit boom: an acquisition originally financed with debt totalling 6 times EBITDA had seen that already high leverage raised to 7.3 times, or above 85 per cent of total enterprise value, by the end of 2009 after three separate refinancing rounds in 2004, 2005 and 2006.[319]

In fact, it is conceivable that if in the first half of 2007 the two equity houses had managed to pull through another recapitalisation – the fourth in as many years – and paid themselves a €600 million special dividend as originally planned,[320] Springer would have collapsed under its debt load instead of finding a more dignified secondary exit. Unable to stand on a strong footing during the negotiations with EQT, Candover and Cinven only engendered an additional 0.2 turn of multiple on the sale, producing a total 1.8 times the original investment. Cinven was not in a position to wait until the credit environment had improved either since it was also confronted with problems on the Gala Coral deal; its Cinven III fund, raised in 2002, needed some good news. Still, at 28 per cent, the gross IRR was very respectable given the market conditions at the time, but we could legitimately ask ourselves whether the LPs in the

Candover 2001 and Cinven III funds would not have obtained an even better return if the German publisher's capital structure had not been so stressed and its owners had not come across as desperate sellers. Looking at Candover's financial information released in its 2009 annual report, it appears that EQT's low bid had forced CIP to recognise an 80 per cent erosion in Springer's equity book value, meaning that until December 2008 CPL had estimated the equity portion to be worth north of €500 million and the company's total EV to top €2.6 billion.

That same month of December 2009, Goldman Sachs and Deutsche Bank led a $1.4 billion high-yield bond issue in order to allow Expro to pay down its term loans. Revenues at the oil and gas service company had waned in recent months due to the combination of the global recession and a slump in the oil price to a low point of $40 per barrel in the first half of 2009.[321] As part of that recapitalisation, Expro's owners had injected further equity in the shareholder loan on which they earned a 14 per cent coupon, but in exchange they had given the company more breathing space by repaying the partly amortising senior debt via the bond issue. The bond, yielding a 9.91 per cent interest, had raised the cost of the company's debt, especially as the pricing on the mezzanine had risen marginally.[322] The trade of private equity post-credit crunch was turning into a tiresome exercise of jugglery.

Besides some successful exits, Candover had just endured the worst year of its existence. Many portfolio companies remained on shaky ground. As proof, Hilding Anders, Technogym, Gala Coral and DX Group would still be valued at nil in Candover's books at the year-end while fall protection equipment manufacturer Capital Safety Group and car information provider EurotaxGlass's would be written down further. The latter for instance had seen its operating profitability drop by almost 20 per cent over the previous two years.[323] Candover was close to breaking point.

As the year wound up, Buffin, aged 52, prepared to leave the company. So much had changed since that *Financial Times* interview on 12 March 2002 when he had commented, referring to the upcoming closing of the firm's €2.7 billion 2001 Fund, that the firm was exactly where it wanted to be and 'did not want to compete in the large high-profile buyout auctions'.[324] Seven years later, after trying in vain to raise a fund almost twice as large as its 2001 vintage, Candover was where it had never contemplated it would ever end.

The last twelve months had been private equity's worst on record, both in terms of the decrease in deal volume and in relation to the number of investee companies facing restructuring. For the whole European market, the number of transactions was down a third on prior year and total deal value was down two-thirds to less than €30 billion, the lowest level since 1996. The year 2008 had suffered a perfect storm, but 2009 had delivered a cataclysm. The buyout sector had genuinely imploded. If 2009 was disastrous for the industry, for Candover the knell had tolled. The following year would bury the coffin.

Chapter 11 - A Sad Anniversary

In 2010, Candover was meant to be celebrating its thirtieth anniversary. It should have been in a position to invest its tenth fund, with a war chest of €5 billion. By then, it was supposed to have become a global fund with a presence across Europe and offices in Asia. Instead, the firm was fighting for survival.

The year began with the announcement that CPL was forced to terminate its 2008 Fund's investment period and cut all LP commitments down to €406 million, including €100 million set aside for follow-on contributions towards Expro.[325] After spending £1.7 million in placement agency fees,[326] the group had finally admitted defeat. Evidently, Candover's strategy had made some investors nervous. Launching a marketing campaign for a very large fund ahead of schedule, in the midst of a catastrophic global banking meltdown while concerns about the world economy were spreading, and the overexposure of CIP had raised many questions. Recent portfolio problems had probably encouraged the last irresolute LPs to withdraw, or for the time being withhold their support to the firm.

The termination of the Candover 2008 Fund was the largest withdrawal of a fundraising process ever recorded in the buyout industry's thirty-plus-year history. From then on, CPL's investment team would only focus on deleveraging and on portfolio realisations to return cash to the limited partners. For testosterone-filled dealmakers, portfolio management had for too long been the second-ranking activity, almost a back-office function. Networking was the noblest activity of their trade. They were now required to enhance, control, monitor their investment holdings.

The group's new decision-makers had already radically scaled back the size of their operations. From fifty-two investment professionals, including the brand new team dedicated to Eastern Europe, Candover had reduced its deal team to nineteen by early 2010, bringing its staff level back to that of 2002. If they wanted to have a future in the industry, Arney and Gumienny needed to find a solution, and fast.

In late April, Alberta Investment Management Corporation (AIMCO), a Canadian fund manager with $70 billion under management, was said to have approached management and to be considering making an offer for the group.[327] These negotiations would of course touch upon the intrinsic value of CIP's underlying portfolio but also the status of the CPL investment team and the role that its key executives would take once under new ownership. AIMCO handled investments for Alberta's provincial government, public pension plans and universities. It allocated funds across a variety of products, including public equity, the property sector and debt markets. It was not dedicated exclusively to PE although it played an LP role in large and mega-funds like Apax, Blackstone, Cinven and CVC. It was seemingly keen to take a more active and meaningful position in that sector if given the chance; especially since the recent market correction had created opportunities potentially to enter at a bargain price.

A year earlier, CPL's senior executives had welcomed the discussions with trusted, long-term deal partners like Goldman Sachs or familiar investment professionals like Coller Capital. But discussions about becoming employees of a Canadian pension fund would likely have been lukewarm. The team must have been aware that many North American limited partners had opened European direct investment operations in the past only to scale back or retreat as soon as reality had failed to meet expectations. Whether or not strategic plans were aligned, there remained significant uncertainty in the European PE market for both sides to choose to tread carefully.

In 2010, Candover was meant to be partying. Instead, the humbled investment firm found itself negotiating with a little-known Canadian investor trying to buy its GP activities and its investment portfolio on the cheap. As negotiations were going on, CIP held its AGM at Founders' Hall, a business centre in the historic part of the City, on Thursday 20 May, and Brooke did not hide his position regarding AIMCO's approach. He had not worked so arduously to build Candover into one of the most revered British buyout firms to see it sold to the only interested party at a low-ball valuation.[328] If until that point AIMCO's management had any doubt, it was now crystal clear that they would have to propose a very high price indeed to convince the other side to let go of its emotionally charged asset.

Also in May, after more than ten months of intense negotiations, the mezzanine lenders of portfolio company Gala Coral, led by US turnaround and distress investor Apollo alongside hedge fund manager Cerberus and mezz specialist Park Square, took control of the casino operator and bookmaker through a debt-equity swap.[329] Only two years after injecting an additional £125 million equity ticket in exchange for resetting covenants, Cinven, Permira and Candover were losing ownership of the business. In truth, over the last eighteen months, it had become a 'zombie' company, as bankers like to label heavily leveraged companies hopelessly kept alive by their owners until the unavoidable, unaffordable interest payout or capital redemption becomes due. Back in March 2009, Permira and Candover had publicly admitted that they had entirely written off the investment.[330] Gala Coral's Internet-based betting activities had held well in the recession, but the bingo halls and casinos had never recovered from the increasing popularity of online bingo, the introduction of a smoking ban in public places and the stricter gambling regulation and tax regime implemented in recent years. Management had done its best to protect EBITDA margins between 2008 and 2010 (they had only fallen from 30.7 per cent to 29.2 per cent between those two fiscal years), but the 11 per cent decline in turnover over that period[331] had hurt profitability and prevented the business from meeting its debt-related obligations. It had been Candover's largest transaction ever, with a total equity ticket in excess of €550 million,[332] accounting for more than 20 per cent of the 2001 Fund's €2.7 billion capital pool. It was the final nail in the coffin, and gave further evidence that making money on a tertiary buyout not only requires a game-changing strategy, like the Coral Eurobet add-on acquisition, but also strong and favourable market conditions. Regrettably for Candover, it not only recorded a 40 per cent loss on the transaction,[333] representing €200 million worth of equity at the lowest estimate, but it also weakened its negotiating position with AIMCO. Already a month earlier, in order to keep control of portfolio company DX Group, CPL had been forced to inject a further £15 million into the business as part of a refinancing following DX's inability to meet its borrowing requirements. The financial restructuring had helped bring down the postal services company's debt-to-EBITDA ratio from a stifling 8.5 times to a more manageable but still taxing 6.1 times.[334] Yet, by admitting that the original equity portion had no value,[335] Candover had crystallised an equity loss of more than €275 million.[336] Prospects for parts of the fund manager's portfolio looked grim.

Information from various limited partners' web sites on the confused performance of CPL's 1997, 2001 and 2005 funds shows that discussions with external parties must have been tricky.[337] The 1997 Fund had achieved a net IRR of 17 to 18 per cent as of 31 March 2010, which was in line or slightly below the average returns yielded by some of Candover's comparable peers: for instance, CVC's 1996 and 1998 funds had netted 23 per cent and 19 per cent respectively, Charterhouse had earned 19 per cent from its 1997 vehicle versus Doughty Hanson's 15 per cent, and BC Partners's 1998 fund had generated a 24 per cent net IRR.

But the 2001 Fund's similar 17 per cent rate of return was not on a par with the vintages of Bridgepoint (+31 per cent), CVC Europe (+43 per cent), Charterhouse (+40 per cent), Apax (+37 per cent), and even KKR Europe (+25 per cent) despite the fact that the latter is known for usually offering below average but steady returns. Advent's 2002 Fund had netted over 50 per cent, but it covered Europe and North America so was not strictly comparable even if still impressive.

It was seemingly too soon to comment on the Candover 2005 Fund's performance, but by March 2010 its net IRR of minus 25 to minus 28 per cent, affected by the loss of Ferretti and various recapitalisations, was also less favourable than Bridgepoint's negative 6 per cent, KKR Europe's negative 8 to 11 per cent, CVC's positive 11 per cent, BC Partners's positive 6 to 9 per cent and Apax's +13 per cent. The returns obtained by CPL on its recent funds were truly discouraging.

Armed with these data points, prospective bidders could not have looked at the achievements of the investment firm in a positive light.

By the summer, CIP had to admit that its discussions with AIMCO had not yielded the expected results. The Canadian asset manager had failed to come up with a proposal to make all parties happy: presumably, CIP's bondholders were not prepared to make a loss, some of its shareholders were looking at the share price in mid-2008 as an indication of where their expectations lay, and the CPL deal team was keen to retain some form of independence from the mother ship. Representing an ultimate but forlorn hope for Candover, officially AIMCO had not even bothered to submit a bid.[338] The board of CIP had to face reality: a trust that had been set up over twenty-five years earlier to take advantage of a tax-incentive regulation specific to the UK was not adapted to today's private equity scenery. Similar tax-efficient but simpler structures could be set up offshore by any GP out of the Cayman Islands, the Channel Islands or from Luxembourg. Many of the intended buyers that had considered acquiring Candover were in reality most likely only interested in the GP's portfolio and its investment team. In the end, a somewhat disjointed CPL team was probably not enticing enough to bid and would almost certainly have required further costly redundancies to end up with the key deal originators and portfolio managers. The existing corporate structure of the Candover Group had shown its limits. CIP and CPL would spend the next few months preparing the divorce papers. Grimstone, one of Prime Minister Gordon Brown's business ambassadors since January 2009, had taken a back seat to let Fallen tackle the unwelcome task of winding up the diseased company.

In late August, CIP publicly announced that its portfolio would be put into run-off mode.[339] Determined to return money to its LPs and to scale down the size of its sickly portfolio, Candover was willing to sell off any of its investment positions at the right price. In July already, baby diaper manufacturer Ontex had been disposed of in a €1.2 billion secondary transaction to Goldman Sachs and US fund TPG, netting a 30 per cent loss on CPL's equity investment in the company.[340] In September, it was even rumoured that Nerio Alessandri, who had sold 40 per cent of his business Technogym to Candover two years earlier, was set to buy that stake back at some point in the future thanks to some sort of contractual pre-emptive rights he held over Candover's holding.[341] In CIP's 2008 and 2009 annual reports, Technogym was valued at nil, indicating that the company was having a tough time. And in October, after a seven-year holding period Equity Trust generated a 6 per cent gross IRR when it was sold off for €350 million to Doughty Hanson.[342] Having noted Candover's intention to unload its portfolio, a few opportunists were queuing up at the door.

In 2010, Candover was reaching the respectable age of 30. There was little for the team to rejoice over, though. There was no reason for the firm's top executives to indulge themselves in the company's traditional bacchanalia. The only excuse Brooke and Curran would have had to take a drink would have been to drown their sorrows. Five years earlier, the firm had thrown a memorable shindig to celebrate its 25th and to mark the successful closing of the 2005 Fund. Hundreds of City high-flyers had attended the party as the industry's explosive growth was in full swing. The year 2010 was different. By December, the Candover story would end in a tragic finale.

In the meantime, by the end of October CPL had completed yet another refinancing by injecting €20 million into automotive data publisher EurotaxGlass's in order to keep ownership of the company, reset covenants and restructure its balance sheet. Part of the original €180 million invested by the fund manager back in June 2006 was, at least temporarily, gone up in smoke.[343] The car information provider's underperformance had worsened over the previous eighteen months and impacted profitability negatively, making the company's lenders nervous. Since its acquisition, the business had been affected by lower advertising revenues from dealers and, even with significant cost-cutting introduced in 2008, EBITDA had continued its downward course, sliding from c. €44 million at the time of acquisition to €37 million in 2008 and €30 million a year later.[344] At the end of 2010, its value would be written down by 70 per cent in CIP's books.

That same month of October, after spending half a year marketing its theme park operator Parques Reunidos, CPL was unable to find an acceptable offer close to its stated price tag of €2 billion and was reported to be looking instead at a recapitalisation.[345] As the debt landscape was brightening up faster than the private and public equity markets, it looked like Candover was bracing itself for another refinancing. That meant more arrangement fees for bankers. Christmas was early for some.

Eventually, Candover got a bit of good news ahead of the final showdown. Its portfolio company Stork had underperformed in the months following its January 2008 acquisition – seeing its sales and EBITDA decrease by 8 per cent and 35 per cent respectively in 2009,[346] and its book value written down by 25 per cent – but CPL secured consent from Stork's lenders to dispose of a small unit. Rival 3i bought out the Materials Technology division for €150 million in November 2010, giving the opportunity for CPL to reimburse some of the company's expensive mezzanine. It looked like Stork's 2010 EBITDA was finally picking up after significant efforts to improve operations.[347] The company was not out of the wood yet, but it could see light in the open field nearby.

Over ten potential bidders were believed to have considered an acquisition of the Candover Group or its underlying assets since March of the previous year. Finally, on Monday 6 December, after months of negotiations with the CPL team and with few third party bidders willing to pick up its troubled portfolio and investment team at anything but a rock-bottom valuation that reflected the prevailing market circumstances, CIP issued a circular explaining that its board had elected to sell CPL to its own management. The listed investment trust publicly stated that its main objective had now become to return cash to its shareholders and not to make any further investments. To generate immediate positive cash flow and reduce the group's debt burden, CPL was being handed over to Arle Capital Partners LLP (Arle) - a new GP formed by Arney, Gumienny and a few of their colleagues - for a nominal amount while 29.1 per cent of CIP's portfolio holdings was sold to Arle and secondary fund manager Pantheon, one of Candover's most loyal LPs over the years,[348] for a total consideration of £60 million. The latter represented a 14.3 per cent discount to the portfolio's book value but a slight premium to CIP's market capitalisation, so it appeared an acceptable trade-off for all parties. It also seemed the appropriate moment for Grimstone to bow out, and he duly announced his intention to stand down as Chairman.[349]

It was the abrupt denouement of a dreadful backbreaking two-year attempt to keep hopes alive. With that press release, the Candover Group officially issued its own death certificate by making a late confession that the strategy it had pursued in recent times had failed. Some commentators did not hesitate to proclaim that the firm's reprieve would likely not be enough to repair the damage done to its reputation or that of the industry.[350] Candover was the biggest private equity victim of the 2008 credit crunch, not just in Europe but worldwide.

Back in January 2008, in the firm's barometer on European PE activity for the fourth quarter of 2007, Gumienny had pronounced that record-breaking times were on hold for an indefinite period, and that success in the down-cycle would naturally be attained by paying close attention to the fundamentals of the businesses PE fund managers invested in.[351] By signing one of the most unforgettable sale and purchase agreements of their career, Arle's remaining senior executives had just decreed their newly found independence, and acknowledged via the demise of Candover Partners Limited that, in recent years, they had at times strayed away from the fundamentals.

On 22 December 2010, CIP's shareholders voted in favour of the sale of CPL to Arle, the newly created entity respectfully named after a river running through the Hampshire's Candover valley. In all fairness, it was long overdue. Candover was simply going through a process that other PE institutions in the UK and Europe had followed many years earlier. The group's investment team was completing its own management buyout just like CVC Europe had carved itself out of Citigroup in 1993, Bridgepoint had done in 2000 in its acquisition of Natwest Equity Partners, and when Permira had acquired Schroder Ventures' buyout activities in 2001.

Unquestionably, the real dilemma for Arle's team was to manage its shrunken reserve of unspent equity. As its portfolio companies continued to sustain harsh trading conditions, some would need additional equity injection in future refinancings. The investment team would have to be very selective in the number of companies it was inclined to back. Having already dropped Ferretti in February 2009, ALcontrol in late

2009 and Gala in early 2010, it had showed that it was prepared to inject fresh equity to keep control of other assets. CIP's 2010 interim financial statements had confirmed that, between 30 June and 31 August, investments totalling £33.6 million had been made in DX Group, EurotaxGlass's, Expro International, Hilding Anders and Technogym. Between debt repayments, capital injections to support the growth of its underlying assets, and equity top-ups to participate in restructurings, CPL's management team needed to play a finely tuned act.

After realising so many exits in recent months, the fund manager had a fairly concentrated portfolio. Following the disposals of Ontex and Equity Trust, oilfield service provider Expro accounted for approximately 30 per cent of the firm's portfolio value and half of CIP's net assets at the end of 2010.[352] The future performance of Arle and CIP would therefore be heavily dependent on Expro's, a business still valued in the books at a 20 per cent discount to its original acquisition cost. Following a change of CEO orchestrated in 2010, the company would be closely monitored by Arle's management, CIP's shareholders, and no doubt by the whole financial community. With the oil price having gone from $144 at the time of acquisition to $90 in December 2010, a price recovery was needed urgently, particularly if interest rates, and therefore interest repayments, shot up. Stork, representing more than 20 per cent of the firm's investment value and a third of net assets, was also one to watch out for. Any trading issues from either of these two companies could have devastating effects.

On a positive note, thanks to its recent spin-off the fund manager was finally in a position to compete on an equal footing with other independent LBO shops. Notwithstanding the difficulties encountered by overpriced Hilding Anders and Expro, Arney was seen as a safe pair of hands to steer the business forward, and to put Candover's recent lacklustre past behind once and for all. He was a younger version of Curran, as meticulous and dedicated though more approachable. And with Leefe departing at the end of 2010, and Gumiennny apparently planning to leave once the portfolio companies he oversaw had been realised,[353] Arney now held undisputed control over the company's destiny.

Hopefully he will be able to benefit from close commercial relationships like the one Candover had enjoyed with investment bank

Goldman Sachs during its last three years of activity. The US bank had acquired the Norwegian cable TV operator Get from Candover in November 2007,[354] was the M&A adviser for the Stork delisting in January 2008,[355] had invested alongside CPL and provided part of the mezzanine to finance the acquisition of Expro International in July 2008,[356] advised the LBO firm on its sale of Wood Mackenzie in June 2009,[357] led Expro's refinancing via a high-yield bond in December 2009, provided part of the debt for and was sell-side adviser on the sale of Springer to EQT also in December 2009,[358] had partnered with Apollo to gain ownership of debt-burdened Gala Coral in May 2010,[359] and teamed up with TPG to acquire Ontex in July 2010.[360] As could be expected, the investment bank was also one of the parties rumoured to be interested in buying parts of Candover's portfolio when the fund manager was in agony in the spring of 2009. As Grimstone would have said, downturns offer great opportunities for the cash-rich investor. Goldman was naturally looking after its various debt holdings and co-investments in the CPL-backed companies. Incidentally, the bank was also generating substantial advisory and arrangement fees.

The market outlook seemed to be improving somewhat in the second half of the year. For the whole of 2010, deals worth a total of €70 billion had been closed in Europe, representing a 145 per cent increase over the prior year, but still sitting below the total deal value of the year 2000. Deals worth over €1 billion were coming back, although most of them were sponsor-to-sponsor transactions, indicating that buyout funds were creating some sort of intra-sector market to realise exits and put money to work. There is a silver lining for Arle. In an ecosystem where financial sponsors are avid buyers, the firm should be in a position to sell investee businesses from its 2001 and 2005 funds, a precondition to any fundraising process.

During Candover Investments plc's Extraordinary General Meeting on Wednesday 22 December 2010, Brooke had wished the Arle team well as he added his vote to the 99 per cent of approving shareholders behind the resolution to sell CPL.[361] He had been very visible ever since the first signs of the group's anguish had arisen in early 2009. Over the previous two years, people at the firm had listened to his wise recommendations. Understandably, his voice retained an unyielding influence. Remaining an esteemed shareholder more than ten years after handing over the chairmanship, and seeing the share price languish at a 70 per cent discount to its all-time high and a third below the level it was at when he had left the firm, Brooke's aim was to witness a fast recovery of CIP's market value, maybe with the ultimate goal of selling out his holding and finally enjoying an unexpectedly delayed retirement in the enchanting Candover valley.

When he had resigned as the group's Chairman in May 1999, he had addressed the shareholders one last time at the AGM. In his speech, he had predicted that despite many obstacles continental Europe was set to provide significant opportunities for Candover.[362] Time had proven him right, but he could not have imagined that a fierce rivalry between financial sponsors to win quality assets across the Continent would lead to overpricing, and would be partly responsible for the firm's eventual downfall.

As Britain was experiencing its coldest and snowiest December in 100 years, the fateful end of the house of Candover was being discussed around the hearth in gentlemen's clubs across London. As any entrepreneur witnessing the failure of his business would no doubt attest, to Brooke the fall of Candover was as excruciating as the loss of a child. A prestigious firm that had seen the light during the hopeless economic conditions of the early 1980s, and that once belonged to the private equity elite, had ruthlessly been crushed by the credit crunch.

POST-MORTEM

Chapter 12 - The End of the Road

Candover's story is the tale of the emergence and fabulous prosperity of the buyout industry in Europe since 1980. What started as a side activity to the venture capital world ultimately became a major provider of funding for mergers and acquisitions across North America and Europe. From the spin-offs and privatisations of the 1980s and early 1990s to the public-to-privates and secondary buyouts of the last ten years, Candover was not just part of it all, it led the industry through that revolution.

Its initial successes and momentum had relied heavily on the visionary strategy of Roger Brooke and on Stephen Curran's methodical and strict operational management. The company that they had diligently and painstakingly built over twenty years was brought down by a sudden funding crisis in the midst of the fiercest financial meltdown in seventy years.

A CORPORATE TRANSFORMATION

From the late 1990s onwards, rising M&A activity led to ever larger fundraises. When in the early 2000s firms like Apax and CVC started attracting funds well in excess of €3 billion,* many mid-market firms chose to follow suit even though performance in private equity is far from being correlated to the size of assets under management. With Brooke's diplomatic style and Curran's detailed, in-control attitude, Candover's culture had developed according to a more conservative pattern. It seems that soon after Curran's departure, Candover launched

---

* See Appendix E: Ranking of the top 10 Europe-dedicated Funds by Candover Vintage

itself into a relentless crusade not only to attempt to recapture the leading position it had once held in the UK and to build a platform across Europe but also to expand into developing Asian markets. That improbable game plan proved the firm's undoing.

And unfortunately for the fund manager's employees and investors, Stephen Curran's retirement in 2006 appears to have opened a void in the company's corporate governance. Where Curran's executive chairmanship had represented an unwavering and skilful counterbalance to CPL's operating team, Grimstone's non-executive duties and his lack of prior investment and operational experience in the PE sector did not give him strong enough a stature to oppose or at the very least restrain the unreasonable vision of turning Candover into a global entity in such a short time. In fact, Grimstone would certainly have relished the opportunity to push the group in Asia, a region on which he was advising Scottish insurer Standard Life and that he had known well during his spell at merchant bank Schroder's Hong Kong office in the mid-1990s. He had himself announced the launch of CIP's Asian activities in early 2008, proclaiming that although Europe would remain the group's main focus, it was time to consider opportunities in Asia, one of the most attractive regions in terms of growth potential, not only for direct capital allocations but also for the benefit of existing European investee businesses.[363]

Whereas the 2005 Fund had been raised in a relatively smooth manner at the peak of the PE bubble, the financial crisis of the late 2000s would not be so kind to the 2008 vintage. Despite all the warning signs accumulating in the debt market and the economy during the second half of 2007, the group had pushed on regardless. Sadly, that decision negatively impacted the lives of many people. Together with 100 CPL staff,[364] the firm handled funds from over 100 investors[365] and a portfolio of companies employing thousands of workers across Europe and beyond.

In the senior directors' defence, the firm had laboured through for several years. It was stuck in the middle, between the select clique of very large, very wealthy pan-European or global players like KKR and Permira and the swarm of strong, dedicated national funds like Electra in the UK, LBO France in Paris, Mercapital in Madrid, Investitori in Italy and Nordic Capital in Scandinavia. Instead of attempting to join the first group, CPL should probably have tried to establish a separate model and find a middle ground. As explained, that approach required a progressive implementation; a course that mid-market investor Bridgepoint, for example, had followed. The City firm could also have chosen to stay focused primarily on the UK market where it had built its credentials over two decades and had an enviable reputation, only every now and then diversifying its portfolio by investing on the Continent. It was the strategy applied with success by mid-market player HgCapital and by old-time challenger Charterhouse. Instead, Candover decided to expand abroad and to try and make it into the big league.

According to industry research, throughout the 1980s and early 1990s, based on the volume of transactions, Candover had been the second most active buyout investor in the UK, just behind 3i. In value terms, it had invested close to £1.9 billion in the country between 1981 and 1993, coming fourth behind Charterhouse, Mercury Asset Management (later rebranded HgCapital) and Cinven.[366] In 1996, it had completed deals with a greater combined value than any other equity arranger in the country,[367] and three years later the firm was still one of the five largest European buyout funds.[368] By 2007-08, in terms of fund size it was finding it challenging to stay in the top ten, having being overtaken by US PE houses like KKR but also by originally more geographically focused firms like PAI Partners.* The group's last few transactions demonstrate however that its investment team was still determined to compete at the top end of the market: CPL executed the largest Italian buyout in 2006, the second biggest in Spain a year later, and the second largest PE deal across Europe in 2008. Beating TPG in the Hilding Anders process and Apax on the MBO of Parques Reunidos or executing Expro's delisting, a transaction briefly considered by KKR, were signs that Candover had unexpectedly made it into the mega-buyout fraternity and was competing head-on with the sector's titans.

Because since 2001 the company had experienced a painful mutation - attempting to catch up with its European rivals by opening offices in countries where some of them had been present since the 1980s - we saw that the implementation of its growth strategy started raising concern

---

* See Appendix E: Ranking of the top 10 Europe-dedicated Funds by Candover Vintage

among observers.[369] Indeed, what appears to have triggered the firm's gradual downfall is that it had embarked on an aspiring expansion project and had decided to enforce it hurriedly.

Until early 2000, the firm was a single-office partnership employing a dozen investment executives managing a sub-£1 billion fund and investing two-thirds of it in the UK, a market that it had dominated for twenty years. Its team was almost entirely British. Six years later, it had become a multinational investor running a €3.5 billion investment vehicle and targeting ten European countries with the help of thirty investment professionals spread across several geographies. Two-thirds of the 2005 Fund's equity would be invested outside the UK, sometimes in countries where CPL had limited or no prior exposure. By the summer of 2008, after the opening of four foreign offices in just over five years and the fresh recruitment of an eastern European team, the company was aspiring to morph into a multinational buyout player investing €5 billion of equity across twenty-five European markets and, on CIP's initiative, dabbling in the two largest Asian markets: India and China. The scale of the metamorphosis introduced in less than eight years, at the heart of Candover's catch-up plans, was a fundamental change in market positioning. The group had attempted to go through a profound multidimensional conversion from a UK-centric mid-market buyout firm into a global large-cap powerhouse. It was the equivalent of a middleweight boxer performing at the national level but aiming nonetheless to make strides in the heavyweight category on the world stage.

Faced with such a fast-paced strategic shift, the firm appears to have struggled to adapt. In the past, it had built a reputation for the stability of its leadership team and the many years its investment executives had worked together – a feature always greatly appreciated by investors. The mid-2000s were to change all that. As seasoned executives started leaving the ship – European Director and co-head of the Paris office Christopher Spencer in 2002,[370] senior Director Hamish Mackenzie in 2003,[371] Head of Germany Kurt Kinzius in 2004, senior French Director Jean-Michel Coulot in early 2006, again Head of Germany and Managing Director Jens Tonn in 2007,[372] and, as already noted, Head of France and Managing Director Cyrille Chevrillon via a transitional Vice Chairman function that same year – the frailty of the company's corporate architecture and governance had become difficult to hide. Although it was following an ambitious strategy and its investment and organisational make-up had become international, Candover had not had sufficient time to remodel its management structure. Despite its modernised headquarters, the eastern European and Asian endeavours, and the growth in headcount, the group seemed to suffer from cultural lock-in. In the last few years of activity, it was closing the vast majority of its transactions in continental Europe and over half of its investment professionals were from outside the UK; it kept on raising funds with over three-quarters of commitments originating from geographies outside its homeland, but when it came to strategic planning, British nationals remained the primary decision-makers at both CPL and CIP.

When Chevrillon had stepped aside, the firm's senior leadership had indeed reverted to being an all-British affair, even though it was by then running four offices on the Continent. The departure of Tonn a few months earlier had confirmed a simple truth: Candover's approach in the two largest European markets outside the UK had come to grief. As a simple comparison, in 2007 five of Permira's seven Executive Committee members were from outside Britain. EQT's Investment Advisory Committee and board of directors offered even more diversity.[373] After seven years in operation CPL's Paris office had only completed two deals and the Düsseldorf outpost had closed none, except for add-on portfolio acquisitions. The firm's decision to expand away from its home market had miscarried. Other better established pan-European PE houses had skilfully demonstrated that, with the right approach, transactions could be executed on a regular basis in the two largest continental markets: between 2002 and 2008, Bridgepoint had closed six LBOs in France and three in Germany, Advent's tally had totalled five and twelve deals, Cinven had racked up five and three buyouts respectively while BC Partners had done three in each country.[374] When some of its competitors had built strong credentials in key geographies, Candover had been left behind.

INVESTMENT DOWNGRADE

Legitimately, it could be argued that the painful experience of raising the latest fund was partly due to the patchy performance of recent transactions.

As the de facto head of investments, Gumienny had naturally been very productive and ended up with his fair share of troubled assets. Out of the last ten deals executed by CPL between May 2006 and July 2008, six had witnessed the involvement of the joint Senior MD: EurotaxGlass's, DX Group, Ferretti, Parques Reunidos, Stork and Technogym.[375] And he could have increased the tally had several negotiations he had entered into in 2007 and 2008 not failed. In March 2007, for instance, he had been outbid on the £685 million carve-out of Jupiter Asset Management from German bank Commerzbank.[376] Similarly, the discussions with Peter Cullum, founder of insurer Towergate, about the purchase of a 25 per cent stake had not gone according to plan. Cullum and Gumienny went way back: in December 1993, Gumienny had led Candover's backing of Cullum's business Economic Insurance. Their most recent conversations had taken place in February 2008 and the fact that they only related to a small minority stake in that publicly listed company maybe shows that CPL was finding it exacting to invest the remainder of its 2005 Fund. Actually Cullum had been rumoured to be in negotiations with various investors, including Candover, to sell Towergate for more than £3 billion back in the summer of 2007, but the process had stalled then because of debt funding uncertainty. The situation was reminiscent of the talks Candover had held with Wellington in the months following the September 11 terrorist attacks; talks that had eventually led to the creation of reinsurance company Aspen in early 2002. It confirms that the firm's executives were interpreting the events of 2007 and 2008 the way they had looked at the economic context in 2001: it was an opportunity to buy and the insurance market was a good point to start from, with the hike in insurance premiums to be expected in a recession. In the end, the talks with Towergate faltered once more as financing the deal was proving impossible in the prevailing debt markets.[377]

Clearly the firm's co-head, who in 2005 had been voted by the readers of weekly paper *Financial News* one of the 100 most influential people in European capital markets,[378] played a pre-eminent role on the investment side. In fact, it was not the first time that scenario had occurred. A few years back, Candover had witnessed a similar period of Gumienny's dominance. Between October 2000 and March 2003, he had led five of the seven LBOs carried out by the firm: Bourne Leisure, Swissport, Aspen Insurance, Ontex and Gala.[379]

By regularly competing for larger and more international transactions, Candover's deal team was getting exposed to more challenging business issues. Whereas the average debt-to-EBITDA ratio for mid-market buyouts was sitting at 4.5 times, in the €1 billion-plus segment it regularly exceeded 6.5 times. What that implies is that in order to bring in respectable returns, the likes of KKR and TPG took a more hands-on approach to portfolio management. They frequently involved operating partners or sector experts to improve processes and corporate efficiency and squeeze every extra penny that they could out of their investee companies. They also employed a myriad of former CEOs and COOs to implement changes quickly via a '100-day plan' immediately post-acquisition, examining anything that could be cut or run more economically. Obviously global businesses like Springer and Ferretti are a lot more complex to supervise than a local or national enterprise like Regional Independent Media or Jarvis Hotels, the type of deal CPL backed in the 1990s. Multinationals call for a solid understanding of various process issues ranging from logistics to offshoring, production techniques, and research and development. Like most professionals employed by European PE firms, Candover's executives were not problem-solvers, they were financial managers and deal doers. For that reason, in the past they had hired the services of operating managers as MBI candidates (as in the case of RIM in 1998) or as troubleshooters when businesses started to underperform (like they had done for Ontex in mid-2006,[380] and EurotaxGlass's in November of the same year[381]). Eventually, recognising that a strong grasp of operational matters was getting as important if not more than financial management, in October 2006 the firm added to its payroll more relevant profiles as Operations Partners to take a pro-active role on the board of portfolio companies.[382]

With their network of senior industrialists and their in-house operations experts, the mega-buyout firms had become some sort of industrial holding companies or modern-day investment conglomerates so Candover had to change its ways if it wanted to defy them.

Without such intimate knowledge of operational matters, high valuations put returns but also the survival of the investee companies at risk. If an equity investor is not capable of systematically executing performance improvement plans, it can only make money from its double-digit-EBITDA-multiple investments in one of two ways. If the business produces strong growth, value creation is derived from profitability enhancement and the corresponding multiple arbitrage (improved margins and fast-growing EBITDA usually warrant a higher earnings multiple); that was the case with Wood Mackenzie, for instance. But value can also originate from high financial gearing, as demonstrated by Springer's serial recapitalisations. However, in the second scenario, the portfolio company is markedly dependent on a positive market environment. Once economic indicators go south, highly indebted, low-growth assets are at risk of default and require cost-cutting measures. The cases of Gala Coral, EurotaxGlass's and Hilding Anders are revealing testimonies. It is no coincidence that these assets, bought out for 10 times EBITDA or more, had been leveraged beyond 6 times earnings[*]: alongside cost management, it was the key ingredient to earn decent returns. The unpredictable consequence of borrowing so much is that portfolio companies are badly exposed to extreme cyclical changes like the drop in mail and parcel volumes at DX Group or to structurally unfavourable market dynamics as was the case for Ontex. Crucially, the key success factor in the large segment of the buyout market is aggressive innovation in deal financing coupled with continuous operational improvement. Candover, which had built its reputation on prudent, diligent investing, was seemingly never at ease in the game of complex structured finance. Its transaction team gave it a go between 2006 and 2008 with the success that we know, but the lenders did not show much consideration when things started going haywire. In view of the events of 2009, it looks like the firm's investors did not either.

---

[*] See Appendix D: Troubled Portfolio Companies in the 2001, 2005 and 2008 Funds

It is instructive that the last strong performer among Candover's funds was its 1994 vintage. With a net IRR in excess of 40 per cent,[383] it leaves all subsequent funds in the shade. CPL's track record since the late 1990s is disconcerting and although it has taken a long time for the 1997 and 2001 Funds to be properly benchmarked against their peer group, by 2009 there was no hiding from it: Candover's performance was lagging. Industry data from research outfit Preqin confirm the information disclosed by various American LPs and show that the Candover 1997 Fund was a third-quartile performer,[384] netting an IRR just short of its European vintage average of around 19 per cent. The bankruptcy of First Leisure presumably hurt returns. The Candover 2001 Fund was also a bottom-half performer, with a rate of return sitting 11 percentage points below the average 28 per cent achieved by European funds raised that year. The complete write-off on ALcontrol and significant losses incurred on Ontex and Gala Coral are behind that outcome. I have already explained that it is premature to comment on the 2005 Fund's preliminary returns, but the value destruction related to Ferretti and the injections of additional equity in EurotaxGlass's, DX Group and Hilding Anders mean that it would require an exceptional revival of the current portfolio for the firm to earn respectable returns on that fund and bring it closer to the median net IRR for that vintage, which stood at +7.5 per cent as of 30 September 2009.

The nature of some of Candover's recent transactions helps explain why the firm's investment performance ultimately suffered.

Over time, the firm became too dependent on secondary transactions. Four of them had been completed by the 2001 Fund (five if one includes Coral Eurobet) and six out of the 2005 Fund. That represents 25 per cent of the 2001 vintage but a staggering 55 per cent of the 2005 portfolio. Again, LPs resented the increasing frequency of secondary buyouts. They certainly must have considered Candover's numbers too high even if they reflected an industry-wide phenomenon. As was the case for all participants in the large-end of the industry, the fact that the 2005 vintage carried out so many secondaries was a sign that sourcing untapped LBO opportunities was becoming a thing of the past. In a survey on the sector published by *The Economist* in 2004 and entitled 'Kings of Capitalism', Michael Stoddart, by then Senior

Business Adviser at British investment firm Fleming Family and Partners, already warned against such sponsor-to-sponsor transactions: 'The results of these deals may prove most disappointing'.[385] Five years later, the shambles within the portfolios of many large buyout firms had underlined the wisdom of one of the industry's most respected founding fathers.

In addition, CPL followed a risky market drift by targeting publicly listed companies. Excluding the £33.5 million delisting of leisurewear and furniture manufacturer Dwek in 1988, the firm had had little exposure to public-to-privates until the late 1990s. Consequently, as was the case for many other European PE firms, its deal team had a limited understanding of such transactions. Looking at it closely, Candover's experience with delistings over the last ten years has been daunting. With the exception of Clondalkin on which it more than doubled its money,[386] all of the firm's other PTPs, which include Lambert Fenchurch, Acertec, Ontex, DX Services, Stork and Expro, put to the test their owner's portfolio enhancement skills.

The Acertec story would make for a disconcerting case study. Following the 1999 delisting executed at a considerable premium to the rival offer from TT Group,[387] and after seven years of ownership, the steel reinforcing rod manufacturer had been relisted expeditiously on AIM on 16 May 2006 after strategic and financial buyers had failed to show any serious interest in the company.[388] Within eighteen months of the IPO, the business's already fitful trading performance was amplified by the discovery of stock accounting errors over the previous three years at one of its UK operations.[389] A company introduced to the market at 148 pence per share was quoted at less than 45 pence per share by the end of December 2007. After two changes at the Finance Director level in 2008, the implementation of several cost-cutting and downsizing measures, the sale of its Asian activities in August 2008, and the appointment of a Chief Restructuring Officer in April 2009,[390] Acertec was finally taken out of the stock market by its management on 30 June 2009[391] when the share price was sitting at 1.25 pence, representing a 99 per cent destruction in market value in just over three years. While, according to Acertec's Finance Director, Candover had made an adequate return on its investment via the £83 million repayment of its loan notes at the time of the flotation,[392] several City institutions including Gartmore, Henderson and Morgan Stanley had lost millions in this wash-out.

The Arle team needs to understand whether it has an execution issue or whether the problem is intrinsic to take-privates. Other LBO shops might want to follow their example in carefully studying the industry's track record when it comes to PTPs.

And with the buyout of oil specialist Expro, the firm showed that, like many of its competitors, it was finding it increasingly onerous to develop angles during auctions. For that reason, it was willing to pursue companies that it had owned in the past. You will recall that the firm had already done a buyout of Expro in collaboration with Cinven back in 1992, admittedly when the target was much smaller. Yet, it was not a first for Candover: I have mentioned that the firm had acquired Fairey's aerospace and defence activities in 1998, after owning its parent company between 1986 and 1988. Also, mail service provider DX Services, which CPL had delisted at a 26 per cent premium to the pre-bid share price for £349 million in August 2006,[393] used to belong to professional services firm Hays plc, a Candover portfolio company between 1987 and 1989. DX had shown little sparkle since the take-private: by mid-2010, sales at the mail services provider were down 5 per cent, but EBITDA was sitting a third below where it had been two years earlier. Margins had fallen from 24 per cent to 15 per cent over the same period.[394]

The Heath Lambert consolidation play had been originated by mid-market buyout firm DLJ Phoenix through a delisting of CE Heath in the summer of 1997.[395] Inviting Candover along for the ride, Phoenix had then combined Heath with the 1999 take-private of a company that CPL owned between 1988 and 1991: Lambert Fenchurch.[396] In fact, the Old Bailey-headquartered group had itself floated Lambert Fenchurch in July 1991, only to take it private eight years later at a time when Roger Brooke was still a board member at the insurer. And if the business had not been confronted with a burdensome pension deficit and a huge debt-related bill, Candover's and Phoenix's intention was to re-introduce the combined entity to the stock market in 2002.[397] Instead, Heath Lambert would default on its debt obligations and would eventually be taken over by its lenders and management in late 2003,[398] in what represented the seventh biggest receivership of an MBO in the UK at the time,[399] providing another proof that repurchasing companies that one used to own and supposedly know well is not a guarantee of success. Far from it.

There were even reports in April 2008 that Candover was in discussions with caravan park manager Bourne Leisure, a company it partly controlled between 2000 and 2004. Eventually, it failed to find the debt finance to support its bid, but the firm had seemed prepared to purchase a business in which it held a stake only four years earlier.

The profile of the firm's last ten transactions, which comprise one tertiary and five secondary buyouts, three take-privates and the acquisition of a minority holding to help an entrepreneur cash out some of its capital, has very little in common with the type of deal Candover (and the whole industry) used to do in the early 1980s. The fund manager's first ten MBOs, completed between December 1980 and September 1983, were essentially divisional carve-outs of big industrial, commercial and financial groups. It is a measure of how much the top end of the sector has changed over the last three decades. The large number of secondaries also betrays a weakness that applies to all financial sponsors entering new markets where they have limited prior experience and therefore no genuine local network. The daring practices used by US newcomers in the 1990s in order to win deals against European incumbents (remember the Hillsdown delisting by Hicks Muse) were, by the mid-2000s, frequently applied by Candover itself. Because it had a short history in Spain and Italy for instance, the City firm had little option but to target companies already owned by a financial sponsor. It was easier for CPL to approach one of its peers than to spend years trying to build its brand in new countries and develop contacts with foreign entrepreneurs and industrialists. The Ferretti secondary buyout had given credibility to CPL in Italy and would have helped convince Technogym's entrepreneurial owner to team up. The firm's misadventure perhaps demonstrates that such a short cut approach comes at a price.

All these factors explain why the group's investment holdings suffered so much in the downturn. Candover's talks with Canadian asset manager AIMCO might well have failed because bondholders were not willing to write off part of their debt or the company's shareholders were reluctant to sell their shares at a 60 per cent discount from their 2008 peak. Nevertheless, we can see from CPL's own heated negotiations with lenders when it tried to work off its overleveraged portfolio companies that CIP's debt-holders were following market practice. It was not their fault if the group's underlying assets – that is CPL's investee businesses – had taken a hammering lately. We can confidently insinuate that it is that same dire portfolio that led Coller Capital, Eurazeo and other interested parties either to offer a modest valuation for the assets or to walk away altogether from the idea of acquiring the fund manager in the first half of 2009. In hindsight, given the setbacks suffered with Gala Coral and the forced recapitalisations of DX Services, EurotaxGlass's and Hilding Anders, it was probably a wise decision.

One of the arguments that some commentators made during the 2009–10 period, when Candover was doing its best to keep body and soul together, to explain its subsequent break-up is that the group and its senior executives had got their timing wrong.[400] Though the timing was poorly considered, it would still have been very challenging to raise the new fund in 2009 or 2010 with a portfolio of underperforming investments affected by the downturn and delaying the launch might not have prevented several assets such as ALcontrol and Ferretti from hitting the wall and being handed over to the banks. With the jittery state of the economy in the US and the credit crunch gaining momentum, many American LPs and global banks had taken a wait-and-see attitude and put further commitments to the industry on hold. The firm should probably have taken more time to address its morass of internal problems before considering going to market.

Candover was not only speeding up its fundraising; it was also shortening its investment period. The 2005 Fund deployed commitments across only eleven transactions and in just over twenty-nine months (between January 2006 and June 2008). It contrasts with the 2001 vintage's sixteen deals completed over a thirty-four-month period (between February 2002 and December 2005) and the 1997 Fund's fifteen transactions executed over thirty-eight months (from January 1998 to March 2001). It looks like the firm was seeking to close larger deals than would have been recommended given the size of its 2005 Fund and it was doing so at a faster pace than ever before, thanks in part to the bullish credit and economic context. In order to invest its equity, CPL frequently invested above its upper range of €1.5 billion in enterprise value: Ferretti, Gala's add-on acquisition of Coral Eurobet, Stork and Expro had price tags exceeding the firm's stated valuation bounds.

Spreading its investments from the 2005 Fund across a smaller number of deals was not just affecting Candover's ability to diversify its portfolio; it was also altering the firm's risk profile since it was investing in the larger-end segment and therefore stretching its in-house capabilities. The fact that CPL had brought in collaborators with the relevant mega-deal credentials on recent acquisitions proves that point: Permira was invited in Gala and helped execute the substantial Coral add-on, and Goldman Sachs supported the fund manager in its delisting of Expro.

Of course, one could argue that the 1994 Fund, which had been invested over a thirty-month period, had equally been rushed if compared to the four and a half years it took to invest the 1989 vintage. However, despite its accelerated timetable, the 1994 Fund had followed the same investment strategy as its predecessor's: a number of transactions (thirteen) close to that of the 1989 Fund (fourteen); an exclusive focus on UK deals with one single foray in France via the MC International buyout; a transaction profile around corporate carve-outs and privatisations, with the notable exception of the eventually doomed CE Heath delisting; and finally a consistent targeting, often on a club deal basis, of businesses worth £10 million to £400 million. So the evolution between the 1989 and 1994 vehicles was progressive, even peripheral. Instead, as we have seen, the 2005 vintage had not only been invested too quickly but also departed significantly from its predecessors' investment philosophy.

In its goal to go up in fund size and vie for larger LBOs, Candover stopped investing in proprietary sub-£500 million British enterprises and targeted more complex transactions. As Chevrillon put it, 'they lost their souls chasing large and pricey deals in competitive auctions'.[401] The 2001 Fund recorded the biggest losses in Candover's history and, along with the 2005 vintage, it will remain synonymous with the firm's sudden loss of focus: an estimated €400 million-plus worth of equity, or almost one sixth of the 2001 Fund's total commitments, were destroyed via the Gala Coral, Ontex and ALcontrol transactions.

Looking further back in time, even though the firm had suffered like many during the early 1990s recession, its prudent investment approach explains why none of its portfolio companies would feature in the UK's top five MBO receiverships of that period. In the first half of the 2000s, at a time when the UK economy was rising, two of the country's five biggest buyout failures had been Candover's: Heath Lambert and First Leisure.[402] And by the time its reorganisation had been finalised in early 2011, the Candover Group had recorded with its Gala Coral loss the nation's biggest LBO restructuring taken over by its lenders, just ahead of Terra Firma's EMI. Even in its home market, where it had for many years earned the respect of its peers, investors, bankers and advisers, Candover had lost its Midas touch. The numerous capital restructurings implemented between 2007 and 2010 would tend to support comments made by journalists that the firm's key dealmakers had grown overconfident in their investment skills. Some had harshly questioned the management team's financial acumen.[403] Ultimately, the decision to launch a fundraising campaign at a time when the world of finance was collapsing brought Candover to the brink of the abyss where the firm's underperforming investment strategy pushed it over.

THE DARK SIDE OF OVERCOMMITMENTS

Looking at it from the fund provider's viewpoint, CIP's setback highlights the risk of making too high a commitment to any new vintage. Limited partners know that expected cash outflows over a short- to medium-term period must always remain lower than expected inflows. The key word here is 'expected'. Because investment realisations from general partners are unpredictable, meaning that it is literally impossible to know whether an asset will be sold in two, five or eight years' time, it is essential for any LP to include some sort of a buffer in its future financial obligations. Should the rate of the GP's realisations slow, the limited partner must not be caught without cash in the event that the fund manager continues to execute acquisitions or recapitalisations and therefore draw down committed funds. The LP must therefore keep some reserve in order not to default on its pledge. There is one easy way to build in that buffer: future commitments, which could be called short- and medium-term liabilities, should remain close to, or ideally below, the net asset value of the LP.

Taking the example of CIP, we can once again praise the cautious methodology followed by Brooke and Curran in the 1980s and 1990s and contrast it with the more audacious approach followed during the recent LBO bubble. In 1989, CIP's £20 million commitment for that vintage was 47 per cent of its net asset value,[404] meaning that the fund provider held twice more assets than future liabilities. In 1991 that ratio was 9 per cent, and it edged up to 83 per cent in 1994, the latter being explained as you will remember by the fact that CIP had to bridge a gap in commitments due to the unusually severe market conditions following the early 1990s recession. In 1997, CIP's £100 million pledge was back to a more conservative 62.5 per cent of NAV.*

In June 2002, as it was closing its 2001 Fund in turbulent post-Internet bubble circumstances, CIP had subscribed €300 million or approximately 75 per cent of its net assets. In the midst of the stock markets readjustment, the group's investment trust had been forced to take a view on CPL's ability to realise its portfolio swiftly over the coming years. Importantly, the group held the cash equivalent of approximately €100 million in reserve on its balance sheet at the end of December 2001, giving it a chance to fund a handful of transactions for the new vintage if needed.[405] The robust health of some of the 1997 Fund's portfolio companies also gave assurances that CPL would be able to exit many of its investments at a nice premium and thereby provide CIP with the necessary liquidity to commit to the next fund.

---

* See Appendix C: Main Features of Candover Funds

196

It might appear that the publicly listed LP had become slightly over-exposed when it pledged €500 million, or 91 per cent of its net assets, to the 2005 Fund, but in reality because the group held close to €275 million of cash and cash equivalent as at 31 December 2005,[406] it was a very manageable undertaking. The problem as we have seen is that CIP chose to return more than half that hoard to its shareholders in 2006 and CPL subsequently invested its new vintage at a record pace. Originally, the 2005 Fund had aimed for a minimum of €3 billion, and a €400 million ticket from CIP.[407] Had CIP stuck to the script, that pledge would have represented 11.8 per cent of the 2005 Fund's total €3.4 billion commitments. It would have been comparable to its 11.1 per cent share of the capital administered by the 2001 Fund and its 11.7 per cent of the 1997 vintage. More importantly, it would have amounted to an even more reasonable 72.5 per cent of the company's NAV. Despite the risk of over-commitment, CIP would still be able to respect its 2005 undertaking.

The real make-or-break scenario would arise in 2008 when it was decided to bet the group's future on the mother of all IOUs: a massive €1 billion cheque from CIP in order to impose a fundraising to a financial market facing complete annihilation. The €5 billion target was a strong attempt to maintain the firm in the leading pack of Europe's largest buyout funds. Unfortunately, the usual readings established to assess the credibility of a fund pledge no longer fitted on the private equity Richter scale. The sensational commitment represented 20 per cent of the target size of the 2008 vintage, making CPL and CIP more dependent on each other than at any time since the 1994 Fund. But CIP was not simply doubling its investment, it was effectively increasing its short- to medium-term liability to the equivalent of 175 per cent its net asset value as at 30 June 2008. Because the underlying portfolio had sustained significant write-offs and write-downs due to weak financial performance and lower market comparables, by the end of 2008 the fund commitment-to-net asset ratio had risen above 370 per cent.[408]

To demonstrate how challenging the €1 billion financial obligation truly was, let us go back to the €200 million yearly contribution it implied. As explained, CIP's cash intakes were essentially derived from CPL's portfolio realisations. It is reasonable to assume that the cash sitting on the group's balance sheet in late 2008 (approximately

£133 million) would have required to be set aside to enable CIP to fund investments on behalf of its Asian operations and of CEEP but also any remaining top-up equity injection in relation to the LP's commitments to the Candover 2001 and 2005 funds. In fact, because one of the two investment objectives of the listed trust was to follow a 'progressive dividend policy',[409] CIP also needed to hold the cash equivalent so it could continue to distribute and increase its dividend payouts. In 2007, that dividend payment had been close to €17 million (£12.3 million). None of that £133 million cash balance could therefore be considered usable towards the new Candover vintage.

On that basis, it looked like the limited partner required at the very least €200 million to feed through annually from CPL.[410] Since CIP accounted for 11.2 per cent of the 2001 Fund's total commitments and 14.2 per cent of the 2005 Fund's, let us assume a blended CIP contribution of 13 per cent (reflecting the fact that the 2005 vintage was bigger). Consequently, in order to give back €200 million a year to its parent company, Candover Partners Limited needed to generate about €1.55 billion of net equity proceeds each year.[411] Over five years (the typical period of investment of any vintage), that represented €7.75 billion. Again, these are net proceeds so the amount is after repayment of any loans used to finance the firm's LBO deals, but it is also after deduction of CPL's management fees and carried interest[*].

By the time the 2008 Fund had had its first closing in August 2008, one of the 2005 Fund investments had already been realised (cable TV operator Get, representing approximately €170 million of equity) and seven of the 2001 Fund had followed the same fate (representing €1.1 billion or so of equity if one includes the partial realisation of Gala following Permira's investment in 2005). It meant that, of the equity invested at that time, c. €1.5 billion of the 2001 Fund and about €2.7 billion of the 2005 Fund remained to be realised. Therefore a total €4.2 billion of equity had to yield €7.75 billion over the following five years.[412] It does not look too demanding until one remembers that £1.1 billion (or €1.47 billion) had been invested by CPL in the preceding eight months. Due to the flat-lining economy and worsening credit terms that would slow down refinancings, realistically most of the €7.75 billion were

---

[*] See Appendix A: Glossary

likely to come initially from the realisation of deals completed before 2008. In any case, to conclude on this slightly long-winded argument, in order for CIP to receive an annual €200 million from its fund manager, between 2008 and 2013 €4.2 billion worth of invested capital needed to generate an average return of 1.84 times the initial investment. That compares favourably with the 1.9 times achieved by the Candover 1997 Fund,[413] a vintage used up during fair economic times.

To stay afloat, the Candover boat would therefore have required the most favourable of tail winds. However, as we have seen, several of the remaining investee companies had already been forced to recapitalise (Ontex in 2007, Gala Coral in April 2008) so the portfolio was not without its challenges. In addition, CIP's €1 billion-pledge made in the summer of 2008 had failed to take into account the impact that over the previous twelve months the deteriorating banking climate was having on the buyout sector and the rate of portfolio realisations. In the end, that oversight wrecked the company.

Table 1 shows that by August 2008, the time when the final decision was made by Grimstone to pledge €1 billion, the LP was already falling way behind its minimum yearly €200 million cash intake indispensable to back its commitment to the 2008 Fund. It is then that CPL's Executive Committee and CIP's board of directors should have taken the difficult but necessary step to scale down CIP's ticket as, based on historical cash flows, even in a strong economic context, CPL would have struggled to realise its portfolio fast enough and distribute sufficient funds to CIP. Perhaps the audit team of Grant Thornton carried out a similar exercise in early 2009 before reaching the self-evident conclusion that CIP had overcommitted itself and CPL had overpromised and under-delivered. Instead of cashing in €200 million each year from its GP subsidiary, CIP only received €60 million in 2008, and eventually €52 million in 2009 and €43 million in 2010, amounting to a cumulative €445 million shortfall over three years, missing its target by 74 per cent.

Table 1: CIP's purchase and sale of investments between 1998 and 2010
(Information shown in € million)

Financial year	Draw-downs	Sale proceeds	Difference	Average outflow	Average inflow	Total outflow	Total inflow
1998	20.5	24.7	4.2				
1999	76.1	41.8	-34.3	50.3	43.3	201.2	173.1
2000	61.5	46.7	-14.8				
2001	43.0	59.9	16.9				
2002	40.4	78.3	37.9				
2003	112.0	59.7	-52.4	76.1	126.1	304.2	504.3
2004	91.1	197.1	106.0				
2005	60.7	169.3	108.6				
2006	139.8	63.7	-76.1				
2007	134.2	240.8	106.6	162.3	121.4	487.0	364.3
2008	213.0	59.8	-153.2				
2009	46.5	51.6	5.1	44.0	47.0	88.0	94.1
2010	41.5	42.5	1.0				

Source: CIP's Group Cash Flow Statements in Reports and accounts from 1999 to 2010
Notes: Original financial information reported in British pounds. Draw-downs = share of CIP in the purchase of investments by CPL. Sale proceeds = share of CIP in the sale of investments by CPL

Between 2006 and 2008, the period during which the 2005 Fund was being invested, CPL had only returned €364 million to its cornerstone investor through realisations whereas it had called upon €487 million worth of equity from CIP. Once again, that €123 million shortfall was financed through CIP's existing cash balance and partly by the issuance of multi-currency loans in 2007 and 2008. Similarly, the €200 million excess cash generated in the previous period (2002–05), when the 2001 vintage was being put to work, had made possible the £100 million-plus cash payout to shareholders enacted by Curran in 2006.

What the table also highlights is that during the 2006–08 period CIP had seen its average annual cash outflows related to investments more than double compared to the 2002–05 term, but its inflows had remained constant. This supports my argument that CPL had invested its 2005 Fund too quickly and had failed to realise portfolio exits at the same pace.

By the time the firm had come to market with its latest fund, some of its investee companies were already feeling the fallout from the credit crunch and the slowing economy; some required serious operational and financial restructuring work. The more troubled companies Candover held in its portfolio, the LPs' thinking went, the more resources it would take away from deal origination and the more time it would consume to achieve realisations. One of the industry's accepted truths, which CIP's board of directors seems to have partly ignored, is that poor performers cannot time their exit and often exhibit valuation multiple contraction.

STRUCTURAL DAMAGE

Too much has been written about the fact that the supposedly dysfunctional two-tier structure of the Candover Group, including fund manager CPL and its owner and listed limited partner CIP, is mainly to blame for the eventual failure of the fund-marketing process and the need to abandon its growth strategy.[414] While there is some truth to this notion, it does not entirely explain why the 2008 Fund had to be terminated. The €1 billion commitment certainly deflected some of the condemnation away from the fund manager, exposing Grimstone to a public grilling from his shareholders during May 2009's AGM. But the successful, though still painful, implementation of various fund downsizings that took place across the industry in 2008 and 2009 demonstrates that GPs can survive even if one or several of their core LPs bow out or lower their commitments significantly. Permira and PAI are here to prove it: their 2008 funds were eventually cut by about 10 per cent and 50 per cent respectively. Charterhouse had even managed to close its latest vintage in March 2009, admittedly a third below its original €6 billion target, but illustrating nonetheless that it was still possible for GPs with a clear positioning and a decent track record to attract sufficient interest from LPs. A cornerstone limited partner like Standard Life had invested in the 2008 vintage funds of Advent and CVC but had apparently withdrawn its commitment or failed to complete its due diligence and willingly stayed out of Candover's latest fund.* If they had considered that CPL was such a tempting investment proposition, its investors would have stuck with it

* There is no mention of any commitment to the Candover 2008 Fund in the Reports and Accounts for the years ended 30 September 2008 and 30 September 2009 of Standard Life European Private Equity Trust PLC

despite CIP's over-commitment fiasco as some observers were quick to emphasize.[415] Instead, they probably felt that the firm had gone astray and the pangs of a financial crisis provided as good a chance as any to walk away from it.

The main issue with Candover's dual structure was that it suffered from inadequate internal governance procedures. And CIP realised this, although too late. The corporate governance section (in which the directors' remuneration report can be included given its direct connection with the running of the firm) never exceeded nine pages in the company's annual reports between 2005 and 2008. In 2009, that section had ballooned to nineteen pages. Having gone through a complete review of the systems and controls in place, the group's newly appointed CEO Malcolm Fallen had concluded, as referred to before, that the relationship between CIP and CPL needed to be formalised but also that the decision process within CIP required a serious upgrade. In the CEO's report section, Fallen had revealed that the group had carried out a comprehensive risk review and upgraded its internal risk procedures with the aim of better protecting shareholder value.[416]

Candover's 2009 annual report was the clearest sign yet given by the company that its resolution to make a €1 billion pledge to the 2008 Fund had stretched its capabilities. Fallen's initiative would prevent a repeat of such misjudgement.

When British mortgage provider Northern Rock had run out of cash and collapsed in the early months of the credit crunch, current affairs and business news weekly *The Economist* had published a YouGov poll asking people who they thought was responsible for the lender's woes. Sixty per cent had responded the bank's management, 15 per cent had named the financial market situation and 10 per cent had pointed to the financial regulator.[417] In the case of Candover we can assume that management would be similarly incriminated.

Curran was greatly admired and respected for his calm leadership and business acumen throughout his practically flawless tenure at the firm. He must now wonder where his succession planning went wrong. In his last statement as Chairman in March 2006, he had observed that Candover had become one of the premier European buyout houses. He had expressed the confident belief that his successors would preserve, even reinforce, such a lead.[418] The following three years would be as destructive as his twenty-five-year reign had been canny and disciplined.

But it is undeniable that Candover often took a commanding role throughout the UK's private equity history and the group's shareholders should pay tribute to Brooke, Curran and Fairservice for the firm's accomplishments during its first two decades of operation. While it collapsed because of very specific managerial, structural and macroeconomic reasons, it should be of concern to many LBO operators and followers that the group fell apart in such a dramatic way. Candover was Europe's most visible casualty of the buyout crash, but it might have just kept up with traditions in showing the way to its peers. It is the end of the road for Candover and most likely the end of an era for the PE industry.

Chapter 13 - Back to Basics

Once upon a time, an LBO transaction process was a thorough affair. A prospective buyer would enter exclusivity with the seller, and carry out detailed due diligence for several months, not just to review the financial accounts of the target or its commercial viability but also to perform insurance and environmental audits, management assessments, and more often than not plant visits. Frequently the price of the coveted business would be trimmed to reflect the various business issues identified. Candover's methodical deal-making skills and analytical rigor were essential in executing MBOs and generating superior returns; they were an integral part of the firm's core values. Buyouts were inherently complex, risky transactions. It was not sufficient to have a comprehensive list of business contacts; scrupulous due diligence work had to be completed to limit the risk of losing one's shirt.

By contrast, in recent years the value engendered by the industry's big hitters owed more to the leveragability of a target company than to the latter's ability to outgrow the market and outperform business plan projections. Fund managers were spending more time looking for the most generous lender than finding and analysing the most promising business to back. Sale processes during the period of 2004 to 2007 were not only more competitive; they were also shorter and the targets were leveraged up more aggressively. Pushy financial innovators had replaced conservative craftsmen. Both the 1987-89 era and the late 1990s were periods of high valuations and pugnacious bidding wars. But to win auctions of €1 billion-plus transactions during the mid-2000s' period of prosperity, you needed to have superior capabilities or you had to cut corners. Building such capabilities required time and a fat wallet. The likes of Apax, Permira, CVC and 3i had anticipated the full potential of the European market and acted accordingly by opening offices in France, Germany and other major countries since the mid-1980s. Many country-focused, mid-sized firms like Candover, which had built their reputation on their almost surgical approach to deal execution, had to change their style if they wanted to do battle with the big guns on the international stage. A team that had proudly emphasised its ability to do proprietary deals was confronted with a world where 'double-digit EBITDA multiple', 'hostile bidding', 'stapled financing' and 'secondary buyout' were the new buzz words. Why else would CPL have engaged into hotly contested takeover battles to delist Stork and Expro when Wreford, Brooke and Curran had generally shunned such aggressive methods? A small group of dealmakers leaning on their rolodex to develop angles and win over the target's management team found that risk-taking and the size of one's wallet were increasingly taking precedent. An LBO shop that had marketed itself as a generalist was losing deals to sector specialists. It is no coincidence that Candover closed four buyouts in the energy sector between 2003 and 2008; specialisation was a way to win savagely fought auctions in an overcrowded market.

Buyout firms are no different from other financial service providers. In the simplest of terms, they compete for a share of the money saved by millions, even hundreds of millions of individuals across the world. Although you might call this view naive, I consider that to be given the chance to manage so much money, whether it emanates from pension funds, banks or other institutional investors, is a privilege. To be entrusted with billions of euros is a huge responsibility. The livelihood of many people depends on such accomplished financial investors; not just because a decent return is expected on their investment but also because many business executives and employees place their confidence in buyout professionals to support their company, be it to implement its development or to consolidate its market position.

During the credit boom, a large proportion of PE investors forgot what they were in it for. Aiming to build their own organisation – a noble cause per se - they lost their ways, chasing more funds and bigger deals with the sole objective of winning higher fees and quick capital gains rather than keeping their focus on prudent deal execution and steady investment performance. By 2007, European PE deals totalled close to €180 billion a year, representing approximately 1,500 transactions. In 2000, the size of that market was only €65 billion, implying an annual growth rate of 13 per cent. Over the same period the number of transactions had only risen at 4 per cent annually. Deal sizes were getting bigger for no apparent reason other than the fact that they represented immense economies of scale and therefore a substantial boost in profits for fund managers. The average LBO transaction in Europe had almost doubled in value over those eight years, reaching approximately €120 million by 2007. That trend was exacerbated by the concentration of funding towards the larger end of the market; it provoked an inflationary spiral in valuation multiples paid on multi-billion-dollar transactions. Benefitting from the reallocation of global liquidity away from Internet start-ups and into more mature sectors of the economy, the buyout community proved incapable of resisting that inflow of easy money and aimed for absolute size instead of strong returns. Suddenly, it was better to have the most capital under management rather than netting the highest IRR. That race for size, prompted by envy, created a gigantic bubble where well-grounded investors had given way to thrill-seeking punters. Industry followers argue that the introduction of the euro in 1999 is behind such M&A frenzy, but in reality it had kicked off with the economic recovery of the mid 1990s, partly encouraged by the recent opening of the communist bloc. In 1995 the European PE industry had executed just short of one thousand deals worth a total of €18 billion. Between 1995 and 2007, volumes were up 3 per cent per annum but values had risen at a staggering 21 per cent compound annual growth rate. To fund these acquisitions, financing structures got more complicated and the tax shield derived from leverage incited both indolent buyout professionals - looking to work the same and earn more - and fee-hungry, volume-driven bankers to pile up the debt. It could only end in tears. Candover's break-up is the symptom of one of the financial industry's worst orgies and we know that its eventful history had seen a few before. Over the years the large and mega-funds had proudly shown off their prowess as deal-makers; their achievements as investors are a different matter and call for a reassessment. Men of Brooke's and Curran's stature, who had spent years mastering the complex craft of LBO structuring and cautious portfolio management, were no longer around to act as the voice of reason.

At the peak of the bubble, because of this irresistible increase in fund sizes many PE firms went through a power shift away from the investment professionals and to the benefit of the fundraising team. In a rush to do deals quickly to keep pace with their fund-marketing plans, the larger LBO outfits piled on the notoriously more challenging secondary transactions and take-privates. Predictably, since 2008 many of them have underscored the importance of portfolio management now that they have to cope with numerous investee companies on life support.

GETTING THE UPPER HAND

Limited partners contributing to LBO funds had few options to act during the recent bubble and its fallout. Some of them were members of advisory committees but they were, in the main, institutions with a long-term relationship with fund managers. Firms like Candover had served them well in the past and internal corporate governance issues coupled with the departures of senior talent, while of concern, were not exceptional in the PE world. As the industry attempts to introduce better bells and whistles, LPs can derive many lessons from the buyout crash.

Performance is, rightly, the most important thing for investors. They should intervene or walk away from a fund manager if investment returns start to slack. They need to act swiftly when they realise that GPs experience hardship. Very often though, by the time performance tumbles, LPs are stuck in commitments and cannot always free themselves from their legal obligations. In most GP structures, investors require a two-third or three-quarter majority vote to be able to withdraw the allocations they made at the time of fundraising. Investors must start building coalitions in order to have the means to impose change at the GP level. Without such a tight collaboration, with typical large PE funds representing commitments from over a hundred investors, the LPs' only option is likely to be a refusal to take part in the following fundraising process. Or they could use the current power shift in their favour to request that the proportion of votes required for recourse be brought down closer to 50 per cent.

To industry outsiders, it might seem odd that investors kept committing funds to an industry that was showing signs of fatigue and excess in 2006 and early 2007, but it is important to keep in mind that it takes many years for any given vintage to show its true colours. CPL's first sign of weakness in relation to the 1997 Fund did not really materialise until First Leisure's bankruptcy in 2004 and even then Candover still held a few investments related to that fund with the potential to yield decent returns. Likewise, with the exception of Ontex the 2001 Fund's portfolio issues did not start showing until the slowdown of 2007. Investors appeared powerless and unable to anticipate the industry's sudden default so it seems that they need to come up with some form of early warning mechanism capable of assessing the risk of failure of a GP. Some LPs underestimated the danger associated with an over-allocation of funds to the large buyout segment.

Primarily, investors should watch out for corporate governance issues within a GP, or between a GP and one of its LPs as was the case with Candover, and should not disregard them readily. Limited partners have little authority to suggest governance improvements or even the removal of senior partners at the GP level, but they are not entirely powerless. In the case of Candover, it was more straightforward since CIP, the group's limited partner, also owned CPL, its general partner. Fallen's initiatives in 2009 and 2010 to rectify internal governance rules helped the group's LP introduce a more formal relationship between the two entities. High-powered institutions accounting for a large portion of a fund manager's capital (CIP's pledge was approximately 15 per cent of the Candover 2005 Fund's total pot) can request that changes be introduced and threaten to withdraw their commitment to any subsequent fund. To state the obvious, taking such a tough stance is only achievable when there are limited conflicts of interest. The problem is that the definition of these conflicts is often woolly. Trade bodies like the European Private Equity and Venture Capital Association (EVCA) only suggest governing principles, not laws or regulations, to overcome the issue. When they propose that 'a fund operator should seek to manage conflicts of interest fairly, both between itself and investors in the fund and between different funds and different investors',[419] no one knows what it encompasses.

Given this lack of clear legislation, in a self-regulated sector like private equity it is up to limited partners to assess and avoid such conflicts as these are likely to restrict their ability to act swiftly and move their money out in times of crisis. We often refer to institutional money as 'smart money' – in contrast to individual investors who lack the information and speed of execution to get out of their investment positions when things go wrong. However, because their funds are contractually committed for up to ten years – usually extendable by one or two years at LPs' discretion – many institutions are frequently not able to act readily due to the poor liquidity of their holdings. In practice, even though they are the ultimate owners of the vintage fund to which they commit capital, LPs cannot take their money and run when disaster strikes. Eliminating conflicts of interest should help improve internal decision-making procedures as was rightly underlined by observers in the aftermath of the Candover Group's reshuffle in the summer of 2009.[420]

Buyout groups are no longer early-stage entrepreneurial businesses like they were in the 1980s; they need to be run like any established company. The traditional model of PE investing had seen LPs play a passive role and be entirely dependent on the ingenuity of the general partners' senior management. But such an arrangement does not preclude limited partners from closely monitoring the financial sponsors' operations. While the existing model of close-ended, legally binding and contractually committed funds is certainly less cumbersome than, and preferable to, the methodology applied in the industry's early days when equity had to be raised each time a GP wanted to complete a management buyout, LPs must somehow regain greater control over the way their money is being used. Investors sitting on the fund manager's advisory board should rise to the occasion and play a more hands-on role. Admittedly it is not easy to implement when the industry is operating in a bubble. The current crisis offers them a unique chance.

As the credit crunch unfolded investors had started to concern themselves with senior management remuneration at some GPs, and so they should. They should indeed ensure that senior partners' total compensation and investment returns remain somewhat correlated. When several senior figures at the mega-funds are rumoured to be taking home €5 million to €10 million a year in fixed emoluments straight from management fees just to administer third-party money, we know that the system has gone awry. I say fixed emoluments because there is nothing variable about them for the simple reason that GPs' managers are their own bosses and set their own annual salaries and bonuses – wouldn't we all love to? Not surprisingly before the financial crisis they kept increasing these at a rate several times that of inflation while at the same time keeping that information under wraps. To call it an all-out money-grabbing feast somehow doesn't quite capture it. Most investors would acknowledge that venture capital investing requires as much work and certainly involves more risk exposure than working in a well-diversified mega-buyout firm. Why a VC executive is paid much less than €1 million a year when some LBO managers earn ten times more is baffling, especially in view of the value destruction the latter have spawned in recent years.

Because they were not managing mega-funds, the members of CPL's Executive Committee were not on such lavish annual remuneration packages, but most industry observers could easily conclude that they had, like their counterparts at other mighty buyout groups, greatly benefitted from the exponential growth in capital committed to the sector over the last ten years. In 2000, based on CIP's financial accounts that year, Buffin and Gumienny had each earned approximately £636,000. In the fiscal year of 2002, the last year their remuneration was disclosed in CIP's accounts, they had each received £1.4 million in salaries, directors' fees, performance-related pay, loyalty bonuses, share options, pension contributions paid by CIP on their behalf, incentive schemes and other taxable benefits.[421] By 2008, their remuneration was evidently higher. Such inflation in personal income was not in line with the performance of the firm but simply reflected the fact that the upsurge in fund size between the 1997 Fund (£850 million) and the 2005 Fund (€3.5 billion) was not followed by a proportional percentage reduction in management fee. And that was the case across the industry. As fund sizes increased, LPs accepted that the same percentage of management fees be applied, even though in some cases funds had become three to four times as large. The fact that a GP is able to charge the same 1.5 per cent[422] to a £850 million fund (let's call it €1.3 billion for argument's sake) and to a €3.5 billion fund, shows that the balance of power in the PE industry was heavily tilted in favour of general partners to the detriment of LPs. The recent financial turmoil has enabled limited partners to negotiate such levies downwards and even close to 1 per cent for some GPs overseeing very large funds so, as stated above, the power of negotiation might have shifted. But thanks to the LBO bubble, a firm that earned c. €19.5 million in commissions annually in 2000 was earning over €50 million each year by 2006.[423] In the meantime, CPL had opened several European offices and recruited forty new staff, but as in all other GP structures, a generous proportion of the upside was certainly shared by its senior executives.

No one truly understands how this industry-wide windfall could ever have been allowed by LPs since these emoluments were paid out of the management fees that they incurred. But what we know for sure is that, in 2008, senior partners at your run-of-the-mill mega-LBO fund, employing at the very most 300 people, with annual income well shy of €500 million, were receiving annual compensations exceeding, often by a wide margin, those of powerful corporate executives like Vittorio Colao, a man earning that year less than £3 million[424] as CEO of Vodafone, the largest mobile telecom operator in the world with 300 million customers and 79,000 employees in twenty-seven countries, generating operating profits of £12 billion on £41 billion of revenues, and incidentally the fourth-biggest market capitalisation in Britain at a very respectable £80 billion.

Quite logically, fee structures are likely to evolve in favour of the limited partners. At the top end of the PE spectrum, the GP's business model looks more and more like that of traditional asset managers. There is anecdotal evidence that their commissions are starting to reflect that fact. In the mid-market, moderate leverage and active financial and operational management of portfolio companies will remain the norm, which should entitle these buyout fund managers to higher fees.

In times past LPs had had no issue with the level of capital gains or carried interest levied by buyout firms, even though it can reach dizzying amounts for each managing partner. More recently, some investors have decided to look at carry levels more closely. With the frequent secondary transactions and refinancings, the high level of debt used to fund some transactions, and the growing number of club deals whereby all the PE firms involved do not necessarily add the same value, investors wonder whether a 20 per cent share of capital gains is justified. They feel that in some instances GPs do not have to work as assiduously to provide returns in excess of the hurdle rate. Usually set at 8 per cent as communicated before, this standard of minimum return guaranteed to the LPs was generally viewed as an appropriate target to keep GP executives motivated and diligent. In the future, it is possible that LPs will decide to pay a different carried interest based on the nature and the leverage of specific transactions. If so, it could be one way to prevent GPs from overleveraging their portfolio companies or taking the easy but lazy sponsor-to-sponsor route.

LBO fund managers who operated during the debauchery of the 2000s received a total compensation well in excess of what entrepreneurs like Brooke earned during the early years of the sector's history. Unlike Cinven, Charterhouse or Bridgepoint, Candover had been established from day one as a stand-alone start-up and was therefore exposed to a much greater risk of failure. Many firms that followed Brooke's example in the early days were gone or acquired within years of their inception. Names like SUMIT, absorbed by Schroders in 1992,[425] and Guidehouse, gone into receivership in December 1991,[426] had long disappeared but Candover had stood the test of time thanks to the unflappable governance of Brooke and Curran.

In principle, liberal theories tell us that markets are efficient and wealth is distributed according to the concept of value creation. Despite hundreds of millions of euros destroyed in recent years, senior partners at large and mega GPs still walked away with a fortune in vested carry, not because of their superior investment monitoring techniques, but because of the sheer size of the funds they were handling in the last decade. The true benefit of the GP business model has been exhibited during the recent market cycle: fund managers get a share of the gains, not a share of the downside. Thanks to yearly and contractually-set management fees, GPs get rich even if they deliver below-par performance. For many years, LBO superstars had fobbed their detractors off with suggestions that their interests and those of their investors were aligned. We now know that it is not quite true. In reality, what the recent debt bubble story teaches us is that it is best to be in the right place at the right time than to faithfully believe in free-market theories.

Investors having been burnt by the market crash will carry out stricter due diligence in the future, especially given the realisation that too much of the general partners' performance during the bubble years was essentially derived from the high leverage used to finance their acquisitions. Many buyout executives allege that most of the value delivered by investee businesses is attained through operational enhancements and top line growth, but such a claim is usually indemonstrable since the data on which these assertions are made are never disclosed. It probably was true in the 1980s, but nowadays, with the numerous secondary buyouts, expensive take-privates of already strongly cash-generative companies, and a marketplace that has become a lot more competitive, it would be surprising if, for transactions with a value exceeding €500 million, most of the wealth crystallised from exits between 2003 and 2010 was not in reality obtained from very high financial gearing. In its 2007 annual report, Candover asserted that three fundamental drivers were responsible for 80 per cent of its value creation over time: revenue growth, improvements in operating margins and cash generation to pay down debt. Bizarrely, no mention is made of rising debt-to-equity ratios and ever lower borrowing cost as factors of wealth accumulation. Since the companies' cash-generation potential is intrinsic and existed before Candover or any of its rivals bought them out, the way large buyout fund managers derived robust returns from their investments during the credit boom must have been primarily by borrowing vast amounts at an all-time low interest rate and settling that debt with the cash produced by these companies, which could be one way of interpreting the third fundamental driver described in the Candover statement above. This however simply requires good cash flow management skills. The more cash a business produces, the more leverage it can bear, hence the numerous refinancings in recent years.

It would be interesting to gauge what proportion of the value engendered by the large and mega-buyout segments during the 2000–08 period was drawn from the excessive debt used to underwrite the deals. In all likelihood, independent researchers will eventually carry out a thorough analysis. I suspect that the findings will be devastating for the industry's reputation and may even help LPs negotiate lower carries from the firms taking part in such transactions. Going forward, LPs will need to do their homework carefully. After all, depending on what survey you rely on, only half to two-thirds of PE funds in any given vintage earn returns above the hurdle rate.

It took seven years for debt-burdened retailer Gateway to emerge from the brink of extinction, ultimately floating itself for £500 million under the Somerfield brand in August 1996. Its bankers had lost their loans in the process and its equity-holders never recouped a penny. And just in case you wondered, yes, Somerfield was delisted during the recent buyout craze by a troop of institutional and private investors, including LBO colossus Apax. Thankfully, this time around the consortium managed to steer clear of any embarrassment by selling out in July 2008 as valuations were about to fall in a downward spiral and only weeks before the Lehman blow-up. It is impossible to determine how many years it will take for the over-indebted companies that have recently been, or will ultimately be, repossessed by their lenders to bring adequate returns to their new owners - assuming they ever do. The real issue relates to the sheer size of the debt overhang currently threatening the buyout industry. Back in 1992, Gateway was the only troubled mega-deal in Europe so it was almost a quirk. Nowadays, there are dozens of Gateway-like zombies being kept alive by their PE backers too embarrassed to admit publicly, as Candover did, that they have messed up and that some of their portfolio companies are virtually worthless. As we slowly but steadily approach the day of reckoning, more GP returns will fall below the hurdle rate and more LPs will reconsider their appetite for king-size buyout funds.

No doubt investors will exercise a lot more discernment in their allocation of funds going forward. They might decide to introduce a ruthless assessment framework, creating therewith a three-tier GP landscape. Top-quartile performers would be allowed to retain the traditional, princely model of 1.5 or 2 per cent in management fees and 20 per cent in carry. Second-quartile funds would have to make do with lower compensation, maybe with a 1 per cent/10 per cent structure. As for the consistently bottom-half players, they would be brutally cast out.

The market is bound to become more dynamic, introducing a much more selective angle to PE investing. It is about time.

REALITY CHECK

For general partners, the takeaways from the industry's distress are of a different kind.

The early 2000s had seen a striking rise in terms of fund size for many of them. At the time, it was fostered by two major trends: the emergence of the buyout market in continental Europe and the end of the technology bull market prompting many LPs to refocus their attention away from VC funding and towards more mature, stable buyout investing. But when the time came for a new fund to be raised in the middle of the decade, LPs tended to agree on one point: target sizes must be realistic and should not represent too much of an increase from one vintage to the next. Most large buyout fund managers failed to listen and ran into overdrive.

General partners must make sure that their investment strategy remains consistent in terms of portfolio diversification and risk management. As we have seen, Candover accelerated its fund-marketing and its investment timetable from one vintage to the next. Moving up in size and reducing the number of transactions carried out from the 2005 Fund was a double whammy on the risk-measurement scale. Financial sponsors must maintain a disciplined schedule in both investing and fundraising and a coherent approach when it comes to the nature and complexity of their deals so that risk can effectively be diversified away: a few PTPs alongside some secondaries together with corporate carve-outs and roll-ups, family succession or entrepreneurial transition opportunities and a handful of turnarounds according to the prevailing environment. Again, these are basic rules, but they were no longer followed during the buyout madness of the mid-2000s.

In the aftermath of the credit crunch, LBO fund managers will need to take time to improve the performance of their portfolio before coming to market with a new fund. The success of upcoming fundraises is bound to depend heavily on the state of the existing portfolio and the number of companies that went under or, more precisely, were abandoned by the GP and taken over by their lenders. As is already the case in many US organisations, portfolio teams will need to comprise operating managers whose purpose is to improve the value-creation potential of the underlying assets. As Gumienny rightly asserted when commenting in the firm's PE barometer for the third quarter of 2007, the focus has moved away from deal making in favour of debt repayment.[427] In some kind of return to the industry's roots, strong demonstrable portfolio management skills will dictate the success of future fundraises. They will also call for some serious pre-marketing work.

GP managers wrongly assumed that, even when heavily geared, larger companies had a lower risk profile than SMEs did. It demonstrates that the world of finance truly suffers from short-term memory symptoms. During the LBO bubble of the mid-to-late 1980s, the transactions that had recorded the lowest returns or gone under were often the most sizeable and aggressively indebted ones. Industry analysts would have known that the fund comprising the 1988 buyout of $30 billion-plus RJR Nabisco had reportedly yielded a net IRR in single digit for KKR's investors;[428] they would have recalled that the $2.5 billion take-private of homebuilder and industrial products manufacturer Jim Walter Corporation by the same KKR would have gone sour less than eighteen months after being acquired, filing for Chapter 11 bankruptcy protection in December 1989 while buried under vast amounts of debt; they would have remembered a similar fate in July 1988 for the $1.3 billion LBO of Revco, America's largest drugstore chain at the time.

The leveragability of a business is not dependent on the size of the target but rather on a diverse set of parameters. When structuring their deals, many GPs failed to apply the most elementary of risk management principles. To add a layer of extreme financial risk (i.e., high indebtedness) to a company implies that other risk elements are held in check. If the business is already exposed to significant operating risks (such as high fixed costs in the heavily unionised car manufacturing industry), technology shifts (for instance, the digitisation of content in music publishing), regulatory uncertainty (like a government's crackdown on gambling) or radical market change (e.g., piracy in the music sector), gearing it up leaves it with little room for error as the

Chrysler, Gala Coral and EMI buyouts showed. The ability to apprehend risk is a fundamental characteristic of a PE specialist's skill set. For all that most LBOs closed in 2006, 2007 and early 2008 neglected to properly factor in macroeconomic uncertainties: the credit crunch and the global recession provided their owners with a valuable refresher course.

Just like Hanson Trust and other members of the conglomerate league in the early 1990s, with ultimately unsuccessful but nonetheless seriously considered bids for FTSE 100 companies such as supermarket chain Sainsbury's or telecom service provider BT, the buyout goliaths of the noughties tried to bite off more than they could chew. The current predicament of many large and mega-deals has shown that size is not an infallible protection to survive an economic recession or a structural market transformation if the indebted business has no headroom to manoeuvre. The story does not say what happened to those workers who lost their jobs because their employer had to choose between redeeming its debt and paying their salaries.

As discussed, buyout specialists are remunerated handsomely because they claim to have superior investment expertise. They can be certain that because of the number of corporate failures they have been responsible for in the first three years of the financial crisis (reported to be more than 100 annual receiverships or over a third of total annual portfolio exits between 2008 and 2010 in the UK alone),[429] they will be closely monitored by investors, regulators and the public at large. The way they handle themselves in these turbulent times might well determine their survival and that of the whole sector. Most fund managers will be unable to go back to their LPs to raise an annex fund in order to support their investee companies. It is telling of the times we live in that this type of structures, once raised to top up vintages and finance add-on acquisitions for portfolio companies, is instead being set up to bail out recent funds and prop up investment positions. KKR's decision to establish such a lifeline for its European Fund II[430] proves that several 2005-to-2008 PE investment vehicles will require patience and significant additional funding if their GPs ever want to receive any carried interest from them.

The majority of LBO firms that have successfully built a sustainable business model over time have been led jointly and collaboratively by a group of individuals. Everyone at the executive committee level must be given equal voting rights. Investment decisions must truly be made collectively without allowing any individual to bulldoze his deals through investment committees. Senior executives share responsibility for the strategic vision and implementation, the running of the organisation, and the preservation of the corporate culture. While the best established firms have also suffered from the recent financial disorder, strikingly when they were at the same time going through succession issues, they still addressed their problems in a collegial manner. To confront the fallout of the credit crunch, GP management teams will need to act in partnership more than ever.

To do so successfully, proper planning will be the determining factor. General partners tend to raise a new fund every three or four years (more like five to six under the credit squeeze conditions), but they rarely have a five-year corporate strategic plan. They tend to rely on the investment scenario defined in their PPM, the main fundraising document, without taking heed of the way the marketplace evolves. Changes in the environment can often, as was the case for Candover, be detrimental to a GP. Their strategy needs to be flexible enough to adapt to a financial crisis, the entry of new competitors or regulatory reforms, for instance. CPL's main fault was to have focused almost exclusively on its internal requirements and on what it would take to deliver on its development strategy without realising that the market conditions were dire and required a postponement rather than a hastening of the fundraising initiative. It is not to say that the firm's management had not acknowledged that the crisis necessitated some adjustment in their fundraising (before the credit crunch, they had reportedly intended to raise a €6 billion fund),[431] but they should have scaled it down further or deferred it altogether when the banking and economic situation worsened in the first half of 2008. Back in March 1991, while announcing CIP's 1990 annual results in an exceedingly unstable economic and geopolitical context, Brooke had shown that fundraising initiatives must take into account numerous factors and that adequate timing is crucial: he had indicated that the recent resolution of the Gulf War had finally given Candover a chance to start marketing a new fund.[432]

All fund managers should naturally follow his example. Nevertheless, as the new generation of GPs tries to institutionalise their operations and formalise their strategic leadership, they must take particular care of preserving the entrepreneurial spirit that is so dear to dealmakers. Creating a common corporate culture does not imply monitoring every single aspect of the investment process. Sourcing transactions will always remain a personality-based activity even if it can be systemised. Its supervision must not make deal originators feel like they are being controlled and not empowered. It is easy for bureaucracy to get in the way of individual initiative. Crucially, establishing an institutionalised framework will require bringing in outside help. In an industry where investment executives frequently press the senior management of portfolio companies to hire all types of consultants, PE executives rarely employ the services of independent advisers to address internal issues. The next wave of GP leaders is likely to be more open to the idea of calling in strategy consultants to surmount future obstacles, assess their competitive positioning and perfect their service offering. The very existence of many fund managers will depend on their proprietary skills and their ability to differentiate their product strategy.

And as is the case for LPs, the fine-tuning of the financial sponsors' business model will invite a serious upgrade in corporate governance. Historically, GPs have despised the idea of having to report to anyone. The advantage of operating in a partnership setting is that you only are answerable to the other managing partners. The only supervisory structure present in most LBO firms is the advisory board on which the cornerstone investors are invited. Rarely more than once a year during the annual investor conference, sometimes on a quarterly basis, this board of LPs meets to discuss and vote on major initiatives including key investment and operational decisions. But the recent financial crisis has shown that large fund managers would benefit from formal supervision, including the establishment of a board of non-executive directors who would bring in fresh opinions. Some have started to operate that way, just like occasionally CIP's board had acted in that capacity for the benefit of CPL. It should become an industry standard for the most prominent funds.

So far the PE industry has failed to acknowledge its role in the recent uncontrolled build-up of corporate debt. Whereas bankers have come under scrutiny, buyout decision-makers have been keen to hide away, missing the opportunity to come to the banks' defence. GPs must learn to accept blame where it falls due. Having the courage to own up to one's mistakes separates the men from the boys. In a way taking reproach on behalf of all those LPs who overcommitted themselves to the industry, Grimstone had the merit of publicly admitting his judgement errors. It cannot have been easy. It must have been even tougher to stay on board when CIP's shareholders chose to keep him to clean up the mess. His grit and professionalism show what he is made of. In 2009 and 2010, there were several instances of general partners waiving their carried interest and reducing performance-related commissions already vested or earned as recognition that if they wanted to raise a fund in the future, they should show their investors that they were prepared to share their pain. I suspect that, regrettably, few will follow suit unless obligated to do so.

Too many GP managers felt that the PE business model was superior to more traditional corporate structures. The last three years have forced industry commentators to re-evaluate this view. Just like the industrial conglomerates of the 1980s, the large and mega-buyout fund managers of the 2000s became too self-assured. Uncontrolled debt-piling will force significant changes. Hopefully the GPs won't need a push to put them in place.

SKILL RESET

Back when it all started, the contribution of venture capitalists and early buyout professionals was essentially to bring in financial management proficiency. For that reason, a strong training in accountancy was a must to be able to run investments. Value creation was derived from making sure that portfolio companies monitored their balance sheet and cash flows professionally. Qualified accountants like Stephen Curran, Philip Symonds, Colin Buffin, and Marek Gumienny were typical recruits for the industry. In the UK and the US, corporate managers proactively looked for financing in order to acquire the subsidiary or division they worked for from its parent company. The best LBO operators were those who built long-term relationships with such businessmen, perfected the due diligence exercise necessary to assess investment opportunities, and introduced efficient cost-cutting practices. By the mid-1990s, deals had become larger, performance enhancement practices in the SME segment had improved and financial engineering was more complex. By now, a background in leverage was often an advantage. In the late 1990s Candover recruited bankers Charlie Green and Ian Gray, both with significant experience in structured finance, but within five years debt funding was increasingly treated as a commodity, notably with the emergence of stapled finance. Operational enhancements of portfolio companies started to deliver superior investment returns as management consultants and operating partners were brought in: it was a remarkable departure from the conventional hands-off methodology. Again, that trend had started in the US a few years earlier. And as the financial meltdown took hold in 2008, GPs used the services of restructuring specialists to help reinvigorate stressed assets. Ironically, with credit drying out GP managers were forced back to their roots, their origins as cash managers. Old-timers like Brooke and Curran could be forgiven for feeling nostalgic.

I mentioned that the average holding period of Candover's first ten transactions had been five years. The average time-to-exit of the Candover 1997 Fund's portfolio was four years, but it fell to three and a half years if problem-ridden investments like Acertec are removed from the sample. If the 2001 Fund had not been affected by the low quality of its underlying assets, the sudden collapse of the public stock and debt markets and the subsequent recession, it is certain that its average holding period would have been shorter still in order to stay in sync with the curtailed fundraising cycle. As they tried to trim the investment holding period and collect funds more frequently, the largest buyout fund managers were no longer taking the time necessary to create value through top line growth and margin improvements like they used to.

It is difficult to ascertain what expertise or training will be needed to successfully run a PE firm and ride the industry's roller coaster over the next ten years, but it is likely to require a mix of the above plus some extra skills. An accountancy qualification, M&A experience or a strong understanding of structured finance would fall way short of the minimum requirements without deep sector specialisation and the well-honed competence of a seasoned operating technician. A solid grasp of international business practices will be a must as a large number of portfolio companies will operate across continents. For that reason alone, as they continue to widen their geographical reach, all the major European and North American LBO groups should have representatives with diverse skillsets and from various nationalities sitting on their executive and investment committees. Many still do not today, in another sign that changes introduced across the sector over the last three years have been, for the most part, cosmetic.

In a more complex and wearisome business context, GPs will need to continue to adapt if they are to preserve their generous emoluments and incentive structures. In particular, as sponsor-to-sponsor transactions represent an ever growing share of the volume of PE deals, creating value and generating superior returns will call upon management techniques all the more sophisticated. The main benefit of the credit crunch is that it has significantly slowed down the pace of deal-making and fundraising, giving time for the executive teams to concentrate on portfolio monitoring, operational enhancements and cost-cutting, all techniques that were in high demand when it all started over thirty years ago.

Chapter 14 - A Wake-Up Call

The party that, one would hope, has learned the most from the recent collapse of the debt bubble is the financial regulator. As widely reported, regulatory authorities, and I would include national governments in this definition since they often play a steering role in that area, failed to identify the risks to which property markets, the buyout industry and other credit-dependent sectors were exposed. They also missed the chance to predict the dangers that over-borrowing represented for the whole economy. For the last twenty years financial self-regulation had been the new mantra of many industrialised nations. Even today, as governments in North America and Western Europe increase their supervisory functions and impose new rules on the investment and banking sectors, many experts and interest groups oppose further intervention and regulation. Those free-market supporters should be ignored. If we have learned one lesson from the last ten years, it is that it is naive and even criminal to expect individuals and corporations managing other people's money spontaneously to exercise caution and restraint. In a self-regulated market where innovation is key and the only barrier to entry is the size of your fund, behaviours can quickly become irrational or, to paraphrase a former central banker, 'irrationally exuberant'.

An industry that had been built on a reputation of rigorous, tight financial control, operational efficiency enhancement and corporate restructurings had become lazy, using all the tricks in the bag – recapitalisations, stapled financing, secondary transactions, club deals, accelerated auctions, sell-side due diligence, reverse break fees – to close larger deals faster and at top valuations. It might sound counterintuitive that they would adopt such a relaxed attitude and take chances as deals were becoming more complex, but industries operating in a bubble usually lose their sanity. Recently, executives in the largest buyout groups have acted with a sense of entitlement, but we should not forget that they are only intermediaries allocating savings and pension money. They have no divine right to keep on taking 20 per cent of capital gains if such profits are achieved via leverage trickery rather than performance improvements of the underlying assets. Many limited partners could see through all the haze but had no real power to effect change. Some, like CIP, even believed the hype. We can be certain that further regulatory obligations, such as the Walker disclosures in the UK and the Volcker Rule regarding restrictions on proprietary trading and private equity investing by banks in the US, will be initiated. The Walker recommendations were only guidelines introduced in 2007 under the supervision of the BVCA after months of protests from trade unions and various politicians regarding the PE industry's extreme asset-stripping and wealth-maximising behaviours since the early 2000s. Other European governments and industry associations have announced or implemented similar proposals. It is the role of industry watchdogs and legislators to make sure that innovation in the financial industry remains a value-creation process, not a destructive force capable of bringing the whole economy to the point of annihilation.

What should worry us all is that during the buyout bubble many industry executives, from LPs to investment bankers and leveraged lenders, publicly expressed concerns about the unreasonable amounts of debt being deployed, yet no one seemed in a position to stop the runaway train. Concerned about the type of transaction that was taking place in 2006 and early 2007, a Treasury Select Committee in the UK had launched an inquiry into some of the industry's dodgier practices,[433] and a congressional Financial Services Committee session had also taken place in the US in the spring of 2007.[434] In all honesty, I do not think that many people within and outside the industry know what the outcome of such hearings was. The effect of the grilling of senior buyout executives on the media had been potent but few concrete resolutions and actions had come out of it. PE has become so pervasive that no one appears truly able to curb its powers. LBO experts showed no more understanding of increasingly complex credit products than the average homeowner in the American Midwest who failed to read the small print on his or her 'subprime' mortgage contract. Yet, regulators have so far proved inept at reining in the excess of testosterone that led the sector into overdrive. Policy makers have been only too keen to rely on the generous but biased advice of professional trade bodies to guide them in their inquiries.

It is not for me to set the parameters of tighter regulation. I do not know if leverage needs to be restricted or whether it should be limited to 40, 60 or 80 per cent of total transaction value, but something needs to be done to control the cyclical excesses that have affected the buyout industry since its inception. The Basel II proposals, which in short are recommendations forcing banks to set capital aside to guard against operational risks, already forced a greater degree of collateralisation on bank debt loaned to buyout firms, and are one way to restrain overleveraging. No doubt the latest version, appropriately named Basel III, will help in that sense even if there is always the risk that the requirement for lenders to establish higher capital conservation buffers might negatively affect non-PE-backed enterprises and the rest of the economy.[435] To those who argue that regulation will slow growth, I will contend that if economic development is primarily dependent on financial innovation then it is not a healthy state of affairs. Funding should also go towards financing new, promising industries and products, and not be dangerously concentrated in debt structuring, a niche and highly flammable area of finance. European and American economies have reached a stage of maturity that predicts a more modest rate of wealth creation than they observed historically. They will definitely rise much more slowly than emerging countries. The sooner we come to terms with the fact that Brazil, China and India are catching up, the easier it will be to reallocate capital to businesses and industries that participate in these countries' development. No amount of financial trickery will sustainably support a faster pace than the natural rate of growth in industrialised economies.

As touched upon, many chief executives and finance directors of a Fortune 500 or FTSE 100 company do not earn a total remuneration anywhere near that of the mega-buyout professionals but still have regularly to withstand fierce commentaries from the press, regulators and legislators. Some industry gurus would be tempted to argue that by adding all the workers of their portfolio companies many buyout groups would easily be among the largest employers in their countries. According to Permira's 2007 Annual Review, the group's portfolio companies employed 220,000 people worldwide. However, it is a misleading view of what PE managers actually are. They do not run their portfolio companies, they fund their strategy. As we have seen, in many cases they are simply hands-off shareholders, and like any shareholders they exercise their right to remove management and vote on strategy or other key decisions. I will not deny that as majority owners they have more influence than the typical minority investor of publicly listed businesses, but as already disclosed they frequently abuse their control position by paying themselves prodigious dividends in order to cash out, leaving the senior management team of the investee company to struggle to keep the ship afloat under an unhealthy debt burden. Senior partners at most of the largest buyout firms supervise very few employees and generate limited revenue but still pay themselves millions of dollars in emoluments annually. For many years their disproportionate financial rewards had been tolerated because there was a widely held belief that the sector's positive contribution to a country's economy was indisputable. According to several surveys, PE-backed companies grew their revenue faster and were more value-accretive than other businesses in the first twenty-five years of the industry's history. It was only natural that senior executives behind such a feat be paid accordingly. However, the last five years have reset the clocks. Because of the debt they stagger under, many buyout portfolios are in such a wobbly position that there will be little job creation at many investee companies in the foreseeable future. As Gala Coral's closures of bingo halls indicated, layoffs are more likely. Sure, the financial sponsors could always argue that such staff reductions would have occurred regardless of the ownership and capital structure, but no one can deny that subjecting a company to extreme leverage leaves little room to manoeuvre when the economy tumbles. Highly geared PE-backed businesses are unlikely to lead the charge in the economic recovery. As limited partners readjust their expectations it would seem appropriate for the general partners' remuneration packages to be reviewed.

The question of determining who should be setting the GPs' remunerations might need to be addressed. Because most of these funds operate under a partnership structure, they do not have shareholders. CPL was owned by CIP, but in the vast majority of cases GP managers are their own bosses. Still, many of them control a fortune in third-party assets. Should they continue to set their own compensation and be expected to apply restraint? Should the LPs take a firmer stance and withdraw from financial sponsors granting their top executives outrageously generous terms? Should governments take a supervisory role? In view of the recent inflation in fees and carry something must be done. GPs' remuneration packages have reached obscene levels.

It would also seem fair for people earning so much money administering the public's savings and pensions to be compelled to reveal their personal income. Regulators could force out the disclosure of the total remuneration, including the carried interest, of the key industry figures even if on a nameless basis. If investors managing public capital such as Warren Buffett, the head of holding company Berkshire Hathaway, and the CEOs of global banks are obliged to disclose their remuneration packages, why should the senior buyout bosses not do the same? Carried interest allocation is no different in nature from the granting of stock options so there is no specific reason why people who handle universities' endowments and insurance money should not let the original investors and savers know how much they are making from commissions and capital gains.

The word 'private' in private equity refers to the nature of the assets in which the funds are invested, as in private companies rather than publicly listed ones. It does not imply that the buyout funds can escape open disclosure and tight reporting on inordinate earnings. In view of the recent crash the industry needs to become more transparent if it is serious about rebuilding its tattered reputation. Given the number of LBO firms alleging to be running top-quartile funds, performance reporting must be standardised to prevent data manipulation, public monitoring needs to be imposed and false claims fined. Regular communication and reporting, maybe on a half-yearly basis, would seem more appropriate for an industry managing hundreds of billions of euros of individual savings, accounting for the lion's share of M&A activity, frequently bidding for blue-chip companies and backing the employment of hundreds of thousands of people in the countries where it operates. In the UK, for instance, PE-backed companies are believed to employ roughly a fifth of the private sector workforce.[436] As governments in

America and Europe have started a process of scaling down the size of the public sector, more workers are expected to come under private equity-management in the future.

Urged by their federal legislators, several US limited partners have started to report on a quarterly basis the net IRRs achieved by the GPs in which they have made fund allocations; more are certain to follow their example. PE groups are reluctant to issue information on their performance on the basis that it would put them at a disadvantage against private trade buyers. Several investment trusts in the UK, mega PE groups in the US and investment holdings in continental Europe are quoted and publish annual accounts. That does not appear to weaken their respective bargaining power. The largest financial sponsors need to come clean about the way they run their funds by disclosing the level of indebtedness of their portfolios, the number of investee companies defaulting on their debt, the extent of their asset write-downs, their corporate governance and the commissions and various compensations they charge for their services. As I have demonstrated PE investing is no longer a niche financial activity; it has become a pillar of the economy, and when an industry encompasses one in five private sector jobs in the country we could not be accused of exaggerating its importance if we said that, for good or bad, it has also evolved into an influential force of our society. With clout and success come responsibility and accountability.

The industry as a whole needs to acknowledge that it does not have to account only to its investors but also to a vast number of stakeholders such as the employees of their portfolio companies, the pension fund beneficiaries and even the public at large. And this time financial regulators, such as the UK's Financial Services Authority (FSA) and the Securities and Exchange Commission (SEC) in the US, rather than trade associations should define the content of these annual or half-yearly reviews, control their accuracy and make them mandatory. I obviously do not suggest that these reports should be as detailed as those of publicly listed companies. One of the key advantages of private equity-ownership is that business managers do not have to spend as much time on irksome administrative tasks and can concentrate on the all-important job of actually running the company. But we need to strike a middle ground. A few disclosures following the UK's Walker-recommended guidelines just won't do any more, chiefly because annual reviews that have been issued in the past by those few general partners who bother with preparing one have more similarities with marketing brochures than performance reports. It is a matter of special urgency as the current lack of transparency is hurting the sector's reputation. As the recent buyout crash has shown, an industry out of public view can get sloppy.

Behind closed doors the very large LBO institutions abused the trust of their investors by moving away from a well-established, prudently diligenced and controlled investment strategy. And by doing so their investee companies lost their traditional edge over the public market. Because of the extravagant level of debt used to finance LBOs, the portfolio companies' managers had to take time away from strategic initiatives and surrender to quarterly earnings reporting to their lenders in order to make sure that their businesses met tight covenants and could reimburse crippling debt obligations. Just like any listed business, by 2007 PE-backed companies were being run for quarterly results rather than longer-term value creation.

Because of the sector's obsession with secrecy – long gone are the days when MBO practitioners advertised in the financial press – it is often a challenge to obtain the most basic of data. When it comes to sizing up the industry, for instance, it is impossible to find consistent information. Deal values are not always disclosed, as in the case of Candover's 40 per cent stake in Technogym, and therefore not included in market surveys. In 2005, depending on what source you believe, the European buyout deal log was worth €116.5 billion, €119.7 billion or €125 billion.[437] Even without the most accurate of information one fact is undeniable: the buyout sector has become big enough for policy makers to take a closer look.

Three years after the world's financial industry crashed, the dreaded regulatory crackdown has not yet occurred, or at the very least it remains unclear which of the proposed reforms so far put forward will truly have a salutary impact on the buyout industry. The provisions on the financial sector's reform introduced by the Dodd-Frank Act and approved by the

US Congress on 15 July 2010 essentially apply to publicly listed financial companies, which leaves most LBO funds unscathed with the exception of the banks' proprietary PE activities that fall under the previously mentioned Volcker proposals. The European Parliament attempted to take the lead in redefining the rules of the game by approving the Alternative Investment Fund Managers Directive on 11 November 2010. But it offers harmonisation principles on regulatory and supervisory requirements at a European level rather than proper legislation. Due to be implemented at a country level by early 2013, it is too early to ascertain whether it will represent an improvement on the existing framework by bringing proper protection to investors and stability to the financial sector. New requests for information to be fed annually to the various national financial regulators might help monitor the PE funds' activity better going forward, but the recommended risk management tools and liquidity stress tests do nothing to prevent abuse in terms of over-leverage or to curb the most overweening behaviours adopted by the very large and mega-buyout segment during the recent bull run unless they are turned into laws. As always after a traumatic crisis like the one we have just gone through, political intent is unwavering. We will need to wait and see if the US authorities introduce more resolute regulatory oversight or if subsequent European guidelines take a stricter position on compensation packages and portfolio leverage policies. If past reforms are any guide, though, the very exclusive private equity club has nothing to fear. The appetite for economic growth has always proved stronger than the desire to repress the extravagant conduct of a small elite. Reporting and recordkeeping standards might become more stringent and low debt pricing might be out for a while, but PE has imposed itself as a crucial participant in our modern economy and financial markets. Even if it offers lower returns than it used to, it will remain an attractive alternative for many companies looking for growth capital. Lending banks and stock markets are good options to raise money, but they are traditionally more risk-averse than buyout investors. No doubt regulators will bear that in mind when they put their thinking hats on.

ALIGNING INTERESTS

It is widely accepted that since the inception of the buyout industry in the early 1980s the top-quartile performers have outshone all classes of investment products. Thanks to that exploit some buyout professionals became very wealthy indeed. Most of the billionaires in the sector reside in the US, but the UK and the rest of Europe have created their share of multimillionaires. Naturally, it raised awareness of the private, almost secretive world of buyouts. It also caught the attention of the media and of many politicians. In 2007, as the wealth creation process of the LBO world was at its apogee after well over fifteen years of almost uninterrupted growth, several pressure groups and politicians raised the issue of the tax treatment of the GPs' share of profits: the famous carried interest. They made a point that, so far, the PE tycoons have failed to address properly: why should carried interest be treated as gains? Critics argued that because fund managers received carry based on the execution of their work rather than the returns achieved on their own investments, carried interest should be treated as a performance bonus and therefore as income. It should consequently be taxed at the top income tax rate.

After a very entertaining consultation period during which retired buyout professional Sir Ronald Cohen, co-founder of Apax, himself criticised the benign UK tax regime applied to the carried interest earned by mega-funds[438] - not without having been reminded by some of the still active PE investors that the same tax regime did not seem to bother him when he worked in the industry - the tax rate applied to carry was finally increased from 10 per cent to 18 per cent from April 2008 on. Importantly, carried interest retained its capital gains tax (CGT) treatment. Not a bad result given that a respectable figure like Nicholas Fergusson, Chairman of investment firm SVG Capital, had cheekily observed that PE executives often paid less tax than the cleaners in their office.[439] In the US, after three years of heated debates and hearings[*] a bill proposed by the Obama administration and passed by the House of

---

[*] Legislation regarding the tax treatment of carried interest had first been proposed during George W. Bush's presidency by members of the US House of Representatives and the Senate in June 2007, and the Senate Finance Committee had held hearings in July of that year on the PE industry's offshore structures and tax avoidance

Representatives, which was considering changing the tax rate from 15 per cent, applicable to capital gains, to 35 per cent, appropriate for income treatment, was dropped by the Senate in late 2010. The buyout industry's lobbying efforts had paid off.

To support such a favourable tax regime, some of the sector's great figures had indicated that carry was some form of risk capital. It is evidently absurd to suggest so. Unlike entrepreneurs, buyout professionals do not contribute any initial funds to earn the right to collect a share of the gains generated from their trade. Instead, carry is a freebie allocated to them as a reward for delivering strong performance. Unquestionably the GP managers participate in the capital draw-downs alongside the limited partners, but again the source of the cash co-invested generally comes from the carry earned on previous funds. I would argue that it is because GPs have no skin in the game that they took inconsiderate risks between 2004 and 2008.

Thanks to the expanding funds under management and the availability of cheap debt in the last ten years, the level of carried interest earned by some individuals in the buyout industry has reached mind-boggling proportions. Cohen himself is reported to have made more than £250 million from his days at Apax,[440] which is somewhat deserved for one of the founders of venture capital in Europe in the 1970s and a key contributor responsible for turning Apax into one of the very few European mega-buyout firms. Based on conservative estimates, like their counterparts at other large funds, Buffin and Gumienny certainly amassed a small fortune in carried interest during their twenty-year tenure at Candover. Should the numbers earned through carry continue to swell, its tax status is bound to be revisited. If so, we will see whether GP managers put into execution their threat of moving to more hospitable tax havens like Switzerland. That is if Switzerland, and maybe even the US, do not hike the tax rate applicable to carry themselves. In the medium term, because of the credit squeeze and the frail economy, the value of carried interest in funds invested over the last five years will remain in negative territory. GP managers are safe for now.

But I am in Cohen's camp and consider that the industry watchdogs know full well that the current tax regime must continue to adapt in order to encourage the right behaviour from investors. Whereas venture capitalists and other providers of growth capital have demonstrated their value to the economy, in particular by backing the development of young entrepreneurial businesses, because of their excessive use of financial engineering the same cannot always be said about mega-buyout funds. If some within the sector are willing to acknowledge that changes are needed, few have come up with concrete suggestions. As always the solution is somewhere in the middle. While the VC and small LBO segments of the industry deserve to be preserved in order to finance the economic recovery sustainably and to foster job growth, it would be quite simple to structure a tax incentive encouraging the more sizeable GPs to hold investments longer (in the UK, capital gains realised on the sale of businesses held for at least two years already benefit from a lower tax rate) and to limit leverage, thereby forcing them to take time to create value rather than benefit from quick flips and refinancings. The best-established PE groups point out that their average holding period is five years, but this statistic is misleading. As the Candover story has shown, many companies stay in portfolio because their owners cannot get a good price for them early on. CPL's inability to IPO Gala Coral and Ferretti in 2008 or to sell Parques Reunidos in 2010 is proof that some of these assets would be sold earlier if the proposed valuations were generous enough. Governments could encourage longer holding periods and lower gearing by adapting the current CGT status accordingly; it would partly address the recurring concerns about the degree of contribution of the large and mega-LBO sectors to the economy. Short holding periods and over-indebted portfolio companies would suffer income tax treatment or a higher CGT rate. I am not a big fan of fiscal tinkering, but this solution is straight forward enough and would bring the buyout industry back to a more controlled behaviour.

This targeted tax treatment would also address a bigger issue. Through many debates I have had in the past with sector professionals, I have come to realise that many of them feel that it is only fair for people who make so much money for their companies, shareholders and society at large to be compensated suitably. As liberal theories go, individual wealth accumulation should be aligned to the level of economic value being produced. Like many theories applied in practice, the recent LBO frenzy establishes that this principle is deeply flawed. What we have seen over the last eight years is that there is a distinction to be made between healthy value creation and selfish profit-making. Looking at what Brooke and his counterparts at Charterhouse and ICFC had done in the 1980s, turning around businesses, improving cash flow management techniques and pursuing consolidation strategies not only benefit the buyout fund manager and its investors but also make the investee companies more competitive and ultimately create jobs. Everyone is a winner. In the 2000s however, some financial sponsors pledged to reap higher IRRs by raising more debt and accelerating portfolio realisations, including through recapitalisations that took cash flows away from the underlying businesses to the exclusive benefit of the lenders, GPs and LPs. Private equity no longer behaved in the interest of the common weal. Starving portfolio companies of valuable growth capital or diverting cash towards debt repayment to the detriment of their senior managers, employees, customers and suppliers culminated in many respectable names like Ferretti and Chrysler joining a catalogue of lifeless assets as soon as the economy took a dive. It is natural to expect governments and regulators to right this wrong.

The surge of the buyout industry has been one of the most momentous trends of the business world over the last thirty years. It revolutionised the way companies were run and financed. It transformed the economic landscape, progressively taking the place of large conglomerates like ITT Corporation and Hanson Trust as the key contributors of corporate development and restructuring. Lamentably, without proper supervision and guidelines, the sector's unstoppable ascent led to numerous excesses and mistakes. The fall of Candover, one of Europe's buyout pioneers, is not just an anecdote. It lays bare the vulnerability of an activity that has remained unbridled and under-regulated for too long.

Let's hope the appropriate lessons have been drawn from the recent market adjustment. Given how closely the property and buyout bubbles followed the technology crash of 2001, I trust that you will forgive me if I express my doubts. In my opinion, the next bubble is almost already in the making.

Chapter 15 - Back to the Future, Assuming There is One

Within months of the debt-fuelled buyout bubble caving in and the economic downturn taking hold, many senior figures of the PE industry were already on the road marketing their business, proclaiming somewhat like Grimstone that they had never been so well positioned to take advantage of the opportunities created by the Great Recession. Ignoring for now the impudence of such a statement made at a time when hundreds of thousands of workers were losing their job, from the outside it appeared wishful thinking. From within, it looks like a scene out of a Tim Burton movie. Not only is the buyout world in torment, but it will take many years for the most aggressive players to get themselves back into shape. And this time, no cheap financing or readily accessible capital will come to the rescue. By their recent haughty attitude, buyout executives did not win many friends. They have a wall to climb before they can contemplate rebuilding their LBO empires.

Which is why many of them have raised distressed debt funds since 2008 in an attempt to buy at a discount the loans that the banks had granted them to finance their now agonising overleveraged portfolio companies. Having lost all or a large portion of their money on the equity side of the transactions they closed in 2005, 2006 and 2007, some are aiming opportunistically to buy cut-price debt on the open market or invite themselves in debt syndicates. They could get themselves into a win-win situation: if the beleaguered company fails to redeem its credit lines, the debt-holders will take control of the defaulting entity and become the new owners, assuming they were not themselves the original equity providers in which case they would simply remain in control of the business. If the investee company can settle the debt, the distressed investor will have made a sizeable profit on the loans acquired at a discount. The most resourceful financial sponsors were thereby able to take advantage of the overpriced buyouts they or their peers had executed two or three years earlier by using a separate cash pile to buy the discounted loans that those same LBOs were unable to pay back. Is it legal? Sure. Is it moral? The limited partners who had backed the GPs' investment vehicles that funded the original buyout transactions might feel otherwise.

A WORLD OF ABUSE

The buyout boom of the mid 2000s was in many ways no different from the one that took place in the US in the late 1980s. It benefitted from an oversupply of debt that culminated in a phase of vast financial innovation. This time around, Europe would take part in the credit binge. The new products were not called junk bonds, but it did not prevent LBOs to be financed with three or four tranches of term loans together with a second lien, to which mezzanine instruments or high-yield bonds would typically be added, topped up by an acquisition facility, a capex line and a revolving facility for good measure. If some of the readers feel lost by the complexity of the whole system, they should not worry; many leveraged bankers and buyout specialists did not understand its implications either, but that did not stop them from stuffing many of their acquired companies with these exotic products in the go-go years of 2004 to 2007.

Whereas most were able to service, i.e. repay, their debt during the years of strong economic growth, things started getting trickier by late 2007. Many deals were being financed with debt packages that accounted for two-thirds or more of total transaction value and, as the Candover situation illustrated, soon portfolio companies began to breach covenants or to default on their interest or capital redemptions. As briefly described before, covenants are commitments that the acquired company enters into at the time the deal is closed. The company pledges that it will perform according to the management's financial projections and that it will meet a set of predetermined performance targets, such as a total-debt-to-EBITDA ratio for example, on a quarterly basis. If management fails to meet the forecasts specified in its business plan by more than a certain percentage called headroom, covenants are breached. If that was the case, the lenders would be able to renegotiate, for a fee, the terms of the debt. The repayment terms and duration could be rescheduled and in the most extreme cases the buyout firm would be forced to inject further equity.

At the very top of the market cycle, as PE professionals were getting even chirpier, they started committing thinner layers of equity and requesting lower headroom on the debt. Headroom on covenants had traditionally been set at 20 per cent to 25 per cent of the management forecasts. During the credit boom years, deals were being signed with 10 per cent or 15 per cent of breathing space, therefore giving less room for error for the management teams running investee businesses. In the early part of 2007, in a sign that buyout fund managers were taking the ascendant over their debt providers, many large transactions across Europe would be executed with hardly any covenant. Called covenant-light (or covenant-lite), these buyouts did not bother with extensive quarterly reports.[*] They did not concern themselves with a sensible debt level or a healthy capital base. As long as the debt was asset-based and benefitted from some form of security or creditworthiness, lenders and borrowers seemed content. It would raise many issues in the following years. The banks would not have any recourse when many of these overleveraged deals would underperform until the day when the companies would prove incapable of repaying a portion of the interest or capital becoming due. When buyouts with covenant-lite structures defaulted on their loan agreements, negotiations between lenders and borrowers proved very interesting. The Terra Firma-Citi saga on the EMI deal is one high-profile case that took place in public view throughout 2010, but many similar scenarios ensued behind closed doors and were sure to continue to occur in the years that lay ahead.

As an aside, it is interesting to note that until Citi took ownership of the business in February 2011, EMI was rumoured to represent a total equity exposure of over 30 per cent of Terra Firma's fund commitments[441] just like Gateway had accounted for a third of Wasserstein Perella's buyout fund back in the early 1990s.[442] One of my economics professors

---

[*] Covenant-lite deals Alliance Boots and EMI, both completed in the first half 2007, reportedly only had one maintenance covenant to be covered on a quarterly basis: the debt to EBITDA ratio

at university used to say that History does not repeat itself, it stutters. He added that, for that reason, it should be studied carefully to help foretell future events and avoid repeating mistakes made by previous generations. In many ways, over a twenty-year period the LBO sector seemed to have come full circle.

In essence, many senior buyout executives had taken the view that if their portfolio companies were to become unable to meet their debt obligations, leverage bankers, bondholders and other mezzanine fund managers would not want to take control of the defaulting companies, as credit documents allowed them to, but would rather leave the buyout magnates in command. Banks would acknowledge, the theory went, that financial sponsors were best positioned to restore debt-laden businesses. After all, monitoring investments was their job. In reality, the last three years have demonstrated that many of today's debt providers, often partnering with turnaround specialists or vulture funds, are more than happy to teach their PE counterparts a thing or two about portfolio management. You can be sure that once these companies currently under creditor-ownership have recouped some of their pep, the banks, mezzanine funds and other lenders will be delighted to sell them back to PE firms for a healthy profit.

Such a long and technical description of the leverage process is necessary to demonstrate how increasingly creative and reckless many GPs got when structuring their deal financing during the credit bubble. These supposedly expert cash managers had forgotten the most basic of rules applicable to debt policy. While it is considered essential for companies to leverage themselves up in order to lower their weighted average cost of capital - that is the combination of the high cost of equity and the traditionally much lower cost of debt - and therefore to refine their value-creation potential, the buyout community had failed to comprehend, or perhaps did not want to remember, that it was meant to be a game of optimisation, not maximisation. Beyond a certain gearing ratio, the debt quantum is so large that any small deviation from the management business plan can jeopardise the service of the loans, and force the company to default. As we have witnessed over the last three years, at a certain point the cost of financial distress is much greater than the value derived from any marginal increase in leverage. The LBO wizards knew that but felt that it was worth the risk. Determining how much a firm should borrow is not an exact science, but we can venture a guess that the PE financiers would have behaved differently if they were investing their own money. For that their LPs will pay dearly and for many years.

Towards the end of the buyout market expansion, as leverage got bolder more portfolio companies started breaching covenants and became unable to meet their debt requirements. LBO firms however had got into the habit of playing what has come to be known as the 'blame game'. Whenever the management team of a portfolio company would fail to meet the projections framed in the business plan, one or several members of that executive team would be replaced. Whether the underperformance of the company was within the management's control was often beside the point. Whether the problems were due to the heavy debt burden imposed by the PE backer was also irrelevant. Financial sponsors are not the most understanding of owners or the type of managers taking responsibility for the consequences of their actions.

At the peak of the bubble, they had even got into the habit of suggesting that they were not to be blamed for the ever higher transaction multiples they were paying. They explained that the trend was only a reflection of the increasingly more bountiful debt packages the banks were granting them, notably via stapled financing. The ultimately unsuccessful lawsuit filed by Terra Firma against its lending bank Citi in 2010 in relation to the EMI transaction is one version of this scenario, with the noteworthy particularity that during that process US bank Citi had acted as lender to acquirer Terra Firma but also as M&A adviser to the seller so that apparent conflict of interest in a way gave credence to the PE firm's suggestion that it might have been manipulated in upping its bid for the music publisher.* Whatever the circumstances of other inflated and over-indebted LBOs, we were expected to believe that debt providers were to be held accountable for the steeper valuations; buyout specialists, supposed to be virtuosos in evaluating businesses and monitoring cash flows, had been arm-twisted into bidding higher

---

* On 4 November 2010, after a three-month trial a New York jury reached a unanimous verdict finding that there was no evidence that Citi had fraudulently induced Terra Firma to overpay for EMI

multiples. We cannot deny that the banks' syndication and collateralisation of loans was not so much a way to diversify risk as the means of spreading it across the financial system like a virus. It is correct that bankers were falling over each other to lend the industry cheap debt, but one would expect professional investors to be able to use better judgement. In 2003, as the PE world was still in convalescence following the Internet and technology crash, leverage accounted for a third of LBO financing worldwide. In 2005, it represented half of transaction values and had reached on average two-thirds by mid-2007. In the last quarter of 2007, in a sign that we had entered the final stages of a bubble, debt had even produced over 75 per cent of LBO financing.[443] This gradual increase in gearing over time was very reminiscent of what the industry had endured during the second half of the 1980s.[444] Once again, investors in the buyout funds and the banks' shareholders would be the ultimate losing parties. Brutal competition between financial sponsors sitting on piles of uncalled commitments had pushed valuations to insane levels, forcing their lenders to resort to new tricks such as covenant-lite, warrantless mezzanine (meaning that unlike their 1980s' equivalents, the mezzanine lenders were not granted any share of the equity upside) or unsecured loans. Buyout firms will find it more of a challenge to pass the blame on someone else this time, though judging from the limited criticism they have sustained so far from regulators and governments, especially by comparison with what the banks have gone through, the LBO maestros might still get away with it.

SURVIVAL OF THE FITTEST

The junk bond madness and the subsequent credit crisis of the early 1990s had provoked few casualties among LBO firms. Similarly, the excesses of the dotcom era had mostly affected the VC segment. This time around, things promised to be different for the more mature buyout sector. In 2009, various pundits predicted that a significant proportion of PE outfits would fall victim to the financial turmoil and the Great Recession. They mentioned mortality rates of 20 per cent to 50 per cent, explaining that inordinate leverage would eventually force investee companies to collapse and buyout shops to close. Some even prophesised that such failures would happen within a couple of years. I agree that some will be incapable of ever raising a new vintage, but it would be surprising if the number of casualties ends up being as high as 50 per cent. In all evidence, the market correction will not happen as quickly as the experts had projected.

First, and in contrast to many of their public investment counterparts, PE funds have a fairly long-term horizon. Investing and administering their capital over ten to twelve years, they have sufficient time to work on their most demanding assets, to restructure them and inject further equity if need be. Since over two-thirds of all European buyout loans contracted during the 2003-07 period mature after 2012, representing close to €200 billion worth of debt,[445] the financial sponsors, distinctly at the more afflicted larger end, will be happy to play a waiting game. Some might want to pre-empt the process to smooth out the maturity schedule but not until their portfolio companies have benefitted from the moderately recovering economic climate. In the meantime, they still earn generous management fees so they can afford to be patient. In addition, while part of their funds were invested at the peak, during the go-go years of 2005, 2006 and 2007, a portion of the funds' commitments often remained undrawn in 2008 so GPs should be able in many cases to yield better returns from it.

Second, PE investment professionals tend to be independent, entrepreneurial individuals. They are unlikely to want to be acquired and start working as employees for their former adversaries. They will do almost anything to retain their autonomy. Presumably the failure of the negotiations between Candover and AIMCO was partly due to the fact that CPL's management was not thrilled by the prospect of losing its independence. The Arle solution was assuredly more palatable. What is likely to happen is that many LBO shops will scale down and remain smaller for some time, even focusing on the less extravagant, but no less competitive, mid-market segment. As for mergers between buyout shops, the Candover case can attest that they will not be made easy; since the financial meltdown of 2008, all buyout fund managers hold distressed assets and might not be keen to add rotten apples to their collection of lemons.

Third, institutions need to invest in alternative products like hedge funds and PE in order to maintain a diversified portfolio. LPs will always need to allocate part of their assets to the buyout segment, if only because in spite of the industry's disastrous performance since 2008, the best performing PE fund managers have shown returns well above those of other types of investment products over a twenty-year period. Selecting those top performers will be a valuable and well-guarded trade secret.

As many able and qualified PE executives see that their current firm is likely to take years to muddle through the post-bubble market and to sort out their overstretched portfolio (implying that carried interest might never materialise), some of them will quit and set up their own buyout shop rather than wait for their existing employer to hit the wall. Some buyout firms will fail to realise lucrative portfolio exits. Others will be unfit to raise a subsequent fund and will be forced to close shop like US firm Forstmann Little had done after the dotcom crash of 2000-02 as a consequence of ill-fated investments in the technology space. Many firms live on borrowed time (no pun intended) and will fall victims to the credit crunch, but because of the incentive to maintain a firm alive in order to keep racking in generous commissions, unlike some industry commentators I will not venture a guess regarding the magnitude and the timing of their demise. All I will say is that should the worst of these predictions prove correct, it would significantly increase the risk profile of the sector as LPs would have fewer options to choose from to diversify their portfolio.

HIGH RISKS, LOW RETURNS

Observers point out that the industry's best returns were achieved during the 1994-95 and 2001-02 vintages. These funds were invested during periods of recovery and followed a market slump. They offered significant upside to investors willing to back the development of businesses during the growth cycle. If we trust their judgement, 2010 and 2011 should be excellent vintages. But this time things might not be so straightforward. The mid-1990s and early 2000s benefited from depressed valuations as investors deserted stock markets and strategic bidders muddled through the recession or were under heavy indebtedness contracted to fund their expensive acquisitions during the technology bull run. But throughout the recent credit boom, corporate buyers were generally outbid by financial sponsors and are therefore today in better shape than many LBOs and their PE backers. Industry data suggest that about €1.5 trillion of capital was sitting on the balance sheet of European companies at the end of 2010.[446] In addition, because of the sorry state of their existing portfolio a large number of buyout groups are eager to redeem themselves by being active during the economic upturn. Despite the banks adopting a more prudent approach to lending, all these factors will contribute to maintaining artificially high company valuations. The magnitude of capital the financial sponsors are sitting on will also make sure that they remain so.

It is indeed somewhat ironic that as the bubble of the buyout market blew up, several reports revealed that the industry had never been so rich. In late 2009, total undrawn commitments supposedly amounted to a startling $1 trillion worldwide across all segments of the PE spectrum, including early stage, mid-market, large buyouts, turnarounds and infrastructure funds. The LBO segment alone represented half of that amount. Approximately a quarter of the capital was believed to be allocated to the European market. Sitting on so much dry powder, as it is called in PE jargon, it was evident that fund managers would take many years to find enough opportunities to invest it. Since typical GPs have a five-year limit to spend undrawn commitments, it was likely that part of this hoard was to be returned to LPs since putting it to work would have implied an average $200 billion of equity being invested globally every year. Approximately $180 billion, $70 billion and $200 billion worth of transactions (including debt and equity) had been completed in 2008, 2009 and 2010,[447] but even if we assumed that equity accounted for half that total deal value, the tally would fall way short of the yearly $200 billion mark. The problem for investors will be to decide how to reallocate these funds into areas where demand exists and expected returns are as high.

Thanks to unprecedented commitments to the industry in 2007 and 2008, when over $600 billion of capital were pledged in each of these two years worldwide, we can safely predict that returns in these vintages will be lacklustre, singularly for the 25 per cent of those allocated to structurally-low-growth Europe. Applying the same old law of supply and demand, so much uncalled capital will lead to higher valuations. Already suffering from depressed 2005 and 2006 funds - negatively impacted by botched investment execution - and therefore from extended holding periods for their existing portfolio, general partners are also expected to record years of underperformance from their 2007 and 2008 vintages due to the high multiples they continued to be paying. This implies that some LPs might decide momentarily to reduce their exposure to a segment of the investment market that shows a higher risk profile than originally estimated and has reached a stage, at least in Western Europe and North America, that leaves little room for the kind of superior returns to which they had been accustomed.

To make matters worse, as is typical when a cycle approaches its peak, the sector had attracted many outsiders from 2002 onwards. Lured by the smell of easy money and the promise of generous commissions, hedge funds such as Och Ziff and Cerberus completed buyout transactions by recruiting LBO professionals, infrastructure funds like Macquarie and Dubai International ventured out of their traditional fields, LPs such as Singapore-based GIC started to invest their funds directly in order to avoid having to pay transaction and management fees to GPs, and wealthy entrepreneurs set up their own investment vehicles with now-defunct Iceland-based Baugur being one of the most enterprising investors in the European retail sector during the early 2000s. Many of these had depressing results, but some are sure to hang on and more will join the industry once the market turns.

Not only is the PE market in Europe more mature and competitive – which explains why average entry EBIT multiples were still at 16x in 2010, more or less the same level as in 2006 – but lending institutions have also scaled back and are no longer willing to provide cheap, un-hedged and infinite financing. Debt-to-equity ratios were 35 to 65 on average in 2010 compared to the reverse 65/35 in 2005. The dilemma for GPs is that too much debt, as we saw in the recent financial meltdown, can kill a deal; not enough debt, however, kills returns. The trade secret is to strike the right balance, assuming the market circumstances will let you. For the time being, with lower amounts of more expensive debt and high enterprise valuations, PE executives are kidding themselves when they portend that the Great Recession will offer dazzling returns. In fact, recent surveys have shown that IRRs in Europe are lower than in North America, a market that encountered even more extreme behaviours than in Europe. Anecdotal evidence, such as KKR's disclosure that its European Fund II and European Fund III were the only investment vehicles in its stable not yet in a position to distribute carry in 2010,[448] also proves that European buyout funds will take more time to restructure their portfolio. A combination of lower structural growth and stricter labour laws might explain why turning around ailing assets will be a tall order.

Rather than return the dry powder mentioned before, financial sponsors have started to use some of it to compensate for the lower debt packages and increase the equity portion in recent transactions. They will also reallocate a portion to bail out their existing stressed investments - like Candover did to keep DX Group and Hilding Anders afloat - unless they are able to raise separate annex funds to carry out that duty as some have done. In any case, that will influence returns but will ensure that GPs continue to collect management, monitoring and other directors' fees. To put it another way, GPs will sacrifice future carry for today's commissions. In such an uncertain market, with many current funds under water and on a net present value basis, it makes a lot of sense for them, less so for their investors.

The nature of certain transactions in recent years also bodes ill for future performance. I have already underlined the proliferation of sponsor-to-sponsor transactions in the last ten years. In 2000, they were estimated to account for 10 per cent of total buyouts by value across Europe, but by 2005 that proportion was 25 per cent. More concerning is the fact that, according to various sources, in 2010 they accounted for about 40 per cent of European buyout values. As indicated earlier, Candover was a key benefactor of that trend. Ignoring companies like Ferretti, Gala Coral and ALcontrol that defaulted on their debt obligations and ended up being repossessed by their creditors, in 2009 and 2010 every single portfolio exit realised by CPL was a secondary buyout. Wood Mackenzie was acquired by Charterhouse, Springer was sold to EQT, Ontex to TPG, Equity Trust to Doughty Hanson, with 3i's carve-out of Stork's Materials Technology division bringing up the rear in late 2010. While 15 per cent of exits from the Candover 1994 Fund had been secondary buyouts, the proportion had been 27 per cent for the following 1997 Fund and so far 54 per cent of realisations for the 2001 vintage with three companies still in ownership at the end of 2010. It is easy to understand why, in an environment where banks are reluctant to let go of their cash, secondaries would gain in market share: lenders already know these assets and can take a more informed view of the lending risk. In essence, a secondary transaction is the equivalent of a simple refinancing, with higher banking fees and margins!

Also, for a PE house looking for a quick and easy exit, a sale to one of its competitors is less cumbersome than a listing. In a secondary process, the seller remains in control as it organises the beauty parade and prospective buyers express their interest. When seeking to float a business the financial sponsor needs to spend time on the road to market the opportunity and convince equity analysts that it is selling a quality asset; not an easy task given the buyout industry's recent track record. A secondary sale is almost certain to go through due to the competitive nature of the process. Listings are often pulled because of unstable market conditions, lack of appetite or a lame valuation. Nowadays, the reluctance emanating from institutional and individual investors comes from the fact that they have been burnt in the past as several major floats of PE-backed companies underperformed post-IPO, in part because the listing was used as a way to deleverage the business and for the equity providers to cash out, not to inject more money to fund future development. All this helps explain why, in the UK, IPOs represented less than 10 per cent of buyout exits throughout the 2000s whereas they were chosen as an exit option by approximately 20 per cent of sponsors back in 1993 and 1994. And once again Candover is a good illustration of that change. An estimated 50 per cent of its 1989 Fund investments were exited via listings. Only 13 per cent of its 1997 Fund and, as of 31 December 2010, 15 per cent of the 2001 Fund's portfolio had followed the same route.[449]

Another factor driving sponsor-to-sponsor deals is the finite life of a PE investment vehicle. As already mentioned, a typical vintage, say the Candover 2001 Fund, has up to five years to invest the funds committed by its limited partners, and usually another five to return the money to those same LPs. It is therefore no coincidence that CPL exited its Ontex, Springer and Equity Trust positions in 2010; they were all investments of its 2001 Fund. And French technology group Qioptiq was also bound to come to market very soon,[450] with a somewhat diminished bargaining power as opportunistic buyers would know that it is approaching its sell-by date. Besides, based on the 2010 CIP annual report, it looked like the 2001 Fund was fully or almost completely drawn down, implying that Qioptiq and Innovia Films (the other remaining majority investment of that vintage) would not be able to receive much financial support from CPL in case of emergency. Luckily for Candover across the table will sit buyout firms equally desperate to put their money to work. Not that the current deals offer compelling returns, but if the GPs fail to make the capital calls during the investment period of five years, LPs are entitled to rescind their remaining commitment. We should not forget that management fees, after the investment period, are usually only levied on drawn-down commitments; that helps explain why GPs are actively pursuing secondary LBOs even though it is well documented that they offer lower returns than primaries.

Additionally, like Candover several PE houses have started acquiring companies that they used to own, implying that they are running out of ideas to escape highly contested auctions or simply that their ability to develop angles through their business networks has run its course. CPL's acquisitions of Expro International in July 1992 and in July 2008 might seem innocent enough: Candover would rightly have argued that the company was much larger than it had been sixteen years earlier. Nonetheless, given that this is far from being a one-off for the industry, such a trend suggests that the top end of the market has reached a degree of competition that is unhealthy for future investment performance. It became such a common occurrence that the practice raised issues among LPs. Whether it is Cinven's November 2005 quaternary buyout of French distributor of plastic pipes Frans Bonhomme, a business it had sold to Apax in September 2003, or Nordic Capital's repurchasing of medical diagnostics company Nycomed in 2005, three years after selling it to Blackstone, or even KKR's March 2011 take-private of pet and food producer Del Monte, a former division of RJR Nabisco at the time of KKR's LBO in late 1988, the deal list is sadly too long to include in these pages, but it predicts difficult times ahead.

People will argue that it is natural for investment managers to target companies that they already know and therefore understand. While this is partly true, there are counter-arguments.

First, the danger is that the fund manager will almost certainly overestimate its ability to run a business it has owned in the past, and risks overvaluing it. Candover's prior knowledge of DX Services when it was part of Hays did not help the business during the recession despite merging it with another company and thereby supposedly strengthening its competitive position. DX was at risk of defaulting on its debt obligations before being recapitalised in April 2010. And Expro too was refinanced in December 2009, less than eighteen months after its MBO. The reason for that was made clear when the company published its annual accounts: in the year ending 31 March 2010, the oil services group's EBITDA was down 16 per cent on prior year.[451] Because they knew the management teams, the company's products and strategy, and the market dynamics, Candover and other buyout specialists felt that it justified outbidding their rivals. Even quality assets have an intrinsic value, though, no matter how well you know them. Based on that evidence, having previously owned a company does not seem to guarantee a strong portfolio performance.

Second, if the market offered many more appealing buyout opportunities, Candover might not have bothered going through the lengthy PTP procedure for Expro. Maybe the fact that the asset management arm of Standard Life held the largest stake in the publicly listed company had reassured CPL that it had every chance of winning the support of institutional investors, especially because insurer Legal & General, one of Candover's long-time investment partners, was also a key shareholder.[452] Nevertheless, delistings are notoriously arduous and expensive since they frequently require offering a substantial premium over the stock price – therefore implying either that public investors are dumb for undervaluing the company or that the PE house has a particular angle such as a game-changing acquisition or merger. Large PTPs in the 2000s also had a different flavour to the smaller ones carried out in the 1990s: they were not driven by a liquidity problem. A take-private usually makes sense if a listed company is so small that its shares stop being liquid, i.e. traded in sufficient volumes, and raising capital is therefore close to impossible for its managers. Delistings were also justifiable in difficult economic times when the public company was underperforming and the pressure of quarterly reporting did not always give management a chance to reverse its fortune. But a PTP of a large company when the economy and the stock market are bullish will often be expensive (if the company is healthy and dominant in its market, as Expro was) or extremely risky (because the company is 'undervalued' for a structural or operational reason, as in the case of conglomerate Stork). And we should not forget that take-privates are not sure to succeed. A financial sponsor might convince institutions looking for liquidity to sell at a premium, but there is no guarantee that the minority shareholders will accept being squeezed out (meaning that they would be forced to sell their stake), a precondition for a company to be removed from a stock exchange. Many failed PTPs turn into private investments in public equity, or PIPE, therefore combining the worst of both worlds: the acquired company must continue to report quarterly to its public shareholders without offering any privacy or the ability to enforce broad operational changes and pay out dividends to its PE owners.

Reading between the lines, you do not need to be initiated to the black arts of private equity to understand that the industry will labour to invest and make attractive returns from a $1 trillion cash pile. It starts being a Herculean task when you consider that new funds obviously continued to be raised every year since the buyout crash. Realising that the floor had caved in, the industry added less than $300 billion to the pot in each of 2009 and 2010,[453] but investment prospects remained gloomy.

During the thirteen years of economic growth between 1994 and 2007, many European corporations took advantage of the generous valuations proposed by buyout firms to exit non-core assets. In all fairness, most of these sizeable spin-off transactions had already taken place by the early 2000s, hence the rise in toxic deal recycling through secondary buyouts, take-privates and acquisitions of previously-owned companies referred to above. Improvements in operational efficiency at many medium-sized businesses have already occurred; that will reduce the number of transactions or at the very least limit the upside potential traditionally derived from process streamlining and cost-cutting. In any case, the SME segment would not solve the equity overhang as it would take an eternity to invest $1 trillion in $100-million individual equity tickets. In 1931 the MacMillan Committee Report had identified a chronic shortage of long-term investment capital for small and medium-sized enterprises in the UK. As we have seen, it led immediately after the

Second World War to the creation of the ICFC and the FCI, both early versions of what had eventually morphed into 3i. Today even the latter supervises a multi-billion-euro asset base. It seems that the 'MacMillan gap' has been filled many times over.

In the 1980s and 1990s, the US, the UK and to some extent parts of the European continent observed a boom in buyouts of divisions of large conglomerates or of companies in trouble during recessions. One of the key forms of exits then was via a listing on a main stock market like the LSE or on a second-tier exchange like the USM in the UK. In the later part of the 1990s and most of the last ten years, as buyout firms built their capabilities and raised giant funds, many ran out of targets to go after and started acquiring larger companies. Many of them were naturally listed on a stock market and had formerly been under PE ownership. The challenge for these big American and European funds will be to find appropriate targets without getting into the issues raised about repeat sponsor-to-sponsor deals and never ending scenarios of listing-delisting *à la* Lambert Fenchurch or delisting-relisting in Acertec-style or any other permutation one fancies. The fact that the number of buyout transactions in the UK was only 10 per cent higher in 2005 than in 1990 demonstrates that growth in that market has mostly come from higher valuations. Of course, continental Europe went through significant development over the last ten years and still has room for growth, but it is also likely to come from the mid-market segment. Very large funds are confronted to a conundrum: how to invest in a market that has too much money chasing too few deals. For now, most of these firms have addressed their predicament by executing mid-market transactions. However, because of the point made earlier regarding the time it would take to invest a multi-billion-euro fund through small equity tickets, they know that it can only be a temporary solution. Like the US funds had done immediately after the late 1980s trough, many European fund managers will have to scale down their next vintages.

With the PE industry reaching maturity, the low-hanging fruit of inadequately priced privatisations and spin-offs of undermanaged corporate divisions have disappeared. Add to this the *fait accompli* that target companies today enjoy external advisory support as well as significantly enhanced corporate governance and operational practices – leaving less room for buyout professionals to produce structural improvements once they have acquired a company and reducing the number of buy-ins of unprofessionally run family businesses - and it is easy to conclude that, in Europe and North America, returns over the next few years will be a shadow of what they were in the 1980s.

A FUTURE OF UNCERTAINTY

There is one number that only a handful of market analysts have reported and it is certainly the elephant in the room that few know what to do about. Between 2001 and 2007, $2.5 trillion to $3 trillion worth of LBOs were executed globally. As of mid-2011, there remained about $1 trillion worth of portfolio companies to be realised in the following five to six years. We can already guess that a large proportion of them will be passed on to that dry powder we mentioned before; I am referring to sponsor-to-sponsor transactions similar to the recent Candover realisations. A significant amount will expectedly end up in their creditors' custody due to repayment defaults, following the example of EMI, Ferretti, ALcontrol & co. Then, there is the possibility that some trade buyers, often representing 40 per cent or more of portfolio realisations, will come to the rescue. But trade buyers have traditionally been more prudent in their valuations immediately after a crash or an economic recession. Warren Buffett's public acknowledgement in 2010 that he would rather stay clear of PE-backed assets could well be a view shared by most strategic bidders.[454] Financial buyers have been so generous on the way in that it is unlikely that they will obtain a similar EBITDA multiple on the way out. That would imply that they will have to see a significant upswing in the operating performance of their holdings or that they will make a loss on part of their portfolio. Some publicly quoted investors like Candover, 3i, KKR and SVG have already reflected this fact in their books, but how many of the privately-held partnerships have been so diligent, no one knows.

To avoid having to record a loss, the GPs might have their sight set on the public stock markets as these progressively regain their composure. Buyout houses might be looking for a greater fool, but we do not know yet what the appetite of public investors for companies valued above 10 times EBITDA will be. Just consider what would have happened to the share price if the 2008 floats of Gala Coral and Ferretti had gone ahead. We might just be about to witness the biggest wave of PE-backed flotations in history as LBO groups and their advisers attempt to hog all the major stock markets. If so, based on the track record of many buyouts post-IPO, I will give you my two cents on the matter: stay well clear. There might be more Midland Independent Newspapers, MFI and Acertec coming to a stock exchange near you very soon.

Over the coming years, the key uncertainty for the industry can be summed up in two words: interest rates. As central banks in the US and the UK have kept their base rate at close to zero and provided a lifeline to many considerably geared LBOs for the last three years, it is only a matter of time before tightening policies get introduced. Since buyout transactions are predominantly financed with debt that is priced at a fixed premium to the variable inter-banking rate, any increase will have two seriously negative impacts on PE activities:

- For large buyout firms in particular, it will reduce the attractiveness of refinancings and consequently alter the IRRs achieved on individual portfolio companies. In recent years, one of the key trends observed by the industry was the systematic recapitalisation of leveraged companies to take advantage of ever lower funding costs. Even though lenders would often charge a 2 per cent to 3 per cent arrangement fee on the refinancing transaction, the improved deal negotiated on interest rates (both on the base rate and the margin charged by the lender) would lower total interest repayments so much that it was worth paying the banks their commission. Candover, like so many, took advantage of these transactions to recover its initial investment early. Again, although from the outside it would appear that CPL took over six years to get back its equity investment in German scientific publisher Springer (since it bought it in 2003 and sold it in December 2009), in reality it had refinanced it several times in that period: in its 2006 annual report, CIP had stressed that Springer had just completed its third refinancing and had already returned cash equivalent of 1.6 times the original investment. During the boom years, recaps were one of the key tools available to buyout funds to realise early partial exits and, somewhat artificially, or at least without having to work too vigorously, beef up their IRR on individual portfolio companies. Since quick flips had such a negative image, GPs had found another way to increase their returns. They are an innovative bunch! Unfortunately, as many banks tightened lending conditions in the days following the Lehman bankruptcy and as central banks' base rates are eventually expected to go up, we can be sure that refinancings, except those forced by the creditors because of covenant breaches or payment defaults, will not be as frequent as they used to be;

- For many portfolio companies, the interest rate hike is likely to coincide with the time in their debt maturity when a large proportion of their capital redemptions also falls due: across Europe, over 75 per cent of debt capital repayments related to the LBOs closed at the peak of the bubble are due post 2012. The combination of higher interest payouts and those upcoming capital reimbursements will force many portfolio companies and their financial sponsors to enter into heated negotiations with their lenders. And in some cases these companies benefit from a covenant-lite structure so there is no trigger to bring PE owners to the table other than the fact that not doing so might well provoke reputational damage beyond repair. We can speculate that this debt overhang sitting in the LBO firms' portfolios is the main reason behind the banks current reluctance to finance further buyouts or at the very least to offer terms that could properly be described as commercial. Regrettably, the rest of the economy and particularly SMEs also suffer from this funding drought. Defaults have built up dramatically since 2007, but the number of investee companies in receivership could rise substantially when interest rates are pushed up.

Interest rate increases will have another, more perverse effect on the buyout industry. Investors' expectations in performance follow changes in the cost of money. When interest rates rise, so should investors' returns. Let's say that an individual gets a 1 per cent interest rate on his savings held in an instant-access account at his local bank when the central bank's base rate is at 0.5 per cent, as it was in 2010 and

2011 in Britain. If the Bank of England raises its rate, the individual will expect to benefit from this hike by seeing the interest he earns on his account go up. This will also hold true for longer term investors like the LPs of a buyout fund. Because their money is tied much longer and is exposed to a much greater risk as the last three years have shown, LPs expect to derive a substantial return. Thus, as central banks' rates go up, LPs will also anticipate an improved IRR. Delivering on such wishes will not be an easy task. Between the mid-1990s and the mid-2000s, GPs had been able to get away with decreasing returns – average net IRRs for large buyouts went from over 30 per cent in the mid-1990s to 20 per cent or less a decade later - because governments and central banks across the world had followed a concerted low-interest-rate policy and tamed inflation accordingly. It is that same low cost of debt coupled with a strong appetite for credit from the PE industry that had encouraged banks to develop innovative products.

Thanks to the above explanations, we can now understand how the large buyout fund managers like Candover were able to generate substantial equity returns during the first half of the noughties. The equation goes as follows:

Lower cost of debt, thanks to low central bank base rates and thin lending bank margins

+

Higher debt amounts, thanks to the 'generosity' of lending banks, bringing down the weighted average cost of capital

+

Earnings multiple expansion between time of investment and time of exit, due to the growing economy and the bullish stock markets

=

Make-you-look-like-a-star equity returns

We now know that the debt amounts have come down whereas loan margins have come up and that multiple expansion has collapsed in line with the economy and the public equity markets - as witnessed by the EV multiple contraction on the Springer deal - and should remain so until the European economies have sorted out their credit problems. The inevitable upcoming interest rate hikes should make the next decade very entertaining for PE investment performance.

Because of the mature state the industry is in today, with more intense competition and lower demand for capital for the time being, even with a more dynamic economy, delivering higher returns as interest rates go up will be a challenge for buyout groups. In the UK, the industry already went through a period of high interest rates and pressure on margins in the early 1990s. Sadly, based on that previous episode, what this implies is that inflation will likely make up for the difference, helping a low-growth PE market earn higher returns in the process. Or, as some critics predicted, the overcrowded buyout industry will start shrinking, taking away some of the competitive pressure and lowering the price of assets.

The truth is, due to the economic rut, the vast sovereign debt overhang, the competitive landscape, the volume of secondary transactions and highly priced take-privates, and the congenital weakness of the euro, the buyout industry in Europe will suffer for many years. This situation explains why most senior executives in the major global PE firms go on and on about the prospects of Asian and other developing markets. Other 'flavours of the month' include the renewable energy sector, life sciences and healthcare products and services. Remember that, back in the 1990s, the PE industry had partly come out of the 1991-92 recession thanks to the emergence of the Internet craze that eventually turned into the technology and new media bubble. As a large portion of the $1 trillion treasure-trove is allocated to emerging markets and clean technology, we should already get ready for the next capital commitment overdose.

The future is not completely bleak, though, for Europe's PE sector. In a slow-pace environment, the public companies' profits are unlikely to increase dramatically, therefore reducing the appeal of stock markets as an alternative to private equity. Institutional investors will continue to look at PE as a way to diversify their portfolio. They might just be more discerning in their selection as there are simply too many underperformers in the industry. Many firms, including well established trailblazers like Candover, were believed for many years to be successful investors, 'top-quartile' performers as the expression goes. Unless they do their homework, future LPs might end up being disappointed.

With so much macroeconomic uncertainty, investment returns will remain permanently lower for the foreseeable future. If we believe the pundits' projections, surviving the next five years will be a triumph in itself. Looking further ahead, can we imagine a world where some European buyout partnerships would get dissolved, their diverse portfolios sold off to a new breed of investors in a way reminiscent to the taking-apart of the industrial conglomerates in the 1990s? As strategic and financial institutional investors, including sovereign funds - many from the Middle East and Asia - start flexing their muscles, we should not take anything for granted. These institutions had entrusted their money to American and European large and mega-buyout funds. When they see what these so-called financial experts have done with it, they might decide to do the investing part themselves next time. The credit crunch might have heralded the end of the buyout industry as we know it.

Afterword

In the 1970s, venture capital was synonymous with funding emerging sectors of the economy or young promising enterprises. The industry had a reputation for risk-taking and its returns were unpredictable, but its contribution to the economy was rarely questioned. Firms like 3i, Electra and Apax in Europe and Advent in America had built their expertise on early-stage financing, investing only equity and progressively replacing government initiatives and corporate venture. It was strenuous work, and not very rewarding since the economy was in the doldrums at the time. M&A activity was the private hunting ground of the large conglomerates. The rise of the leveraged buyout changed all that.

In the US and the UK, and later across Europe, market-oriented policies, and the deregulation and globalisation of financial markets, helped the buyout industry raise constantly larger funds and close ever bigger deals, fuelled by cheaper debt, flourishing stock markets, and positive economic conditions. By the middle of the 2000s, owing to the technology slump, VC funding had shrunk significantly to the benefit of buyout financing. In the UK, pension funds were believed to contribute 85 per cent of their PE-related money to buyouts and this shift was still amplifying before the LBO crash of 2008. The risk-return relationship of buyouts had become economically too enticing for investors to ignore. Every man and his dog wanted on the action. The captains of industry had been supplanted by the barons of finance; big money had replaced big business. Without noticing it, Europe's buyout industry had just gone through 15 years of unimaginable growth fed by an explosion in credit. Nowadays, the word 'conglomerate' is almost unknown to the new breed of investment professionals. Who knows whether the term 'mega-buyout fund' will not ultimately suffer the same fate? These entities are today more akin to financial engineers extracting maximum short-term value from their portfolio companies than to traditional MBO backers or initiators trying to significantly enhance the target's long-term operational and strategic potential.

For individuals not familiar with the world of private equity and high finance, it would be easy to conclude from this book that the behaviour of some financial sponsors during the 2004-08 period was heedless, if not outright unprofessional. Their jumbo deals executed through aggressive bidding and in a speedy, sometimes hostile manner, reminiscent of the style adopted by corporate raiders like Sir James Goldsmith and Carl Icahn in the 1980s, were headline-grabbing stuff, so that is all we read in the papers. We are all familiar with property deals signed in just two hours instead of the customary 3-to-5-day timetable. At the top of the market, desperate people often make snap decisions. They rarely prove judicious. Still, it is one thing to act that way when you are investing your own money and another when you are administering other people's hard-earned savings. We expect our local bank to handle our cash accounts with care and diligence. Similarly we trust that professional investors watching over part of our retirement savings take all the necessary precautions. One would be right to expect a more disciplined, informed and mature decision-making process from supposedly financially savvy individuals, even if they are bidding for assets against ten or twenty other interested parties, as was regularly the case back in 2006. By then, unfortunately, due diligence was frequently being replaced by undue negligence.

Keep in mind, however, that many of the most daredevil deal execution practices that took place during the bull market were restricted to the larger end of the industry, for transactions with an EV in excess of €500 million. The small and mid-market segments, representing between two-thirds and three-quarters of the number of transactions, were largely unaffected by that craze. Not that some of their GPs were not tempted by high multiples of cheap exotic debt. But the banks, despite all the bad press they have been subjected to post-Lehman, were unwilling to lend money with the same generous, or rather aggressive terms. They considered rightly that medium-sized businesses represent a greater risk of default in case of a downturn.

I would therefore contend that the small and mid-market buyout groups have a real chance to thrive. And to be brutally honest, if it wants to get back on track the world economy needs them to do well. With small stock markets like AIM showing once more, like they had after the collapse of the Internet and technology sectors in 2000, that they represent unreliable liquidity pools, and with the banking system stuck in first gear for years to come, until it has nursed its real estate and buyout hangover, European SMEs are only left with PE investors to fund their growth. Knowing that in the mid-2000s, across Europe only 3 per cent of the active population was believed to work in a PE-backed company,[455] compared to 8 per cent in the UK,[456] we can expect further gain in capital deployment once the economic upturn has kicked in.

If this book gave a lot more importance to the UK market than to the rest of Europe, or even the world, it is not just because Candover originally started operating there and was culturally a very British institution. The emphasis on the UK buyout landscape also reflects the fact that the country was a key contributor to Europe's buyout frenzy. London is the Continent's undisputed capital of private equity, investment banking and credit markets. As the Candover case proves, even if it is hard to quantify, the vast majority of European LBOs, be they of UK companies or from other European countries, were frequently sourced, executed or led from the London districts of Canary Wharf, the City and Mayfair.

In addition, buyouts of British businesses accounted for a much bigger share of the nation's GDP and corporate activity than in any other country in the world, including the US. Although industry commentators had often argued that it was normal for the more elaborate and ripened UK market to regularly account for 30 per cent to 40 per cent of total European LBO transactions, when we benchmark the British and American markets against one another, something looks decidedly peculiar. According to data published by the World Economic Forum,[457] between 2001 and 2007 the UK accounted for almost 29 per cent of the world's LBO transaction volumes and over 15 per cent of deal values. Over the same period, the share of the equally advanced and time-honoured American market was 35 per cent and 43 per cent respectively. A country with an economy 6 times smaller than that of the US, and a population a fifth that of its American cousin, was generating 80 per cent as many LBOs and a third of its transaction value. The British marketplace was not so much mature as saturated.

Europe had been spared the junk bond madness of the late 1980s, mostly because it was still emerging and too small a market for its transactions to warrant such complex instruments. Some buyouts in the UK retail sector had suffered from high interest rates and aggressive gearing between 1989 and 1992, but with the exception of the Gateway embarrassing episode, the Continent had never experienced the supersized LBO phenomenon so prevalent in America. This time around, Europe reached a level of development that justified using all the innovative products and short-cut mechanisms developed in the US, exposing the Old Continent's PE industry to systemic risks embodied by its thirst for excess leverage. Second-lien debt and covenant-lite facilities were 'imported' in 2004 and 2007 respectively as tools to help buyout firms pile on more debt in their portfolio companies, in a last foolhardy attempt to maximise returns. They are bound to play a marginal role in the immediate future. Luckily for this global industry, the Middle Eastern and Asian regions were still too small to get affected by the latest financial innovation fury. We can be sure that when the industry goes through another one of its extravagances, say fifteen years from now, these emerging markets will have grown in stature and will be ready to take some abuse. The real concern is that the sector might have become so large and omnipotent at that stage that its credit glut, not that of the property market, might be the one tipping the world economy into financial chaos.

At a time when the global financial system is still wrestling with an enormous debt overhang, such a scenario might seem unlikely, until you consider that a sector that accounted for 3 per cent of M&A activity in 1997, 12 per cent in 2002 and 24 per cent four years later now regularly represents half or more of corporate deals across Europe. In what has now become a tradition, the buyout specialists are also the first back into the ring after an economic crisis. In the first nine months of 2010, in a context that remained uncertain and strenuous, PE accounted for three-quarters of all mergers and acquisitions in the UK.[458] In 1992, when Britain was in the middle of a recession, that share was also over 50 per cent. Above all, it demonstrates that the industry has become a major force of the economy. Whereas PE represents only 2 to 3 per cent of most UK and European limited partners' fund allocation, many North American institutional investors, like CPL investors Canada Pension Plan and CalPERS,[459] hold close to 15 per cent of their assets under management in that space. As European pension funds are forecast to move away from state-management and into private ownership, the PE market is very likely to benefit. The recent arrival in the sector of government-backed investment vehicles, sovereign funds and hedge funds will only increase the influence of private equity in the world economy. The industry as we know it is unlikely to survive beyond the next decade, but whatever replaces it will carry more weight on the global stage than ever before. Whether it is a force for good will depend on the quality of the resolutions that governments and legislators will have taken to redress its current failings. In any case, an industry handling trillions of dollars in debt and equity cannot realistically continue to operate below the radar. There seems little logic in reinforcing the regulatory and supervisory framework for debt lending, as American and European authorities have done over the last three years, while keeping equity funding self-regulated and open to excess through misleading performance reporting and dubious investment management techniques. As no doubt regulators know, a job half-done is not worth doing at all.

As Brooke looked on while the Candover Group was fighting for survival, he must have wondered how the matter could have gone so much out of control and how a business he had cautiously built up could be taken apart so easily. Back in September 1980, as he was announcing the creation of the business, he had been asked by a *Financial Times* journalist to explain the choice of the company's name. Brooke had commented, in reference to the Candover Valley: 'The house I bought there is probably my best investment. I hope this is a good omen'.[460] It had taken thirty years for him to find out.

When going through my research and during my conversations with various contacts, I frequently thought about Candover's early days and Roger Brooke's contribution. I never had a chance to meet the man during my tenure at the firm, but after months of investigation I have come to admire an individual who was not satisfied with living just one life like most of us do. On 2 February 2011, as he was celebrating his 80th birthday, Brooke surely reflected fondly on his international experience in the Foreign Office, his highly influential career in the corporate world, his entrepreneurial ventures at Candover and several other VC-type organisations, all complemented by an abundance of charitable work to express his desire to make a difference, which had landed him an O.B.E.[*] in 2005 for services to medical research and to the Hampshire community. It is an imposing CV, but his true legacy had been to provide Candover with a symbiotic leadership structure thanks to the combination of Curran's and Fairservice's wise expertise and the energetic personalities of Buffin and Gumienny. Back in 1999, the firm was left with a clear leader, a focused strategy and a unified organisation. Ten years later, much of that was lost.

In an article published by *Bloomberg Markets* in November 2010,[461] in a rare moment of public outburst the key figures behind the group's past success vented their frustration and let out at the leadership team responsible for the firm's undoing. From Curran's peeved view on the sudden change in strategy − 'If you expand too much too quickly, you can lose control' − to Fairservice's opinion of his and Curran's style of management − 'We were hands-on managers of the companies we owned but also, more importantly, of Candover itself. Some of the later guys at Candover were not' - it was clear what they thought the problems were. For the firm's founder, who had demonstrated such moderation over the previous two years despite the fact that watching his business going down the drain must have been more painful than undergoing root-canal surgery without anaesthetic, it was time to ponder glumly: 'It's not a particularly happy situation for me where, having started the business, it's going apart'. Days before Candover's official break-up, no matter where responsibilities lay, Brooke was already in mourning. No doubt he reminisced about a time when the company still enjoyed a reputable brand, an unrivalled network, and a disciplined and sensible investment approach. By imperceptibly moving to the larger end of the market and to geographies further afield, the firm had lost the benefit of its strong competitive positioning. Unequivocally, the underlying portfolio had suffered from that upheaval. Judging from his remark to those same

---

[*] Officer of the Order of the British Empire. Honour granted to individuals as a recognition for their service to Britain or to their community

264

Bloomberg journalists, it is a sentiment shared by Grimstone: 'The real issue of this firm has been poor investment performance'.[462]

The choice of the Candover name eventually turned out to be of evil portent for the investment firm, but the collapse of the latter - a FTSE 250 company at the height of its fame in 2008 - will have implications for the rest of the profession. Undoubtedly, many factors behind the Candover Group's disintegration, such as its shaky corporate governance, badly timed fundraising and deficient international strategy execution, are specific to the firm. But beside such self-inflicted wounds, excessive transaction leverage, ineffective pre-deal due diligence and loose (the exact PE terminology is 'hands-off') portfolio supervision methods, are industry-wide issues that put into question the mode of operation of the large and mega-buyout fund managers. Because in mature markets like the US and the UK, the vast majority of transactions will continue to be secondary buyouts or take-privates of companies, it is expected that GPs will no longer be allowed to charge commissions two to three times higher than those of traditional asset managers. The golden days of shameless individual wealth accumulation in private equity might well be behind us. The dynamic and innovative, but uncontrolled and ill-managed, ways of the last ten years will need to be replaced by a more structured organisational model with strict operating and reporting systems. This is bound to produce lower but hopefully more predictable returns. PE investors in Europe had better be setting their expectations lower than ever before, and in all likelihood permanently. As always, the investment industry's warning disclosure applies: past performance is no indication of future returns.

While I have drawn many parallels between the industry's problems in the late eighties and those of 2007-10, it would be dangerous to underestimate how much more serious the recent LBO crash was. Earlier, I likened the junk bond era of 1986-89 to the awkward phase of puberty, but the credit crunch represents a much more problematic mid-life crisis for the sector. In view of their preliminary results to date, the LBO vintages of the mid- and late 2000s are unlikely to deliver the type of performance that their LPs had come to expect. When the scaled down buyout groups come to market with a new fund, their executives are likely to blame the disgraceful display of the last ten years on their departed colleagues. Harsh and somewhat unfair but so is life in the City. It is a shame that the entire industry's reputation has suffered from the misdeeds of a small minority, albeit a very visible and powerful one, but it is now up to those executives operating at the lower end of the sector to demonstrate that they are still strong, positive contributors to the economy.

At a time when governments around the world take tough measures to cut down their national borrowing and the size of the public sector, it is PE investors focused on providing financial backing to the small and mid-market segments of the economy that will no doubt plug the hole and boost GDP growth for the next ten years. The real challenge for those fund managers and their truncated investment teams emerging from the crisis is to win back the confidence of their investors so that, one day perhaps, they will again enjoy the aura of prestige that their predecessors had earned under the visionary leadership and prudent guidance of fatherly figures like Stoddart, Cohen, Brooke and Curran. Before they can aspire to such honour however, they will need to demonstrate their commitment to their LPs by defusing the sector's ticking time bomb: the wall of outstanding portfolio debt maturing over the next five years. Maybe then will they be allowed to jump back on the buyout bandwagon and raise a new vintage, demonstrating by the same token that they have learned their lesson.

APPENDICES

Appendix A: Glossary

AIM
Britain's Alternative Investment Market. Created in June 1995 to replace the USM. For the benefit of smaller businesses, AIM offers easier listing requirements than the main market of the LSE

Break fee
Also formulated as termination fee. Inducement fee paid by the seller to the buyer if a rival offer is accepted by the target in lieu of the original proposal made by the buyer. Can also be payable if the buyer's offer is rejected by the seller's shareholders. A reverse break fee implies that the buyer must pay the seller if the former fails to deliver a bid on pre-agreed terms

Buyout
Also known as leveraged buyout (LBO) or management buyout (MBO). In short, the acquisition of a company financed by bank debt (hence the term leveraged) and equity. The equity portion is invested by the GP while the debt is provided by banks and other lending institutions

Carry
Also called carried interest. Represents the GP's share of capital gains achieved on a given fund. Typically, in the buyout industry, the GP's share is 20 per cent of total capital gains earned over the hurdle rate

CIP
Candover Investments plc, the listed trust set up for tax reasons in 1984. One of CPL's key fund providers (LPs)

Club deal
Transaction carried out by a syndicate of buyout firms

CPL
Candover Partners Limited. The fund manager or GP of the Candover Group. A wholly owned subsidiary of CIP

EBIT
Earnings before interest and tax. Like EBITDA, it is used as a proxy for the company's operating cash flow generation

EBITA
Earnings before interest, tax and goodwill amortisation

EBITDA
Earnings before interest, tax, depreciation and amortisation. An accounting proxy for the cash generated by a company

EV
Enterprise value, also known as transaction value, including the equity portion and the debt quantum used to finance the acquisition

Fund closing
Procedure by which a new fund's commitments are confirmed and can no longer be withdrawn (except under specific and exceptional conditions) by Limited Partners. Initially, commitments from LPs are only indicative; they become firm and cannot therefore be withdrawn once closing has occurred

GP
General Partner, or fund manager. Also called financial sponsor, it is the investment fund's management company, i.e., the entity that invests the equity into leveraged buyouts and that manages the funds committed by the LPs

High-yield bond
A rebranding of the 1980s' infamous 'junk bond'. This debt instrument is subordinated to loans with a higher-priority repayment schedule. Also, it is unsecured, meaning that it exclusively relies on the borrower's creditworthiness. This gives it a higher risk of default, hence its higher interest rate than the ones earned by term loans

Hurdle rate
Minimum rate of return guaranteed by a GP to an LP before the GP can earn its carry. The hurdle rate is usually set at 8 per cent

IPO
Initial Public Offering, also called introduction, listing, float or flotation. Introductory placement of a company's shares on a public stock exchange

IRR
Internal Rate of Return. The key indicator of a GP's investment performance. It is reported gross or net of the GP's management fees and carried interest

Leverage
Borrowing, in layman's terms. Also known as financial gearing

LP
Limited Partner. The term commonly used to describe the provider of funds to the GP, i.e., the GP's investor. LPs include in particular pension funds, universities' endowment funds, insurers, bankers, funds of funds and sovereign funds

LSE
London Stock Exchange, Britain's main stock market

MAC clause
Material Adverse Change clause. A legal provision included in sale and purchase agreements that enables the acquirer to withdraw its offer in the event of an unforeseen material adverse change in business or economic conditions. Legal challenges can occur as to what constitute a 'material' change

Mezzanine loan
A type of high-interest debt instrument used in the financing of buyouts as a top-up to the senior debt. Because rights held by the mezzanine lenders over the assets of the acquired company are subordinated to those attributed to the term loan holders, mezzanine is said to be part of the junior debt

NAV
Net Asset Value. An increase in NAV is a measure of the value being created for investors. It is an accounting value assessed on a quarterly or half-year basis

PE
Private equity. This term often refers to both the buyout and venture capital segments although in this book it more frequently only applies to buyouts

PTP
Public-to-Private, also called take-private or delisting. The buyout of a publicly listed company and its subsequent removal from the stock exchange

Quartile
Represents 25 per cent of a vintage in performance benchmarking surveys. A top-quartile fund is therefore in the top 25 per cent of performers among all buyout funds raised in the same year

Refinancing
Also called recapitalisation. Process of changing the capital structure of a company. Transaction carried out by buyout firms to negotiate better terms with the banks than the ones originally obtained when financing the acquisition. In short, refinancing is paying off existing debt with new debt just like a house can sometimes be remortgaged. Post-credit crunch, because of chronic undercapitalisation of portfolio companies, this procedure was often imposed by the lenders to take control of defaulting/distressed assets or to force financial sponsors to re-inject equity in the business

Second lien debt
A form of term loan that is subordinated to other term loans with a higher priority of repayment. Second lien debt usually has a maturity and an interest rate falling between those of conventional term loans and mezzanine debt

Secondary buyout
Also known as a sponsor-to-sponsor transaction. A management buyout executed by a financial sponsor of a company already under PE ownership. In principle, when a company is acquired by a private equity firm for a third time, we speak of a tertiary buyout, for a fourth time, of a quaternary buyout. In short, a secondary is a buyout transaction where both the buyer and the seller are PE firms

Stapled financing
Pre-arranged and often pre-negotiated debt finance available to the winning bidder of an auction. It enables a faster execution and completion of a transaction

Term loan
Bank loan with a specific repayment schedule. Its interest is set at a fixed rate above the interbank rate (e.g., LIBOR, Euribor). Often referred to as senior debt because it is

secured on the company's assets and has a higher priority repayment schedule than that of unsecured loans

USM
Unlisted Securities Market. Second-tier stock exchange created in 1980 to address the need for liquidity of small and medium-sized enterprises in the UK

VDD
Vendor due diligence. Also called sell-side due diligence. Due diligence is the evaluation process typically carried out by a potential buyer to assess the risk profile of an investment. A VDD report is instead commissioned by the seller

Vintage
The year when a new fund has its first closing and can start being invested. The performance of a specific buyout fund is benchmarked against all other funds in its vintage year

Walker report
Guidelines for Disclosure and Transparency in Private Equity recommended by Sir David Walker and introduced in the UK in 2007

Appendix B: Key Dates of Candover's History

1980
September: Brooke sets up Candover Investments Limited with funding from Electra Investment Trust, Globe Investment Trust, Finance Corporation for Industry, Prudential, British Rail Pension Fund, BP Pension Fund and four investment trusts from Murray Johnstone in the form of £2 million low-coupon loan capital and £100,000 of equity
December: the company closes its first buyout alongside ICFC

1981
May: Curran joins the firm from the National Coal Board Pension Fund where he was a project finance manager
Candover closes 5 MBOs, including Ansaphone, one of the largest buyouts in the UK that year

1984
Candover raises its first fund, the Hoare Candover Exempt Trust, totalling £7.5 million of commitments
December: The company floats on the LSE under the name Candover Investments plc. It has a market capitalisation of £11.45 million

1985
The Electra Candover Direct Investment Plan is set up with £260 million of capital commitments

1987
The firm's third investment vehicle, the Candover 1987 Fund, receives £30 million of commitments to invest in small buyouts

1989
Candover Partners Limited raises £319 million, including £20 million from CIP, for the 1989 Fund

1991
January: Curran becomes Candover's CEO, replacing Brooke who becomes Chairman

1992
September: The firm raises £37.5 million for its fifth fund, the Candover 1991 Fund

1995
February: The Candover 1994 Fund raises £307.5 million, including £70 million from CIP, after 21 months of fundraising

1997
March: CPL controversially sells its stake in train-leasing company Eversholt at a huge profit one year only after buying it from the British government
September: the Candover 1997 Fund is launched with a £650 million target

December: CPL closes its 1997 Fund with £850 million in commitments, including a £100 million ticket from CIP

1998
The group employs 28 people

1999
May: Curran steps down as CEO and replaces Brooke as Executive Chairman. Fairservice steps down as Deputy CEO to become Deputy Chairman. Buffin and Gumienny take on day-to-day operating leadership
That year, CPL completes nine buyouts worth a combined £1.5 billion

2000
The firm has 30 employees

2001
March: the Candover 2001 Fund is launched with a €2.5 billion-to-€3 billion target size
October: CPL opens an office in Paris

2002
July: The firm closes its 2001 Fund with total commitments of €2.7 billion
CPL employs 43 people

2003
March: CPL closes its first secondary buyout by paying £1.2 billion for casino operator Gala (actually in a tertiary buyout)
July: CPL opens an office in Düsseldorf
The firm completes 6 transactions worth a total of €6.6 billion

2004
May: investee company First Leisure goes into administration in the fourth largest UK bankruptcy of a PE-backed business
Candover employs 54 staff including 22 investment executives

2005
May: Faiservice retires as Deputy Chairman and serves a 12-month term as director on CIP's board
November: The 2005 Fund has a final closing at €3.5 billion

2006
May: Curran retires and Grimstone, a non-executive director of CIP since 1999, becomes CIP's non-executive Chairman. Arney, Gray, Green and Leefe named Managing Directors
September: The firm opens an office in Milan
The number of employees reaches 71 including 37 investment professionals
Headquarters renovated
CPL closes €4.3 billion worth of deals

2007
Managing Director Cyrille Chevrillon takes his distance from CPL's operating leadership and becomes Vice Chairman

July: The Madrid office opens
October: CIP raises two 7-year loan notes, one of $200 million, the other one of €30 million to help prepare for the 2008 Fund
December: with the €800 million tertiary buyout of Alma Consulting, CPL completes its sixth secondary buyout in 19 months
That year, three buyouts worth a combined €2.1 billion are completed

2008

January: CIP issues a third 7-year loan note of £30 million
February: CPL launches its tenth fund, Candover 2008 Fund, setting a target of €5 billion
March: Candover opens a Hong Kong office. The same month, Candover, Cinven and Permira inject £125 million of equity into Gala Coral to keep ownership of the company
July: The firm takes Expro private for a total EV of *c.* £2 billion
August: CPL announces that it has received €2.8 billion for the first closing of its 2008 Fund. Candover Eastern Europe Partners is fully operational. The same month, the Candover Group opens a Mumbai office
December: Managing Director Charlie Green quits
The firm employs 100 people including 52 investment executives

2009

February: Following its annual audit, CIP admits that it cannot fulfil its €1 billion commitment to the Candover 2008 Fund. CPL gives out that it is reducing its target size for the 2008 Fund to €3 billion
March: Candover enters into negotiations with possible acquirers
April: CPL loses control of portfolio company Ferretti
June: Talks with potential buyers end. The same month, in a management reshuffle, Arney becomes Managing Director of CPL, Gumienny moves to the Chairman position while Buffin transitions out. Over the summer, the group closes its German, Italian and Asian offices and fires investment professionals, including the newly recruited Asian and eastern European teams
September: after an interim period, troubleshooter Malcolm Fallen is brought in as full-time CEO of CIP
October: CPL loses control of 'zombie' portfolio company ALcontrol. The same month, the firm puts SEK 400 million of additional equity into Hilding Anders to retain a 50.1 per cent stake in the company
December: portfolio company Expro is refinanced while debt-laden Springer is disposed of
After a major headcount reduction CPL employs 42 people including 19 in the investment team

2010

January: CPL terminates its 2008 Fund as the majority of its limited partners have decided to withdraw their support
April: Canadian asset manager AIMCO enters into discussions to acquire the Candover Group. The same month, CPL injects £15 million of equity into DX Group to keep 51 per cent of the company
May: Candover and its co-investors Cinven and Permira lose control of Gala Coral to the benefit of the mezzanine lenders
July: Talks with AIMCO fall through. CIP reveals that the company enters wind-down mode

October: CPL injects €20 million into EurotaxGlass's to keep ownership and reset debt covenants. Equity Trust is sold off for €350 million to Doughty Hanson
December: CIP announces that CPL is being sold together with a 29.1 per cent share of CIP's underlying investments to Arle, a new entity led by the remaining CPL management team, and fund of funds Pantheon for a total consideration of £60 million. Grimstone announces his upcoming retirement in 2011 after the completion of the group's break-up
35 full-time employees including 12 investment executives remain in the firm

Appendix C: Main Features of Candover Funds

Table 1 – Commitments and Draw-downs

Vintage	Size (million)	Change on previous fund	CIP Commitments (million)	% of CIP's NAV[1]	CIP's Share of fund	Drawn down from fund (million)	Percentage drawn down
1989	£319		£20	47%	6.3%	£255-£270°	80%-85%°
1991	£37.5		£5	9%	13.3%	£26	69.3%
1994	£307.5	-3%	£70	83%	22.8%	£176.4	57.4%
1997	£850	+176%	£100	63%	11.7%	£686 or £750*	80.7%/ 88.2%
2001	€2,700	+110%¬	€300	75%	11.1%	>€2,600^	>96%^
2005	€3,500	+31%	€500	91%	14.3%	€3,245^	92.8%^
2008	€ 406^	-89%^	€100^	N/A	24.6%^	€306^	75.4%^

[1] Net asset value at the closest interim or annual reporting
° Estimate based on press reports and CIP Chairman's statement on 3 May 1994
¬ Depends on the £/€ exchange rate used
* CIP Reports and accounts 2005 and 2006 disagree on what amount has been drawn down
^ Estimated as of 31 December 2010, based on CIP's press release 8 January 2010 and CIP 2008 Report and accounts

Table 2 – Investments Made

Vintage	Number of deals completed	UK deals	Non-UK deals	Club deals	PTPs	Secondary buyouts°
1989	14	14	N/A	11	Nil	Nil
1991	Fund used for co-investments. Incomplete data					
1994	13	12	1	7	1	Nil
1997	15	11	4	7	2	Nil
2001	16	6^	10^	6	1	4
2005	11	3	8	3	3	6
2008	1	1	0	1	1	0

^ Several transactions had a truly international nature. Deals like Aspen, Innovia Films and Wellstream were treated as UK because originated and run from there but they had global operations
° Includes tertiary transactions

Table 3 – Realised Exits

Vintage	Total Number of Exits (as of 31.12.10)	Number of Trade Sales	Number of IPOs	Number of Secondary buyouts	Number of receiverships or loss of ownership
1989	14	7	7	Nil	Nil
1991	Fund used for co-investments. Incomplete data				
1994	13	7	2	2	2
1997	15	6	2	4	3
2001	13	2	2	7	2
2005	2	0	0	1	1
2008	0	0	0	0	0

Appendix D: Troubled Portfolio Companies in the Candover 2001, 2005 and 2008 Funds

Portfolio Company (CPL Fund)	EV / EBITDA	Debt Multiple¬	Date of Acquisition	Refinancing(s)	Outcome (as of 31 December 2010)
Ontex (2001)	8.0x	5.0x$^\Omega$	January 2003	€50m equity injection in early 2007	Sold at a 30 per cent loss in July 2010
Gala Coral (2001)	>10.0x°	>6.5x°	March 2003 (Gala) and October 2005 (Coral Eurobet)	Permira, Cinven and CPL injected £125 million in April 2008	Gone to lenders at a 40 per cent loss in May 2010
ALcontrol (2001)	>11.0x#	>7.0x#	December 2004	Recapitalisation in July 2007	CPL lost control when lenders took over in October 2009
EurotaxGlass's (2005)	10.7x	7.9x&	May 2006	CPL injected €20 million in October 2010	Still in portfolio
DX Group (2005)	>9.0x∞	>6.0x∞	August 2006	CPL injected £15 million in April 2010	Still in portfolio but CPL ownership dropped to 51 per cent
Ferretti (2005)	12.7x*	7.8x*	October 2006		CPL lost the business when lenders took control in January 2009
Hilding Anders (2005)	11.5x^	7.5x^	October 2006	CPL injected SEK 400 million in October 2009	Still in portfolio but CPL's ownership reduced from 81 per cent to 50.1 per cent
Expro (2005 & 2008)	>11.0x	>6.0x	July 2008	High-yield bond issued in December 2009 to repay term loan	Still in portfolio

¬ Total debt at time of acquisition over the historical, last-twelve-month (LTM) or prospective EBITDA. Total debt includes senior debt, second lien, mezzanine and high-yield bonds but excludes revolving credit facilities, acquisition facilities and capex facilities

Ω Based on senior debt of €500 million and mezzanine of €165 million (Financial Times, 16 November 2004) and EBITDA of €133 million (De Tijd, 7 July 2007)

° Based on EBITDA of £394.5 million as of 30 September 2006 (CIP 2006 Report and accounts)

Based on EBITA data released in CIP 2006 and 2007 Reports and accounts

& Financial Times, 20 June 2006; Euroweek, 23 June 2006

∞ Estimated blended EBITDA multiple of DX Services and Secure Mail Services based on data for fiscal year 2007 reported in DX Group Limited 2008 Annual Report. DX Services was taken private in August 2006 at an enterprise value multiple of 12.6x pre-exceptional EBITDA for the twelve-month period ended 31 December 2005 (Candover press release, 6 July 2006)

* Based on the last-twelve-month EBITDA at time of acquisition. Multiple paid on EBITDA of financial year ended 31 August 2006 was 14.35

^ Based on EV of SEK 9.2 billion and EBITDA of SEK 852.7 million as of 31 December 2006 as disclosed in CIP 2007 Report and accounts

Appendix E: Ranking of the Top 10 Europe-dedicated Funds by Candover Vintage

	UK and European Funds				European Funds					
	1994		1997		2001¬		2005¬		2008¬	
		£m		£bn		€bn		€bn		€bn
1	3i (1994)[a]	N/A	CVC II (1998)^	2.1	CVC III (2001)	4.65	CVC 2005 + 2007[1]	10.1	Apax VII (2007)	11.2
2	CINVen ±	N/A	Doughty Hanson III (1997-98) *	1.65	Apax (2001)	4.4	BC Partners VIII (2005)	5.5	Permira IV[3] (2006)	11.1
3	Doughty Hanson II (1995) *	410	Cinven II (1998)±	1.5	Cinven III (2002)	4.4	Permira III (2003)	5.1	CVC VI (2008)	10.8
4	Baring PE (1994)	350	Candover	0.85	BC Partners VII (2001)	4.3	KKR Europe II (2005)	4.5	Advent (2008)[2]	6.6
5	Candover	308	Charterhouse VI (1997)	0.8	Permira II (2000)	3.5	Cinven III (2002)	4.4	Cinven IV (2006)	6.5
6	Charterhouse V (1994)	300	Carlyle Europe (1998)	0.7	Candover	2.7	Apax (2005)	4.3	KKR Europe III (2008)	6.0
7	Morgan Grenfell (1994)	300	BC Partners VI (1997)°	0.67	Charterhouse VII (2002-03)	2.7	Charterhouse VIII (2006)	4.0	BC Partners VIII (2005)	5.5
8	Advent (1994)[2]	280	NatWest PE Bridgepoint I (1998)	0.65	Bridgepoint II (2002)	2.0	Candover	3.5	Carlyle III (2006)	5.4
9	NatWest Ventures	250	Schroders /Permira I (1997)	0.6	3i Eurofund III (1999)	2.0	3i Eurofund IV (2004)	3.1	PAI V[4]	5.4
10	EQT I (1995)[Ω]	240	Advent (1997)[2]	0.6	EQT III (2001)	2.0	PAI IV (2005)	2.7	Terra Firma III (2007)	5.4

¬ List only indicative and non-exhaustive. Excludes global funds such as those of Apollo, TPG, Blackstone, Warburg Pincus and Bain Capital

± Until 1994, CINVen acted as an adviser to pension funds rather than as an investor in its own right. The newly branded Cinven raised its first fund in 1996 with total commitments of €1.5 billion but the firm was investing funds on call from its LPs before that. The Cinven II raised in 1998 managed €2.2 billion

Ω EQT I raised SEK 3.2 billion

ᵃ 3i managed third-party money so its total firepower was much larger than its peers'. Its Eurofund II of ECU 650 million, raised in 1997, fails to include third-party money

° BC Partners VI raised $1.1 billion in 1997

* Doughty Hanson's 1995 Fund raised DM 1 billion and its 1998 Fund had raised $2.7 billion

^ CVC 1998 Fund had €3.03 billion under management

[1] CVC raised a €6 billion fund in 2005 plus a €4.1 billion tandem fund in 2007

[2] Advent Global Private Equity II (1994), III (1997) and VI (2008) target America and Europe

[3] Permira IV scaled back to €9.6 billion in 2009

[4] PAI eventually halved its fund during an internal reorganisation in 2009

About the Author

Sebastien Canderle was born in the outskirts of Paris. Educated in France and the United States, he has over twenty years of work experience in London and New York, twelve of them in the private equity industry. He is a fellow of the Institute of Chartered Accountants in England and Wales and holds an MBA from the Wharton School. Sebastien lives in London.

Index

N

O

P

T

Y

Notes

Chapter 1 – The Harsh Reality

[1] International Monetary Fund

[2] Office for National Statistics

Chapter 2 – Humble Beginnings, Ambitious Goals

[3] Electra Investment Trust, Annual Report, year ended 31 March 1981, Chairman's statement

[4] Financial Times, 30 October 1981

[5] The Times, 19 December 1980

[6] Financial Times, 18 February 1981

[7] Financial Times, 17 July 1981

[8] Financial Times, 29 May 1981

[9] From July 1982 onward (source CIP 1999 Report and accounts)

[10] Financial Times, 30 October 1981

[11] The Times, 18 February 1982

[12] Financial Times, 1 December 1984

[13] The Times, 22 August 1981

[14] The Sunday Times, 19 June 1983

[15] The Times, 16 September 1983

[16] Financial Times, 22 June 1982

[17] The Times, 18 February 1982

[18] Financial Times, 24 July 1984

[19] Financial Times, 27 March 1984; CIP 1999 Report and accounts

[20] The Times, 10 February 1984

[21] Financial Times, 10 May 1984 & 8 December 1984

[22] The Times, 22 November 1985; Wall Street Journal, 22 November 1985

[23] The Sunday Times, 23 February 1986; Financial Times, 8 December 1986

[24] The Times, 18 February 1982; Financial Times, 3 December 1985

Chapter 3 – A Small Club of Like-minded People

[25] Financial Times, 6 July 1987 – source: Venture Economics

[26] Financial Director, 2 August 1988

[27] Financial Times, 1 July 1986

[28] Financial Times, 18 January 1986 & 12 March 1986

[29] Financial Times, 25 June 1987

[30] The Times, 2 January 1987

[31] Financial Times, 27 January 1987

[32] Financial Times, 25 March 1987

[33] Financial Times, 6 July 1987, 25 September 1987 & 14 October 1987

[34] Financial Times, 1 May 1987

[35] Daily Mail, 14 March 1990

[36] The Times, 21 October 1987

[37] The Times, 12 October 1998

[38] Based on the CIP 2002 Report and accounts, the original £30 million investment only returned a total of £37 million

[39] Financial Director, 2 August 1988

[40] Financial Times, 6 September 1990

[41] Financial Times, 12 March 1986; CIP press release - 1989 annual results, 13 March 1990

[42] Financial Times 15 October 1988 & 14 March 1989; The Independent 22 July 1989

[43] International Monetary Fund

[44] Office for National Statistics

[45] Organization for Economic Co-operation and Development

[46] The Guardian, 8 January 1995; The Independent, 10 May 1995

[47] Financial Times, 14 March 1989

[48] Financial Times, 6 June 1989

[49] Financial Times, 13 October 1988

[50] Financial Times, 8 July 1988

[51] Office for National Statistics

[52] The Times, 6 February 1989

Chapter 4 – A Period of Transition

[53] CIP press release, 13 March 1990

[54] The Guardian, 2 January 1991

[55] Financial Times, 19 March 1991

[56] Financial Times, 9 December 1989, 5 July 1990 & 3 January 1991

[57] The Independent, 17 March 1992

[58] The Times, 17 February 1990; Financial Times, 26 November 1990

[59] Financial Times, 9 September 1989

[60] CIP press release, 29 December 1992

[61] The Independent, 14 January 1994

[62] The Times, 23 November 1989, 21 January 1990 & 24 December 1992

[63] The Times, 16 July 1992

[64] CIP press release - annual results for the year ended 31 December 1993, 7 March 1994

[65] Financial Times, 9 September 1992

[66] CIP press release, 15 April 1994

[67] The Times, 24 September 1995

[68] The Times, 4 March 1994, 7 September 1994 & 19 September 1996

[69] The Observer, 10 February 1991; Financial Times, 12 June 1992

[70] CIP 1994 and 1995 annual results press releases, 13 March 1995 and 6 March 1996

[71] The Independent, 6 March 1994

[72] Financial Times, 20 July 1990 & 6 June 1996

[73] The Observer, 17 June 1990; CIP 1990 annual results announcement, 27 March 1991; Evening Standard, 11 November 1991; The Observer, 14 June 1992

[74] The Times, 13 October 1994; The Independent, 13 October 1994

[75] The Times, 5 May 1992

[76] The Times, 19 January 1995

[77] CIP press release, 13 September 1993

[78] Financial Times, 12 May 1993

[79] Financial Times, 14 March 1995

[80] The Guardian, 20 November 1994

[81] CIP press release, 28 February 1997; UK Venture Capital Journal, 1 April 1997

[82] Financial Times, 5 December 1996

[83] The Independent, 4 January 1997

[84] The Independent, 2 February 1995

[85] Financial Times, 12 September 1995

[86] Financial Times, 7 March 1996

[87] The Independent, 3 July 1996

[88] Financial Times, 11 January 1997

[89] The Guardian, 7 August 1996

[90] The Independent & The Times, 20 February 1997

[91] Financial Times, 11 March 1997

[92] Financial Times, 18 September 1980

Chapter 5 – Shifting Gear

[93] Candover press release, 17 December 1997

[94] Financial Times, 26 September 1997

[95] CIP 2000 Report and accounts

[96] CIP Preliminary results for the year ended 31 December 1997, 9 March 1998

[97] Financial Times, 3 July 1998

[98] The Times, 18 December 1997

[99] The Times, 8 September 1998

[100] CIP 1999 Report and accounts

[101] The Guardian, 28 February 1998

[102] CIP 1999 Report and accounts

[103] Financial Times, 23 October 1997

[104] *ibid*

[105] 3i Group plc Annual Report and accounts for the year ended 31 March 1998

[106] The Guardian, 31 October 1998

[107] Based on a £360 million EV and a £31.5 million EBIT for the year ended 31 December 1998 as per CIP 1999 Report and accounts

[108] Financial Times, 28 February 1998

[109] The Guardian, 28 February 1998

[110] CIP - Statement by Roger Brooke at the Annual General Meeting, 11 May 1999

[111] CIP 1999 Report and accounts, Ten-year record

[112] The Independent, 4 June 1999

[113] Financial Times, 5 June 1999

[114] CIP 1999 Report and accounts

[115] CIP Preliminary Results for the year ended 31 December 1998, press release 8 March 1999

[116] In its 2002 report on The Economic Impact of Private Equity in the UK, the BVCA stated that 35 per cent of IPOs on the Official List of the LSE between July 1992 and December 2001 were PE-backed

[117] CIP 1999 Report and accounts

Chapter 6 – Into the Big League

[118] CIP 1999 and 2002 Reports and accounts

[119] CIP 1999 Report and accounts

[120] The fund was 60 per cent invested at the 1999 year-end (CIP 1999 Report and accounts) and had already called on £48.6 million of equity to buy nightclub operator First Leisure in the first half of 2000

[121] The Times, 9 November 1998

[122] The Times, 28 September 2000

[123] CIP 2004 Report and accounts

[124] Curran would reveal that the 1994 Fund had only invested 3 per cent of its assets on the Continent. Financial Times, 9 September 1997

[125] Candover press release, 19 June 2001

[126] CIP press release for annual results for the year ended 31 December 1990, 27 March 1991

[127] Financial Times, 10 March 1993

[128] Dumrath & Fassnacht, 11 August 1998

[129] Financial Times, 11 December 1986; CIP press release, 1992 annual results, 9 March 1993

[130] The Times, 6 January 2001

[131] Evening Standard, 20 February 2001

[132] Data on receiverships from the Centre for Management Buy-Out Research

[133] Financial Times, 31 August 2001

[134] Financial Times, 1 July 1997

[135] Candover press release, 10 September 2001

[136] The Daily Telegraph, 9 February 2002

[137] Financial Times, 13 March 2001

[138] Financial Times, 7 July 2003

[139] CIP 2002 Report and accounts

[140] Financial News, 2 August 2003

[141] CIP 1999 Report and accounts

[142] Candover press release, 13 May 2002

[143] The Times, 14 May 2003

[144] Financial Times Deutschland, 11 October 2004

[145] Financial Times, 19 April 2002

[146] Financial Times, 29 July 2002

[147] Centre for Management Buy-Out Research

[148] The Times, 30 December 2003

Chapter 7 – Identity Crisis

[149] The Independent, 21 April 1990

[150] BVCA, UK venture backed flotations (London Stock Exchange) New issues; Financial Times, 17 January 1995; Keller Group PLC - year ended 31 December 1994 - Final Results, 31 March 1995

[151] The Independent, 2 June 2003; Financial Times, 16 November 2004 & 2 April 2007

[152] Candover press release, 26 February 2003

[153] Sunday Business, 11 August 2002

[154] Based on EBITDA of €133 million and EV of €1.1 billion as disclosed in De Tijd, 7 July 2007

[155] Based on total leverage of €665 million - Financial Times, 16 November 2004

[156] De Tijd, 7 July 2007

[157] The Times, 29 December 2003

[158] Based on 2003 EBITA of £105.3 million as disclosed in CIP 2004 Report and accounts

[159] The 1997 Fund was 85 per cent drawn down after the Picard deal, as disclosed in CIP

2000 Report and accounts

[160] Financial Times, 15 November 2004

[161] CIP 2002 Report and accounts

[162] CIP Preliminary results for the year ended 31 December 1999, press release 13 March 2000

[163] Based on 1980s press articles and on data from the Centre for Management Buy-Out Research, report on Management Buy-outs 1986-2006, Past Achievements, Future Challenges, June 2006

[164] CIP 2004 Report and accounts

[165] Financial Times, 25 October 2004

[166] CIP 2005 Report and accounts

[167] The Herald, 29 April 2005

[168] Gala Group Limited – Report and Accounts for the year ended 25 September 2004

[169] Gala Group Limited – Report and Accounts for the year ended 24 September 2005

[170] The Guardian, 20 August 2005

[171] Sunday Business, 25 September 2005

[172] Based on EBITA disclosed in (Coral Eurobet) CE Acquisition 1 Limited – Report and Financial Statements, 25 September 2005

[173] European Venture Capital Journal, February 2006

[174] According to CMBOR data released in a Sunday Times article dated 6 March 2005, only the MEPC/Leconport (in 2000) and Spirit Amber/S&N Retail (in 2003) MBOs were larger

[175] Evening Standard, 4 December 1998

[176] Financial Times, 3 August 2002

[177] Private Equity News, Annual Review 2005, 30 January 2006

[178] Candover press release, 10 November 2005

[179] European Venture Capital Journal, February 2006

[180] The CIP 2001 Report and accounts state that they were among the beneficiaries of the 2001 Fund Employee Benefit Trust and the CIP 2002 Report and accounts confirms that they had beneficial interests in the 2001 Fund's carried interest arrangements

[181] Candover press release on internal promotions, 2 May 2006

Chapter 8 – Bubble Trouble

[182] Private Equity News had published its 2005 Annual Review on 30 January 2006 with the title "Over inflated"

[183] Centre for Management Buy-Out Research

[184] Bloomberg Markets, 21 November 2010

[185] Lloyd's List, 16 November 2006, refers to two weeks but the Chairman of Ferretti had confirmed approaches by PE firms at a press conference in early October, which would indicate that the secondary sale process had lasted three to four weeks

[186] Based on EBITDA of €118.4 million – Candover press release, 27 October 2006

[187] Candover press release, 21 September 2006

[188] Standard Life European Private Equity Trust PLC 2008 Annual Financial Report

[189] Grimstone was Deputy Chairman of Standard Life PLC (the ultimate parent company of SL Capital) at the time of Parques Reunidos's completion. He became Chairman in May 2007, having been a director of The Standard Life Assurance Company since July 2003 (source: Standard Life web site)

[190] Based on €492 million of senior and €125 million of second lien - Euroweek, 11 May 2007

[191] Based on EBITDA of €74 million – Expansión, 20 January 2007

[192] The equity invested in ONO represented 1.5 per cent of the 2001 Fund (source: CIP 2005 Report and accounts)

[193] Bloomberg Markets, July 2007

[194] CIP 2007 Interim results for the year ended 30 June 2007, press release 7 September 2007

[195] Les Echos, 27 November 2007

[196] Candover press release, 7 June 2006

[197] Based on EBITDA of €71.2 million for the year ended 31 December 2007, as disclosed in CIP 2008 Report and accounts

[198] La Tribune, 23 November 2007

[199] Institutional Investors, 12 June 2007; Financial Times, 16 July 2007

[200] Dow Jones International News, 27 November 2007; L'AGEFI Quotidien, 30 November 2007

Chapter 9 – All Bets are Off!

[201] Dealogic data, The Economist, 29 September 2007

[202] Council of Mortgage Lenders

[203] Financial Times, 26 July 2007

[204] CIP 2007 Report and accounts

[205] EBITDA of €210 million for the year ended 31 December 2006 as per Stork N.V. Annual Report 2007

[206] Candover press release, 10 August 2007

[207] Financial Times, 11 August 2007

[208] Stork B.V. Annual Report 2008

[209] Stork N.V. Annual Report 2007

[210] Financial Times, 29 November 2007

[211] Based on *c.* £345 million disclosed in CIP 2008 Report and accounts

[212] CIP 2007 Report and accounts

[213] Candover-Unquote" Private Equity Barometers Q1 2008 and Q4 2007

[214] The Independent, 9 February 2008

[215] Financial Times, 13 July 2007

[216] Euroweek, 5 October 2007

[217] The Independent, 8 September 2007

[218] Evening Standard, 7 September 2007

[219] Standard Life European Private Equity Trust PLC Report and Accounts for the year ended 30 September 2009

[220] Candover's press releases, 13 June 2002 & 10 November 2005

[221] Gala Coral Group Limited, Annual Report 2007

[222] The Guardian, 5 January 2008

[223] Based on information disclosed in Gala Coral Group Limited, Annual Report 2007

[224] Financial Times, 4 April 2008

[225] Organization for Economic Co-operation and Development

[226] Real Deals, 11 April 2008

[227] CIP 2008 Interim financial statement

[228] Financial Times, 14 June 2008

[229] Based on underlying EBITDA of $330 million for the 2008 fiscal year as disclosed in Expro International Group Holdings Limited's Report and financial statements for the period ended 31 March 2009

[230] Expro International Group PLC – Annual Report and Accounts, Year ended 31 March 2008

[231] Expro International Group PLC – Annual Report and Accounts, year ended 31 March 2008

[232] Reuters News, 6 May 2008

[233] CIP press release, 8 January 2010

[234] The Guardian, 18 April 2008

[235] The Independent, 24 August 2003

[236] Vetco's entry EBITA multiple was 11.9 times based on EBITA of $77.4 million released in CIP 2005 Report and accounts. According to Expro's 2008 and 2009 annual accounts, Expro's EBITA for the year ended 31 March 2008 was $230 million, implying a multiple of about 16 times

[237] Candover-Unquote" Private Equity Barometer Q2 2008

[238] SVG Capital plc Annual Report and Accounts 2007

[239] AlpInvest Partners Annual review 2008

[240] Candover implied that Standard Life had participated in this closing (Financial Times, 28 August 2008) but Standard Life Capital Partners failed to mention it in its Annual Report for the year ended 30 September 2008

[241] As disclosed in March 2008 in CIP 2007 Report and accounts Chairman's statement

[242] Organization for Economic Co-operation and Development

[243] The Sunday Telegraph, 17 August 2008

[244] Candover press release, 17 December 1997

[245] AlpInvest Partners Annual review 2008

[246] CIP Interim results for the six months ended 30 June 2008, 27 August 2008

[247] CIP's share price had reached 2,294 pence on 14 February 2008 (source: FT.com/Marketsdata)

[248] The Daily Telegraph, 28 August 2008

[249] *ibid*

[250] Financial Times, 4 March 2008; Reuters News, 28 October 2008

[251] Wall Street Journal, 21 November 2008

[252] Evening Standard, 10 September 2001

[253] Financial News, 16 March 2009

[254] Trends/Tendance magazine, 5 April 2007; De Tijd, 7 July 2007

[255] Private Equity News - Annual Review 2007, 28 January 2008

[256] Based on information disclosed in Gala Coral Group Limited – Annual Report 2008 (for the year ended 29 September 2008)

[257] Milano Finanza, 18 October 2008

[258] Les Echos, 27 November 2007; L'AGEFI Quotidien, 21 August 2008

[259] Centre for Management Buy-Out Research

[260] CIP 2007 and 2008 Reports and accounts

[261] BVCA – Private Equity and Venture Capital Report on Investment Activity 2008, July 2009

[262] 2007 and 2008 Annual Reviews published by Apax and Bridgepoint

[263] Bloomberg Markets, 21 November 2010

[264] Annual Financial Report of Standard Life European Private Equity Trust PLC for the year ended 30 September 2008

Chapter 10 – Annus Horribilis

[265] Reuters, 21 May 2007; Music Week, 11 August 2007

[266] Terra Firma Annual Review 2008

[267] Wall Street Journal, 18 March 2009

[268] The Observer, 3 May 2009

[269] Financial Times, 17 January 2009

[270] Financial Times, 27 January 2009

[271] CIP 2009 Report and accounts

[272] In its 2008 Report and accounts, CIP admitted that although covenants were not expected to be breached, there was a need to renegotiate the terms with the lenders. Later in the year, several press articles would claim that a covenant breach was possible, including The Independent on 3 June 2009

[273] The US are mentioned as a possible target market in Les Echos, 10 March 2008

[274] CIP 2007 Report and accounts, Chairman's statement

[275] Financial Times, 10 March 1998

[276] CIP Preliminary results for the year ended 31 December 2005, 13 March 2006

[277] CIP press release, 17 February 2009

[278] CIP 2008 Report and accounts

[279] Reuters, 14 May 2009

[280] Candover-Unquote" Private Equity Barometer Q1 2009

[281] Il Sole 24 Ore, 5 February 2009

[282] Reuters 26 March 2009; Mercati Finanziari, 9 April 2009

[283] Il Sole 24 Ore, 11 September 2008

[284] Based on the original equity drawn down of £226.4 million, per CIP 2007 Report and accounts

[285] CIP Interim Financial Statement, 6 April 2009

[286] The Observer, 12 April 2009; Financial News, 20 April 2009; Il Mondo, 24 April 2009; The Independent, 25 April 2009; The Express 30 June 2009

[287] CIP 2008 Report and accounts

[288] Investors Chronicle, 16 March 2007

[289] Reuters, 14 May 2009

[290] Bloomberg Markets, 21 November 2010; Gerry Grimstone was up for re-election that year (as disclosed in the Form of Proxy included in the CIP 2008 Report and accounts) in line with the company's corporate governance rule requesting that each year a portion of its non-executive directors retire by rotation while still being eligible for re-election through a vote at the AGM

[291] Financial Times, 14 May 2009

[292] Financial News, 19 June 2009; CIP 2009 Interim financial statement

[293] Candover press release, 31 May 2007

[294] Candover press release, 20 July 2007

[295] Candover press release, 20 November 2007

[296] As disclosed in the board of directors section of the Springer 2008 Annual Report

[297] Financial Times, 15 April 2009

[298] CIP 2004 Report and accounts

[299] CIP 2009 Interim financial statement

[300] Candover press release, 19 June 2009

[301] Proceeds from the Wood Mackenzie sale reportedly enabled CIP to meet its debt covenants – The Express, 22 August 2009

[302] CIP 2009 Report and accounts

[303] The Herald, 10 June 2009. At the time of Wood Mackenzie's buyout by Candover, over 150 employees were believed to be invested in the business – The Herald, 29 April 2005

[304] Financial News, 6 July 2009

[305] CIP 2009 Report and accounts

[306] *ibid*

[307] The Daily Telegraph, 27 February 2009

[308] The Independent, 19 July 2009

[309] Based on £113 million originally invested, CIP 2004 Report and accounts; Financial News, 8 October 2009

[310] Financial News, 30 October 2009

[311] CIP 2006 Report and accounts

[312] Hilding Anders is valued at nil in CIP 2009 Report and accounts

[313] Yorkshire Post, 24 November 2009; Springer Science + Business Media Annual Report 2008

[314] Based on EBITDA of €278 million disclosed in EQT's 2009 Annual Review and €275 million in Springer Science + Business Media's Overview 2009

[315] Based on EBITDA of €150 million as disclosed in Candover's press release, 11 December 2009

[316] CIP 2008 Report and accounts

[317] The Guardian, 27 March 2009; Yorkshire Post, 30 June 2009

[318] €450 million per EQT's 2009 Annual Review; €435 million per Springer Science + Business Media's Overview 2009

[319] European Venture Capital Journal, February 2004

[320] Financial Times, 13 July 2007

[321] Expro International Group Holdings Limited – Half-year review – 6 months to 30 September 2009

[322] Expro International Group Holdings Limited – Reports and financial statements for the years ended 31 March 2009 and 31 March 2010

[323] EBITDA numbers for the years ended 31 December 2007 and 2009 as disclosed in CIP 2008 and 2010 Reports and accounts

[324] Financial Times, Candover fund targets Euros 2.5bn, by Katharin Campbell,12 March 2002

Chapter 11 – A Sad Anniversary

[325] Candover press release, 8 January 2010

[326] CIP 2009 Report and accounts

[327] CIP press release, 27 April 2010; Bloomberg, 28 April 2010

[328] Financial Times, 21 May 2010

[329] Financial Times, 13 May 2010

[330] The Guardian, 6 March 2009; SVG Capital plc Annual Report and Accounts 2008; CIP 2008 Report and accounts

[331] Gala Coral results for the years ended 27 September 2008 and 25 September 2010

[332] Based on data released by CIP in its 2003, 2005 and 2008 Reports and accounts

[333] CIP 2010 Interim financial statement

[334] DX Group Limited – Report and financial statements for the year ended 30 June 2010

[335] CIP 2009 Report and accounts

[336] Based on an original £197 million equity injection, CIP 2006 Report and accounts

[337] Including from CalPERS (as at 31 March 2010), California Teachers' Retirement System (as at 31 March 2010), and Washington State Investment Board (as at 30 June 2010)

[338] CIP statement re possible offer, 16 July 2010

[339] CIP 2010 Interim Results Statement, 31 August 2010

[340] CIP 2010 Interim financial statement

[341] Il Sole 24 Ore, 2 September 2010

[342] CIP presentation to analysts, 1 March 2011

[343] Based on £122.9 million invested as disclosed in CIP 2006 Report and accounts

[344] CIP 2009 and 2010 Reports and accounts

[345] Financial Times, 19 October 2010

[346] Stork B.V. - Annual Report 2009

[347] Stork B.V. – Annual Report 2010

[348] Pantheon was LP in the Candover 2001 Fund according to Candover's press release, 13 June 2002, and secondary investor in the Candover 2005 and 2008 vintages as reported by Bloomberg, 6 December 2010

[349] CIP press release - Proposed change of investment policy, disposal of Candover Partners Limited and sale of a strip of investments, 6 December 2010

[350] The Telegraph, 7 December 2010

[351] Dow Jones International News, 28 January 2008

[352] CIP 2010 Report and accounts

[353] Bloomberg, 6 December 2010

[354] Financial Times, 21 November 2007

[355] Candover press release, 28 November 2007

[356] Financial Times, 18 April 2008

[357] Scotsman, 12 June 2009

[358] Candover press release, 11 December 2009; Financial News, 11 December 2009

[359] Financial Times, 13 May 2010

[360] Candover press release, 15 July 2010

[361] Candover press release on Results of General Meeting, 22 December 2010

[362] CIP - Statement by Roger Brooke at the Annual General meeting, 11 May 1999

Chapter 12 – The End of the Road

[363] CIP press release – CIP to explore opportunities for investment in Asia, 25 February 2008

[364] CIP 2008 Report and accounts

[365] The 2005 Fund had 106 investors according to Candover's 10 November 2005 press release

[366] Financial Times, Survey of Management Buy-Outs, 8 December 1993

[367] CIP press release for the preliminary results for the year ended 31 December 1996, 10 March 1997 – source Acquisitions Monthly magazine

[368] Based on size of investment fund and deal value

[369] The Times, 30 December 2003; Financial News, 21 August 2006

[370] PR Newswire, 24 October 2002

[371] Financial News, 12 October 2003

[372] Business Wire, 14 November 2007

[373] Permira 2007 Annual review and EQT 2009 Annual review; Permira and EQT web sites

[374] Advent, BC Partners, Bridgepoint and Cinven web sites and press releases

[375] As disclosed in the board of directors sections in the 2008 Annual Reports of Stork B.V. and Gala Coral Group Limited

[376] The Daily Telegraph, 5 March 2007

[377] The Sunday Telegraph, 30 March 2008

[378] Financial News, 29 June 2005

[379] CIP 2003 Report and accounts

[380] De Tijd, 7 July 2007

[381] Ots, Orginaltextservice Schweitz, 27 November 2006

[382] Candover press release, 5 October 2006

[383] CalPERS data, Pensions & Investments magazine, 23 December 2002

[384] Preqin Private Equity Benchmarks: Buyout Benchmark Report – As of 30 September 2009

[385] The Economist, 27 November 2004

[386] The Guardian, 2 February 2004

[387] Birmingham Post, 2 April 1999 & 30 April 1999; The Independent 30 April 1999

[388] Financial Director, 26 April 2007

[389] The Times, 22 November 2007

[390] Acertec plc press release, 21 April 2009

[391] Acertec plc – Result of General Meeting, 22 June 2009

[392] Acertec PLC Annual results for year ended 31 December 2006, press release 22 March 2007; Financial Director, 26 April 2007

[393] Candover press release, 6 July 2006

[394] DX Group Limited – Reports and financial statements, years ended 30 June 2008 and 30 June 2010

[395] The Times, 28 June 1997

[396] The Express, 23 November 1999

[397] The Sunday Telegraph, 20 January 2002

[398] Financial Times, 11 November 2003

[399] Centre for Management Buy-Out Research, report on Management Buy-outs 1986-2006, Past Achievements, Future Challenges, June 2006

[400] Financial Times, 1 September 2010

[401] Bloomberg Markets, 21 November 2010

[402] Centre for Management Buy-Out Research, report on Management Buy-outs 1986-2006, Past Achievements, Future Challenges, June 2006

[403] Investors Chronicle, 18 March 2009

[404] As of 30 June 1989 – Financial Times, 14 September 1989

[405] £61.7 million in net current assets per CIP 2001 Report and accounts

[406] £189.4 million per CIP 2005 Report and accounts

[407] CIP 2005 Interim financial statement

[408] Net asset value had dropped from £448.3 million to £224.3 million between June and December 2008 (source: CIP 2008 Interim and Annual Reports)

[409] CIP 2007 Report and accounts. The other objective was to achieve above average capital gains

[410] It is more typical for only *c.* 85 per cent of total commitments to be drawn down in the

first five years with the rest being called upon for follow-on injections

[411] A 13 per cent share of €1.55 billion represents approximately €200 million

[412] Assuming that CPL did not intend to actually invest its 2008 Fund within three to three and a half years as it had done with its 2001 and 2005 vintages, in which case the realisation timetable would have had to be shortened

[413] CalPERS Alternative Investment Management Program Fund Performance Review as of 31 December 2010

[414] The Express, 22 August 2009; The Daily Telegraph, 1 September 2010; Daily Mail 4 September 2010; The Times 7 December 2010

[415] Evening Standard, 6 September 2010

[416] CIP 2009 Report and accounts

[417] The Economist, 21 February 2008

[418] CIP Preliminary results for the year ended 31 December 2005, press release 13 March 2006

Chapter 13 – Back to Basics

[419] EVCA Guidelines, Governing Principles

[420] Reuters News, 21 August 2009

[421] CIP 2000 and 2002 Reports and accounts

[422] The percentage assumed in Real Deals, 22 September 2009

[423] CIP 2000 and 2007 Reports and accounts show £12 million and £37.4 million respectively although these amounts are a blend of fees levied over two vintages (the 1994 and 1997 Funds in the 2000 annual accounts and the 2001 and 2005 Funds in the 2007 annual accounts)

[424] Vodafone Group Plc – Annual Report for the year ended 31 March 2009

[425] The Independent, 17 November 1992

[426] The Times, 16 December 1991

[427] Candover-Unquote" Private Equity Barometer Q3 2007

[428] Based on data released by CalSTRS and Washington State Investment Board regarding the KKR 1987 Fund

[429] Centre for Management Buy-Out Research, UK Private Equity - Exit Trends

[430] The Times, 25 April 2009

[431] Les Echos, 12 March 2007; Les Echos, 10 March 2008

[432] The Independent, 19 March 1991

Chapter 14 – A Wake-up Call

[433] House of Commons, Treasury Committee, Private Equity, Tenth Report of Session 2006-07 – Volumes I & II, 24 July 2007

[434] Private Equity's Effects on Workers and Firms - Hearing before the Committee on Financial Services - US House of Representatives, 110th Congress, First Session, 16 May 2007

[435] Bank for International Settlements, Basel Committee on Banking Supervision, Basel III: A global regulatory framework for more resilient banks and banking systems, December 2010 (rev June 2011)

[436] BVCA report on The Economic Impact of Private Equity in the UK - 2007

[437] Bridgepoint/Incisive Media survey, 21 February 2006; CIP 2006 Report and accounts; Evening Standard, 31 January 2006

[438] Financial Times, 14 June 2007

[439] Evening Standard, 4 June 2007

[440] The Sunday Times Rich List, 2005 and 2006

Chapter 15 – Back to the Future, Assuming There is One

[441] Evening standard, 3 February 2011

[442] Sunday Times, 13 December 1992

[443] Based on analysis from data provider Dealogic

[444] According to analysis from KPMG Corporate Finance and reported in the Financial Times on 8 December 1993, the gearing of UK MBOs with a transaction value exceeding £10 million had been approximately 70 per cent during the four-year period ended in December 1988 but had reached on average 75 per cent of EV in the six months leading to June 1989 and even 85 per cent in the six months to December 1989

[445] Fitch Ratings data. Only relates to loans contracted to finance LBO transactions in the years leading to the 2008 credit crunch

[446] Dow Jones Newswires, 21 December 2010

[447] Preqin Research Report – 2010 Private Equity-Backed Deals

[448] Financial News, 11 August 2010

[449] Based on press articles and Candover press releases

[450] The Sunday Telegraph, 31 October 2010; Financial Times, 17 July 2011

[451] Expro International Group Holdings Limited – Report and financial statements, Year to 31 March 2010

[452] Expro International Group PLC – Annual Report and Accounts, year ended 31 March 2008

[453] Preqin data

[454] Bloomberg, 8 October 2010

Afterword

[455] EVCA Research Paper, Employment contribution of Private Equity and Venture Capital in Europe, November 2005

[456] House of Commons, Treasury Committee, Private Equity, Tenth Report of Session 2006-07, Volume I, 24 July 2007

[457] World Economic Forum, Globalization of Alternative Investments, Working Papers Volume 1, The Global Economic Impact of Private Equity Report 2008

[458] Financial Times, 21 December 2010

[459] Canada Pension Plan was an investor in the 2001, 2005 and 2008 vintages as per Candover's press releases, 13 June 2002 and 10 December 2005; and Financial Times, 28 August 2008

[460] Financial Times, Financial backing available for company managers, by Richard Lambert, 18 September 1980

[461] Bloomberg Markets, 21 November 2010

[462] ibid

Printed in Great Britain
by Amazon